Contemporary Spanish Gothic

Contemporary Spanish Gothic

Ann Davies

EDINBURGH
University Press

To Sue and Martin Rich
and to Jean and David Airey
for their support in difficult times.
It is never forgotten.

Edinburgh University Press is one of the leading university presses in the UK.
We publish academic books and journals in our selected subject areas across the
humanities and social sciences, combining cutting-edge scholarship with high editorial
and production values to produce academic works of lasting importance. For more
information visit our website: edinburghuniversitypress.com

Edinburgh University Press Ltd
The Tun – Holyrood Road
12 (2f) Jackson's Entry
Edinburgh EH8 8PJ

First published in hardback by Edinburgh University Press 2016

Typeset in Monotype Ehrhardt by
Servis Filmsetting Ltd, Stockport, Cheshire,
and printed and bound by CPI Group (UK) Ltd
Croydon, CR0 4YY

A CIP record for this book is available from the British Library

ISBN 978 1 4744 0299 6 (hardback)
ISBN 978 1 4744 3193 4 (paperback)
ISBN 978 1 4744 0300 9 (webready PDF)
ISBN 978 1 4744 1792 1 (epub)

Contents

Figures

Acknowledgements

I have learnt the hard way that writing a book while moving institutions is never a good idea. I must therefore acknowledge the patience and support of my colleagues at the University of Stirling while I carried out both the writing and the moving. I would particularly like to thank my Gothic colleagues Dale Townshend and Matt Foley for their advice, encouragement and collegiality, the students on the Gothic Imagination programme who allowed me to try out and discuss some of my ideas with them, and my colleagues in Spanish who gently guided me around the practicalities of teaching on the Spanish programme while my head was full of ghosts and monsters. Cristina Johnston, my counterpart for the French programme, deserves a mention here too.

Beyond Stirling I must give particular thanks to Beate Müller and Rosie White who listened kindly to my anxieties about THE BOOK, Sarah Wright and Duncan Wheeler for allowing me to see drafts of forthcoming work, Xavier Aldana Reyes who not only allowed me to see drafts of his work but also pointed me to important sources, Carlos Aguilar for his generosity, the Universities of Aberdeen and St Andrews which invited me to try out my ideas on postmodern Gothic heroines on unsuspecting audiences, and to Chris Perriam and Rob Stone whose continued support over the years goes above and beyond. Richard Strachan and Rebecca Mackenzie of Edinburgh University Press were helpful and unflappable when dealing with my questions and concerns. Finally, the members of my family are my foremost supporters, through thick and thin and the cryptic mutterings of the youngest. There can be no limit to my gratitude to them.

Parts of this book were previously given as papers at the conferences of the Association of Hispanists of Great Britain and Ireland, the European Cinema Research Forum, the Society for Cinema and Media Studies, and the 'Reading Architecture' conference at Stirling. The Carnegie Trust provided funding for travel to archives in Spain.

All translations from French and Spanish are my own.

CHAPTER 1

Introduction

Somewhat belatedly, Spanish cultural critique is beginning to catch up with the Gothic. Certainly there have been Gothic texts produced in Spain for at least the last two centuries while arguably earlier productions, such as the tale of Don Juan and its ghostly statue, prefigure the start of what we consider to be the Gothic in the eighteenth century. It is just that recognition of such texts as Gothic has occurred only recently. This state of affairs is not only the result of a process of catch-up as Hispanic Studies follows the paths of disciplines such as cultural studies, paths already well trodden by others. Abigail Lee Six, herself one of the few scholars writing on Spanish Gothic, observes that 'Hispanic Studies has tended to be excessively isolationist in its approach to certain literary trends' (Lee Six 2010, 11), and I fully concur with this. I would extend this criticism still further to argue that such isolationism can apply to wider cultural trends. This perhaps follows from Spain's history over the past two centuries, somewhat semi-detached from events elsewhere in Europe, such as the two World Wars, in conjunction with a tendency to read texts only in terms of national history. Genre, as a mode that crosses national borders or indeed takes no notice of them, is often neglected even though genre can prove a ready vehicle for bringing ideas into a national culture while also allowing that culture to contribute to the sum of the genre.

Nonetheless, in terms of the Gothic, such neglect in Hispanic Studies also arises from Gothic's overwhelming focus on British Gothic texts, with some space allowed for American texts as well. There are good reasons for this: the Gothic as we know it today is generally thought to have begun with Horace Walpole's *The Castle of Otranto* (1764), followed fairly swiftly by the works of Ann Radcliffe and then Matthew Lewis. Yet a consolidated scholarly interest in Gothic production from other nations and cultures and in other languages has recently come to fruition in the last decade or so, as has interest in Gothic cultural flow, defined as globalgothic by Glennis Byron (2013a) and Justin D. Edwards and Fred Botting (2013). It is, I find, ironic that the new focus on other countries arises just at a time when the idea of a nation and of national identity has come into doubt. I am not sure I agree with the idea that we are in a post-national world but I do recognise that, in contemporary society, borders can be crossed more easily and that ideas can circulate beyond national boundaries. Indeed, such circulation is hardly a new thing. It is this circulation that is one of the elements that interests me here, and I am considering Spain as a nexus or crossing point of the circulation of Gothic ideas.

The initial, and perhaps rather dubious, contribution of Spain to the rise of the Gothic text from the eighteenth century has been to provide a setting and context of Roman Catholic superstition, with Lewis's *The Monk* (1796) and Maturin's *Melmoth the Wanderer* (1820) the best-known examples. Chris Baldick and Robert Mighall argue that, in the traditional Gothic narratives, the setting was Spain, Italy or southern France

> because, to the Protestant mind, they were firmly associated with the twin yoke of feudal politics and popish deception, from which they still had to emancipate themselves. Put simply, Gothic novels were set in the Catholic south because [. . .] Gothic (that is, 'medieval') practices were believed to still prevail there. (Baldick and Mighall 2001, 219)

Joan Curbet argues that Spanish contribution to the genre was weak but that Spain itself inspired British writing (Curbet 2002, 161). As I have already mentioned, Spain in fact offered a more active contribution in the tale of Don Juan with its macabre end – Don Juan dragged to Hell by a statue of a man he murdered – that both predates and prefigures the rise of the Gothic elsewhere. It is odd that Don Juan's story is not normally considered a Gothic tale: perhaps this is because much of the story deals with Don Juan's serial sexual conquests but it is certainly because the framework of Gothic as a form of literature did not exist at the time the first Don Juan play was written (in the early seventeenth century). What is also worth noting, in terms of the framework of the circulation of cultural ideas, is how the tale of Don Juan spread beyond the confines of Spain, notably to France with Molière's play and then further afield with Mozart and da Ponte's opera *Don Giovanni*. Spain itself reworked the story to fit changing cultural values, in particular the Romantic version of 1844 by Zorrilla (in which Don Juan is saved from Hell by the intercession of his dead lover). Another Spanish writer, José de Espronceda, offered in *El estudiante de Salamanca* (The Student of Salamanca, 1837) a variant tale of a young rake brought to a moment of reckoning by the dead but this time it is his lover, cast away by him and now dead, who returns to haunt him and claim his promise of marriage.

It is true, nonetheless, that the Gothic in Spain did not take hold until the nineteenth century and, even then, production of Gothic texts remained at a low level: texts with Gothic sensibilities were, in addition, not always recognised as such. Few translations of English Gothic were available in Spanish, and those that arrived did so via a French version. Ann Radcliffe was not popular, and Maturin's *Melmoth the Wanderer* remained untranslated throughout the nineteenth century (Hale 2002, 32). Nonetheless, there were forerunners bridging the eighteenth and nineteenth centuries. Perhaps the most notable contributor to a Gothic sensibility was the artist Francisco de Goya (1746–1828) whose work includes many paintings that embrace the macabre: his Gothic influence is recognised worldwide (Goya as cinematic subject will form the focus of discussion in Chapter 2). His Gothic approach derived in great part from his observations of a corrupt and venal Spanish society. Goya's Gothic eye was rendered sharper by the political events he lived through: the exile of King Carlos IV to make way for Napoleonic rule; the violence of Napoleonic occupation; and the political oppression under Ferdinand VII, once the occupation ended and the Bourbon monarchy returned. Nonetheless, Curbet warns us not to assume a Gothic divide in Goya's work into a 'before' and 'after' the Napoleonic occupation, with the Gothic confined to the latter (Curbet 2002, 169). Goya's Gothic style was well developed before these events took place.

Curbet suggests José Blanco White (1755–1841) as a Gothic writer and, in particular, his narrative *Intrigas venecianas, o Fray Gerundio de Jerusalén* (Venetian Intrigues, or Fray Gerundio of Jerusalem, 1823–5), first published in London, as a rare example of Gothic literature before 1850 (177). He further observes that both Goya and Blanco White veer between the Gothic and didacticism (169), and concludes:

> Such an oscillation suggests conflict between the critical perspective and a deep fascination exerted by the object of this critique. The few instances of the gothic that appear at the turn of the century are the work of specific, isolated individuals who operated in a state of extreme ambiguity towards their own culture. (170)

Curbet's suggestion of the Spanish Gothic as an isolated phenomenon renders figures such as Goya and Blanco White somewhat Gothic themselves. Yet this ambiguity is what distinguishes these outputs from the Gothic predecessors mentioned above, in their criticism of a society that was, by the beginning of the nineteenth century, well on a slide to political decadence that would become more pronounced as the nineteenth century progressed, ending in entrenched political positions that would ultimately lead to the Spanish Civil War (1936–9), the Franco dictatorship (1939–75), and the Basque separatist campaign (1960s–2011). The politics of the turn of the century, and the Gothic gaze upon them, thus form an unbroken line with the contemporary period that will be the subject of this book.

Curbet concludes that, between Goya and Blanco White and the emergence in the nineteenth century of Gustavo Adolfo Bécquer (1836–70), there is very little sense of the Gothic in Spain (178). José Monléon has argued strongly for Bécquer as a critical conduit for the Gothic in Spain:

> Bécquer articulated a situation similar to the one registered by Gothic literature: when reason seemed to have finally overcome a history of frustrations and setbacks, when it had finally secluded the last remnants of the old feudal society, unreason appeared. And it reappeared following the same patterns erected by the Gothic. Unreason emerged from the margins, from the periphery of the social and cultural horizon. (1990: 115)

These ideas echo those of Goya, particularly his well-known etching from the *Caprichos*, 'El sueño de la razón produce monstruos' (The Sleep of Reason Produces Monsters), a painting we shall have cause to return to in Chapter 2. Monléon goes on to argue, however, that 'as soon as the Gothic found a voice in accordance with the Spanish reality, it faded away' (121) because of belated but rapid economic development in the second half of the nineteenth century. Instead, Bécquer's *Leyendas* (Legends) are arguably the starting point for the Spanish fantastic, a category Monléon distinguishes from the Gothic though he recognises some isolated predecessors of the fantastic with Eugenio de Ochoa and Gertrudis Gómez de Avellaneda (108). The full-blown Spanish fantastic emerges only in the 1850s, 'after the consolidation of a bourgeois society' (109).

Lee Six suggests that Spanish novelists became aware of the Gothic from the late nineteenth century, and draws attention to the process of transfer involved, through the translation of novels from elsewhere, through reading such novels in the original language, and through the adoption of appropriate techniques in these novels by Spanish authors (Lee Six 12–14). The Gothic lacked recognised cultural value, however, and authors tended to use Gothic motifs 'cautiously and selectively, deploying a range of strategies to keep them at arms [*sic*] length' (15). Lee Six goes on to say that this tentativeness continued into the twentieth century but, by the end of that century, the Gothic had come out of hiding to be used as an explicit point of attraction as popular culture has become increasingly respectable (16). With the arrival of the twentieth century, a new version of an old tradition appeared. Spanish literature has frequently emphasised the grotesque and cruel humour. The best-known examples occur in the picaresque tradition in which Spanish literature had already

Figure 1.1 Francisco de Goya, *El sueño de la razón produce monstruos.*

produced masterpieces such as the anonymous *Lazarillo de Tormes* (1554) or Francisco de Quevedo's *La vida del buscón* (The Life of a Swindler, 1626), to say nothing of some of the adventures of Cervantes's Don Quixote. The grotesque and cruel humour are also a part of Goya's work. In the twentieth century, grotesque humour acquired a new political tone and a new label, *esperpento*. The term was coined by playwright and writer Ramón del Valle-Inclán as a way of describing the sense of distortion and warping in his work that represents the tragic situation of Spanish society in the early decades of the twentieth century. *Esperpento*'s link to Spanish politics makes it culturally specific but there are, nonetheless, clear links to the macabre and monstrous elements of the Gothic (where humour is not unknown).

The Gothic and the grotesque seemingly disappeared as Spanish politics reached such high levels of tension that it was hard to exaggerate it still further. With the outbreak of the Civil War and the onset of Franco's dictatorship, the times were too extreme for the excesses of the Gothic to hold much sway. For that reason among others, for much of the twentieth century the presence of the Gothic in Spanish culture was neglected in favour of realism: fantasy literature was rarely considered worthy of attention (Roas and Casas 2013, 7–8). Social realism, in particular, has held sway as the canon of Francoist literature, often used as a way of resisting Franco's dictatorship. Nonetheless, as Lee Six has noted (2010, 15–16), some authors did write in a Gothic mode even if it was not explicitly recognised as such. And, by this time, of course, literature had a competitor in Gothic narratives: film. Monleón argued for Gothic and fantasy as distinct in Spain, confining the Gothic to a particular historical period prior to the rise of the bourgeoisie, while fantasy is more pervasive and free floating. (Monleón 1990, 14). The above discussion, to say nothing of the entire premise of this book, clearly indicates that I do not agree with Monleón regarding the Gothic. I am not sure he is correct about fantasy either, as Spanish writing on Gothic, horror and fantasy tends to conflate the terms (as the titles of Aguilar 1999 and 2005a, and López and Pizarro 2014 suggest); but the wider question of fantasy lies outside the scope of this book. Spanish cinema does not, however, follow the distinction that Monleón posits: Gothic tends to be subsumed under horror, as also happens with Gothic films in other countries, and, as such, has had a fairly consistent presence in Spanish culture though, as we shall see, some Spanish horror historians do observe declines in the Gothic at certain times.

This may surprise those more familiar with the realism and neorealism often used obliquely as a form of resistance to Franco's regime, though even those sometimes carry their own Gothic, such as *El espíritu de la colmena* (Spirit of the Beehive, Víctor Erice 1973) (see Chapter 4 and also Davies 2015a, Fiddian 2013, Labanyi 2001). Ángel Sala claims Carlos Saura's *Ana y los lobos* (Ana and the Wolves, 1973) as another example (Sala 2010, 338–9), while Diego López and David Pizarro (2014, 631–2) would add the same director's *Peppermint Frappé* (1967). Nonetheless, Gothic cinema has existed from the very start of Spanish film history. Carlos Aguilar points out that silent film in Spain included horror and fantasy offerings, and even sci-fi of a sort (Aguilar 1999, 17). López and Pizarro posit Segundo de Chomón as a pioneer in making fantasy films, deriving in great part from his apprenticeship with George Méliès (López and Pizarro 2014, 20–7). They also suggest the early film-maker Nemesio M. Sobrevila as an example (35–8). Contrary to that which we might expect from a regime keen to exert ideological control over cultural product, the Franco era saw the rise of horror film-makers even from the 1940s (42 ff.), in particular with the work of Edgar Neville, including films such as *La torre de los siete jorobados* (The Tower of the Seven Hunchbacks, 1944), *Domingo de carnaval* (Carnival Sunday, 1945) and *El crimen de la calle Bordadores* (The Crime on Bordadores Street, 1946): López and Pizarro point to international and to Spanish sources for Neville's inspiration (48–9).

Cinematic horror and, to a lesser extent, Gothic really got going in the 1960s, however. As Aguilar observes, the classical motifs of Spanish horror did not really develop until the 1960s, well after similar movements in Hollywood and the rest of Europe. Even then, horror films were permissible only on the understanding that the action did not take place in Spain (Aguilar 1999, 15) so, while the Franco regime permitted horror to be made, there were implicit restrictions. In addition, the Gothic was not a primary focus for Spanish horror at this time: as Aguilar observes, the common denominator of Spanish horror was and is 'crudeza', a crudity based on the interaction between eroticism and violence, sex and death (16). The prime and best-known example of 1960s and 1970s horror is Jess Franco who has come to stand for the exploitation cinema of the 1960s and 1970s in a rather reductive way. Gómez and de Felipe (2013, 198) speak of the 'fantastic' genre, a label often applied to horror and/or Gothic: they talk of the rise of the fantastic in the sixties and seventies while also noting the turn to exploitation cinema within the genre as a specific reaction to the Francoist politics of the time. As they go on to observe, some Spanish auteurs, such as Carlos Saura (whose *Goya en Burdeos* (Goya in Bordeaux, 1999) we shall discuss in Chapter 2) and Víctor Erice used an allegorical style to oppose the regime and thus offer a different form of protest from 1960s exploitation, which went into decline (202). While I think the notion that auteurist cinema simply replaced horror film as an outlet for resistance overly simplistic, auteurist influence on the Gothic can be detected in films such as *El espíritu de la colmena* mentioned above which, in particular, fed into some of the ideas for Alejandro Amenábar's first feature film, *Tesis* (Thesis, 1996), a slasher thriller with its own Gothic labyrinth. There is also the stand-alone example of *El extraño viaje* (The Strange Journey, Fernando Fernán-Gómez, 1964) which López and Pizarro identify as the first full-blown Spanish Gothic film (2014, 626). Spanish cinema was producing Gothic auteurs of its own, however, such as Narciso Ibáñez Serrador: his films *La residencia* (The Boarding School, 1969), and *¿Quién puede matar a un niño?* (Who Can Kill a Child?, 1976) as well as his television series *Historias para no dormir* (Stories to Keep

You Awake) are strong examples of a Gothic strain of horror (see Lázaro-Reboll 2012, Ch. 3). López and Pizarro specifically identity Eloy de la Iglesia and Pedro Olea as Gothic film-makers, particularly the latter's *La casa sin fronteras* (The House Without Borders, 1972; López and Pizarro 2014, 8). Any political aspect to Gothic film-making was itself diminished by the advent of television and a more liberal approach to the film industry (Gómez and de Felipe 2013, 208). Aguilar argues that the real horror boom started in the early 1970s, and this coincided with the decline of the Gothic tradition in other countries (Aguilar 1999, 30). Instead, this boom emphasised the grotesque, in line with the style in comic books in the United States and Italy.

Gómez and de Felipe observe a decline in horror film-making in the 1980s (2013, 203). Aguilar expands on this, arguing that fantasy and horror genres suffered under the socialists in the 1980s and 1990s: at best, the genres were tolerated, given the emphasis on 'racionalismo', realism. Aguilar argues that such an official attitude to horror continues and is endemic, as horror is despised by both Right and Left (Aguilar 2005b, 13). As government funds were at that time an important source of revenue for film producers, the decline therefore may not be surprising though, as the funds for sixties and seventies horror often came from abroad or through co-production arrangements, this suggests a certain turning inward of the industry that is not totally explained by politics or policy. Iván Gómez García associates the rejection of the fantasy genre with bourgeois values: potential for subversion in the genre was ignored and genre cinema took no political part in the Transition as a result. Fantasy cinema did not chime with the emphasis on a rupture with the past. Nor was there an interest in the magical because of the links with primitive rural superstition (Gómez García 2013, 203). According to Ángel Sala, however, the 1970s and 1980s featured a more specifically Spanish Gothic which included:

> Las cocinas infernales, las celebraciones en torno a las matanzas de animales para el alimento (los cerdos) o la diversión (los toros), el sentido de la caza en la España rural, la avaricia, las tinajas de vino rancio llenas de sorpresas, los rostros enlutados en calles bañadas por un sol severo, la pobreza, ignorancia y represión sexual formando un *cocktail* explosivo, campos en barbecho y unos siniestros ritos religiosos (sobre todo procesiones e imágenes de santos torturados y Cristos crucificados). (330).
>
> (Hell's kitchens, rituals based on the killing of animals for food (pigs) or sport (bulls), the enjoyment of hunting in rural Spain, avarice, jars of sour wine full of surprises, faces in mourning in streets bathed in harsh sunlight; poverty, ignorance and sexual repression forming an explosive cocktail, fields lying fallow and religious rites (in particular processions and images of tortured saints and crucified Christs).)

Sala suggests the early films of Eloy de la Iglesia as the high point of this specifically Spanish thread (336): *Algo amargo en la boca* (Something Bitter in the Mouth, 1969), *El techo de cristal* (The Glass Ceiling, 1971) and *Juego de amor prohibido* (Game of Forbidden Love, 1975). In the 1990s, Agustín Villaronga's work is also classified by Sala as specifically Spanish (346), citing the 1997 film *99.9* as an example of 'esa España ignota' (that undiscovered Spain).

If the Gothic really has a boom period in Spain, however, both in terms of film and literature, it would be now. The surge in Spanish film production in the mid 1990s included a new emphasis on popular narrative alongside new forms of art-house cinema: new directors, such as Amenábar, Álex de la Iglesia, Juanma Bajo Ulloa and Enrique Urbizu, directed films that drew on the Gothic, horror and film noir. The 1990s also saw an increase in 'intelligent' detective fiction with noir and Gothic elements, influenced by such bestsellers as Umberto Eco's *The Name of the Rose* (1980): this included Arturo Pérez-Reverte, one of the authors discussed in Chapter 3. The increased emphasis on genre narratives in both literature and film is also a result of one of the key elements for discussion in this book: the international trade in popular narratives that has played a great part, for good or ill, in the shaping of such narratives in Spain as it increasingly detaches itself from the emphasis on difference and on looking inward that shaped many twentieth-century Spanish texts.

Not all would necessarily see this as a good thing, prefiguring the anxiety expressed by many in the face of the postmodern Gothic that I shall return to below. Of *cine fantástico* at the turn of the century, Aguilar notes that, while genre production improved to some degree in the (right-wing) Partido Popular (Popular Party) era of the late nineties, cinema was generally in crisis, given the change in government policy:

> esta producción carece, por lo corriente, de aquel peculiar espíritu de mestizaje cultural que podía apreciarse positivamente en los decenios anteriores, al desdibujarse su cualidad dentro del fenómeno de la globalización; en consecuencia, muchas veces procede hablar preferiblemente de imitación. (Aguilar 2005b, 25)
> (this production usually lacks that special spirit of cultural miscegenation that we could appreciate in previous decades, as its quality fades within the phenomenon of globalisation; as a result, it would be better to talk of imitation.)

And Hollywood provides the model for such imitation. For Aguilar, the priority for contemporary horror is thus to leave behind the Gothic forms of the 1960s and 1970s, finding horror instead in the contemporary realities of Spain in order to aid identification with a younger generation who do not know about the older forms and do not care (26). Sergi Ramos

Alquezar (2011, 45) offers an opposing argument that claims that the monsters of this era were situated as much in the *esperpento* tradition as in classic fantasy; and certainly directors such as de la Iglesia, with *Acción Mutante* (Mutant Action, 1993) and *El día de la bestia* (The Day of the Beast, 1995), would bear this out. Ramos Alquezar further observes that these monsters became true fantasy monsters in the 1990s and 2000s (46); that is, monstrosity no longer symbolised something else but existed in its own right as pure horror. As we shall see in Chapters 3 and 4, critics still look to interpret and critique Gothic novels and films as symbolic of something else. Ramos Alquezar's remarks suggest, however, that such films (and perhaps the novels as well) are beginning to detach themselves from a specifically Spanish cultural context.

Circulation and Cultural Exchange

From the very beginning, the Spanish Gothic was subject to international circulation, not simply by providing appropriate settings for eighteenth-century Gothic but also by forming part of an international market for Gothic novels. Apart from a few sentimental Gothic novels, most translations of English Gothic into Spanish (always via a French translation) were usually published in Paris for a readership of Spanish exiles. In particular, this applied to the 'dangerous' ones such as Lewis's *The Monk* (Hale 2002, 32). Curbet (2002, 174) argues that the lack of circulation of European Gothic can be ascribed to censorship (so that many key Gothic novels from outside were not translated or circulated) while historical novels tended to the epic and the idealisation of the Spanish past as one of unity. Clearly, however, some Gothic novels made it into the hands of Spanish readers. Curbet's association between the Gothic and exile suggests a Spanish interest in the Gothic based at least in part on dissidence and resistance but which encompasses a semi-detached relationship with Spain itself. It is intriguing that the association of the Gothic with opposition to the prevailing order once again involves travel, just as Goya and Blanco White exiled themselves in France and England respectively.

I wish to look at these aspects of the Spanish Gothic, the ways in which it circulates and the way in which one country serves as a nexus, in addition to analysing contemporary texts for their Gothic qualities. Using Spain as an example of how Gothic might travel and how a particular locus can function as nexus is, of course, hardly coincidence: Hispanic Studies is my primary field of research. Nonetheless, I think Spain an intriguing example for my purposes. In that regard, the case studies I use involve texts that are often fairly readily available outside Spain: they are available, clearly, precisely because of the circulation of Spanish Gothic. In a couple of cases the circulation has gone so far that the texts themselves are not immediately recognised as Spanish. While Spanish film critics and Hispanists like to claim *The Others* (Alejandro Amenábar, 2001) as a Spanish film, this is open to challenge (see, for example, Triana-Toribio 2003, 162–3), as the film also has its roots in Hollywood: and, indeed, in Chapter 5 I question the insistence on interpretations that cling too closely to Spanish history. On the other hand, no one would consider the *Twilight* series of films (based on the novels of Stephenie Meyer) as having anything to do with Spain, yet *New Moon* (Chris Weitz, 2009) shows the clear influence of an approach to lighting derived in part from previous experience in the Basque and Spanish film industries. I discuss *New Moon*, too, in Chapter 5 where I also discuss the contempt with which such texts as *New Moon* are received, a disdain for the popular with which the Gothic has long been familiar. These examples will demonstrate, I hope, just how far contemporary Spanish Gothic can circulate.

Films form a key part of this circulation, and they feature strongly in this book, in part because my background is in Spanish film studies in the first instance. But there are other reasons. Firstly, as Samuel Amago observes, 'In the contemporary Spanish cultural context, cinematic reflexivity almost always draws the viewer's attention to the global–national dialectic, making visible national industries and audiences situated within their local and global contexts' (Amago 2013, 3). Amago further adds:

> Spanish filmmakers are also in constant negotiation with an array of global forms, market strategies and national and regional interests, working to position themselves within the global market. Present in the formal and thematic structures of their films we can see how global film culture comes into contact with the nationally circulating film culture as images of Spanish national identity similarly move out, into, and through the global cinemascape. (7)

Antonio Lázaro-Reboll makes similar claims specifically for horror film, arguing that

> Over the last forty years, horror film has formed a significant part of Spain's local and transnational filmic production and is part and parcel of the international and global circulation, reception and consumption of horror cinema [. . .] any critical history of Spanish horror film must extend beyond histories of Spanish cinema and must be seen as part of transcultural flows and international traditions of horror cinema. (Lázaro-Reboll 2012, 3)

The circulation of Spanish Gothic cinema began at an early stage with Segundo de Chomón's *Souperstition andalouse* (Andalusian Superstition,

1912) but Chomón was himself influenced by Méliès and, unsurprisingly, Spanish cinema received more influence than it gave out, in particular from German Expressionism. Later influences included, unsurprisingly, the United States (223–4). Aguilar (1999, 38) notes that Spanish horror even made its own versions of films such as Friedkin's *The Exorcist* (*Exorcismo*, Juan Bosch, 1974) while Gómez and de Felipe suggest early American influences such as Poe and Browning (2013, 201). López and Pizarro argue that Spanish Gothic – and here they are being careful to distinguish this from Spanish horror more widely – derives specifically from the American Gothic from the late 1960s to the early 1990s:

> el *Spanish Gothic*, intentando asemejarse a su homónimo estadounidense, reformula sus bases principales, haciéndolas propias y, de este modo, asimila la desintegración del núcleo familiar, implantación de engendros verídicos, la confrontación entre lo rural y lo urbano, la disgregación entre clases sociales, las diferentes culturas y nacionalidades . . ., pero añade toques castizos propios del cine de los cincuenta, cimentado por ese gusto por lo perverso y truculento, lo prohibido y amoral, lo arcaico y retrógrado . . . (López and Pizarro 2014, 625: ellipsis in original).
>
> (Spanish Gothic, aiming to resemble its American namesake, reformulates its basic principles, making them its own and, in this way, it absorbs the collapse of the nuclear family, the implantation of real freaks, the confrontation between the rural and the urban, the breakdown of social class, different cultures and nationalities . . . but it adds local touches typical of 1950s cinema, reinforced by a taste for the perverse and cruel, the forbidden and amoral, the archaic and retrograde . . .)

Lee Six (2010) has discussed examples of the Gothic novel in Spain's democratic era and, indeed in recent years, there has been a minor boom in Gothic publishing, following the successes of Arturo Pérez-Reverte and Carlos Ruiz Zafón, authors who will be discussed in Chapter 3. Those who have adopted the Gothic as a framework are not, however, necessarily adopting a local model, as the Spanish variants on Dan Brown's bestseller *The Da Vinci Code* (2003) attest. A similar move can be seen in some detective novels which are also experiencing a minor boom. Spain is also involved with the related steampunk movement, with a website that celebrates steampunk writings in Spanish (http://www. mundosteampunk.net/). Television is getting in on the act, too, with series such as *Luna: el misterio de Calenda* (Luna: the Mystery of Calenda, 2012–13) and *El internado* (The Boarding School, 2007–10). Some might argue that the 'infiltration' of elements from outside Spain thus renders such production 'not Spanish': this ignores the fact that the Gothic is arguably all about infiltration anyway, of the present by the past, of the rational by superstition, of the sane by the insane, and so on. Included in that is the influence of other cultures, going right back to the ways in which British Gothic literature drew on its own perceptions of southern European cultures.

In this respect, Gothic film, and horror film more widely, became part of a transnational Gothic flow that film-makers and scriptwriters adapted to their own ends. Thus, Ángel Sala (2010, 322) suggests the influence of *Wuthering Heights* (William Wyler, 1939) and *Rebecca* (Alfred Hitchcock, 1940) on Rafael Gil's *El clavo* (The Nail, 1944), and *The Phantom of the Opera* (Rupert Julian, 1925) and James Whale's *Frankenstein* (1931) on Edgar Neville's *La torre de los siete jorobados*. Examples of co-production include the unusual collaboration of Spain and Japan in Jacinto Molina's *El carnaval de las bestias* (Carnival of the Animals, 1980): Molina was also influenced by late Hammer and Mario Bava (Sala 340, 342). Later, we have Amenábar's *The Others* (2001), discussed in Chapter 5, which Sala likens to Henry James's *The Turn of the Screw* (346) and Guillermo del Toro's Spanish films (347). Co-production featured early: with France (López and Pizarro 2014, 33), Germany and Switzerland (68). Aguilar observes that the Nuevas Normas para el Desarrollo de la Cinematografía (New Norms for the Development of Cinematography) of 1964 favoured co-production (1999, 19): this, in turn, broadened the Spanish experience of horror, as European horror was by then well developed (20). Jess Franco took an international approach to his horror. López and Pizarro's chapter on his work is a recital of foreign influences, co-productions, international locations and studios, as well as stars from other countries such as Christopher Lee and Klaus Kinski (López and Pizarro 2014, 75–85). Influence in the 1960s was also forthcoming from the Italian *giallo* and the British Hammer films (Sala 2010, 326), of which *La residencia* (Narciso Ibáñez Serrador, 1969) was a zenith of both, with perhaps a central European touch as well (327). Gómez and de Felipe point out that 1960s horror, with the help of co-production, allowed Spain to come out of its cinematic isolation (2013, 199) but they also observe how Spanish horror seems to merge into a stateless realm of horror production in which personnel from different countries mingle (200).

As Paul Julian Smith has observed, some of the more successful Spanish films, including Gothic ones, have been castigated for deriving from foreign influences. Amenábar, whose Gothic film *The Others* will be discussed in Chapter 5, was certainly not immune: even his biopic *Mar adentro* (The Sea Inside, 2004), a story of the paraplegic Ramón Sampedro's struggle to legalise assisted death, was described by one reviewer as 'Spielbergized', 'claiming it is identical in its aesthetic to mainstream horror films' (Smith 2012, 65). Smith, however, concentrates on that Gothic success *El orfanato* (The Orphanage, J. A. Bayona, 2007) which a critic of Spanish film magazine *Fotogramas* accused of 'Hollywood-style pseudo-mimesis' (ibid.). Smith, however, argues that it is Bayona 'who is attempting to introduce a new aesthetic regime to the Spanish audiovisual establishment, one which champions an impure aesthetic and unconsecrated genre filmmaking over the European art-house tradition' (67). Smith's perception moves us away from Gómez and de Felipe's statelessness to one that suggests Bayona's position as a crossing point of international Gothic influences and traditions nonetheless based within the cinema of a specific country.

Circulation and Gothic Theory

According to some Gothic theorists, the exponential circulation of the Gothic in the present day serves to render the Gothic as empty and meaningless, a victim of late capitalism, and I should like to address this idea before considering how Spain's role as a nexus of Gothic circulation fits with such fears. The concerns of these theorists derive from different definitions of what the Gothic actually is but the end point is the same. One example is Alexandra Warwick's article 'Feeling Gothicky?' wherein she discusses what she sees as the problem of the Gothic's contemporary ubiquity: 'the Gothic is everywhere, out in the light and at the centre of things, which already might be thought strange, given that it is usually characterised as being, in the most general terms, at the dark margin of culture' (Warwick 2007, 5). For Warwick, the Gothic is intricately bound up with trauma and loss. Contemporary Gothic, on the other hand, 'is the manifestation of the desire *for* trauma, not the trauma of desire that finds itself prohibited, but something of a sense that trauma itself is the lost object, that the experience of trauma, and not the healing of it, is that which will make us whole' (11). For Warwick, then, the popularity of Gothic offers trauma as an indulgence (though that is not the term she uses), a spectacle for entertainment that ultimately avoids the pain: 'Gothic becomes a surface texture that indicates the presence of the process, but not, I would argue, of the loss' (12). If the increasing presence of the Gothic in contemporary culture devalues our understanding of trauma and loss, then clearly this is a problem. This question will reappear in the Spanish context when we come to consider the Gothicisation of the Spanish Civil War and the Franco dictatorship, something I shall look at in more detail in Chapters 3 and 4; and, in addition, we shall intermittently see how the Gothic is in danger of being reduced to spectacle. For now, I wish to stay with the idea that trauma and loss lose their depth, that they are rendered as simply surface experiences, and thus, in a literal rending of surface, superficial.

Warwick considers that the Gothic, once concerned with keeping things hidden, now opens up everything to our gaze. She remarks: 'if Gothic speaks the unspeakable through coded representation, there seems to be little left in contemporary culture that is unspeakable' (12).

Fred Botting suggests something similar when he argues that 'to live in gothic times at present means that Gothic loses its older intensity, shedding some of the allure of darkness, danger, and mystery' (Botting 2002, 287). It is now a thing of fashion or lifestyle choice. The Gothic is not so much surface as veneer. In perhaps the most despairing position on contemporary Gothic that I have come across, Botting also describes Gothic as indulgence and spectacle that cannot quite disguise its lack of meaning:

> A sense of cultural exhaustion haunts the present. An inhuman future is shrouded in old Gothic trappings emptied of any strong charge: past images and forms are worn too thin to veil the gaping hole of objectless anxiety [. . .] Gothic figures, once giving form to the anxieties surrounding the transition from aristocratic to bourgeois culture, now disclose only the formlessness, the consuming void, underlying the flickering thrills of contemporary western simulations. (Botting 2002, 298)

Jerrold Hogle (2001) observes similar phenomena to Botting in his discussion of the Gothic as essentially counterfeit. The Gothic has been based on counterfeiting ever since its rise in the eighteenth century because that rise was a revival of what was perceived to be an earlier Gothic style in medieval times (293). The continuation of the Gothic then becomes pastiche upon pastiche, a construction of so many layers that, in the end, the 'authentic' fake of Gothic can no longer be discerned. By the time we arrive at what Hogle calls the neo-Gothic:

> The counterfeit, or more precisely the Renaissance counterfeit of the medieval, has now become the evacuated 'signified' of the Gothic signifier, which is thus the ghost of the counterfeit. The neo-gothic is therefore haunted by the ghost of that already spectral past and hence by its refaking of what is already fake and already an emblem of the nearly empty and dead. (298)

Hogle goes on to add:

> as the counterfeit becomes its ghost in western thinking, it is already moving, in the Gothic and elsewhere, towards the early industrial view of the signifier as a *simulacrum*, as a symbol repetitiously manufactured from a pattern or mould (which is itself a ghost of the counterfeit. (299)

Though Hogle is less apocalyptic than Botting, nonetheless, he, too, sees the contemporary Gothic as collapsing into nothing but simulacra. Eventually, the Gothic and its ghosting of the counterfeit will 'dissolve itself into sheer *simulation*, the (un)grounding of western discourse in a hyperreality of signs referring to other signs that cannot root itself even in quasi-industrial moulds' (300).

As we can see, in the views of these scholars, the contemporary Gothic is always at risk of moving irrevocably from depth to surface (though, in Botting's view, this is not so much risk as certainty). Yet this is hardly a new fear: Monleón observes that, at the beginning of the twentieth century, 'Unreason was present everywhere; emptiness had no form, but was capable of assuming them all; meaning seemed to be inapprehensible . . . how could otherness be distinguished from the self? (1992, 99: ellipsis in original). Baldick and Mighall, happily taking potshots at shibboleths of Gothic academe, argue that 'it is likely that an awareness of bourgeois complacency is precisely the irritant that impels the modernist intelligent-sia to *wish* paralysing dread upon the bourgeoisie [. . .] The figure of the terrified bourgeois in Gothic Criticism is a fantasy projected by vengeful frustration' (Baldick and Mighall 2001, 226).

Glennis Byron, on the other hand, suggests that the globalised circula-tion of the Gothic can be considered in positive ways:

> Gothic has energetically participated in the cultural flows and deterritorializations that characterize globalization, and if one of the most striking features of Western Gothic has always been its propensity to prey upon itself, to delight in consuming and recycling certain persistent motifs, then the transnational flows that characterize globalization have functioned both to reinvigorate and intensify this tendency by opening up multiple new fields of play: the literature and film of different countries are feeding off each other to produce new forms of Gothic that reveal the increasing cross-cultural dynamics of the globalized world. (Byron 2012, 373)

What does this shared sense of despair at the vapidity of the Gothic mean for a culture that is still coming to terms with a Gothic culture at all? I am not so readily inclined to assume that the Gothic has become meaningless and toothless simply because it is widely circulated. On the contrary, I would argue that what we are seeing is the Gothicisation of globalised circulation, so that the latter is what is rendered uncanny. As Byron observes:

> the contemporary emergence of these [gothic] motifs is provoked by new kinds of disturbances to identities and borders, and these motifs are familiar and yet unfa-miliar, simultaneously global and local. Increasingly detached from any specific historical, social, or cultural 'origins', Gothic as it travels nevertheless inevitably incorporates, and necessitates attention to, different historical, social and cultural specificities at the same time as it produces figures of collective fears and traces the outlines of a growing global darkness. (Byron 2012, 376)

Byron argues here that the Gothic is increasingly globalised while nonetheless retaining elements of local specificity, though I would add that such specificity is itself compromised by its incorporation into a global flow. That compromise is in itself one of the fears of a global Gothic. Her reference, however, to 'a growing global darkness' implies not simply that Gothic tropes and figures are recognised worldwide but that globalisation itself *is* Gothic. As we shall see in Chapter 3, Byron herself is not immune to some of the fears posited by Warwick, Botting and Hogle, as she reacts in horror to a vision of Victorian London apparently imposed on present-day Barcelona. Byron's point here, however, is that the fear which is an integral part of a Gothic mode has not vanished in the face of a globalised postmodernism but rather that such postmodernism carries with it precisely those globalised fears of which Byron speaks.

Contemporary Gothic may not simply be demonstrating vapid pleasures but dealing with sociopolitical conflicts and contradictions much as eighteenth-century Gothic did. Hogle observes, in a later piece:

> the creative Gothic as pre-postmodern (*Frankenstein*, for example) and post-modern (in *Lot 49* and much more) uses the uprooted and circulating signs that enable capitalist globalization – frequently the ghosts of earlier specters – to give form to the fears and irresolvable conflicts now underlying that very globalization [. . .] (Hogle 2014, 10)

The very circulation of the Gothic, far from instilling passivity in its observers, might just as easily render international and transnational circulation uncanny. Yet the ability to derive readings of national, social and political traumas may still derive from forces such as national identities and cultures though those forces themselves are rendered uncanny through our ability only to half recognise a national identity such as Spanishness without really being able to define exactly what it consists of. Readings of Gothic texts in terms of national traumas occur in the Spanish case as elsewhere, as Chapters 3 and 4 show in relation to the Spanish Civil War (to the extent that other traumas become invisible), and Chapter 2 in the case of Francisco de Goya's portrayal of the Spanish society through which he moved. Of course, simply reading a Gothic text in terms of national identity carries its own dangers, as we shall see in the texts discussed here that have some narrative connection to the Civil War and Franco's dictatorship. If we accept Hogle's definition of the Gothic as fakery and pastiche, then it is not the best vehicle to metaphorise a real trauma. The Gothic as a tool to represent national trauma is an unreliable one, given that its role is also to thrill and entertain. Such entertainment is not necessarily the vapid circulation dismissed by Botting: Gothic was ever thus, right from Walpole's *The Castle of Otranto*.

Part of the critical fear of the state of contemporary Gothic seems to arise from Gothic's commercialisation. Baldick and Mighall claim that 'the true bourgeois can afford to regard his "Others" not with terror but with equanimity or even delight, because, from opium fiends in China to wielders of "Pink Dollars" in California, they represent what he loves best – a new market' (Baldick and Mighall 2001, 226). Byron explicitly links the globalisation of the Gothic with commerce:

> Certainly, what is identified as Gothic today is something increasingly detached from any specific historical, social, and cultural 'origins', and many of the changes we see in contemporary Gothic, including the proliferation of national and regional forms and the production of Gothic as a lucrative global business, would appear to have much to do with the social, cultural, and economic impacts of globalization. Contemporary Gothic both registers and is impacted upon by the new world order in which people and products move with increasing ease and speed across national boundaries. (Byron 2012, 371)

Justin D. Edwards and Agnieszka Soltysik Monnet argue for commercialisation as the ghost that haunts the Gothic:

> If [. . .] the waves of Goth/ic from the 1980s and 1990s disseminated a discourse of anti-commercialism which is also being driven by commodification and market-oriented consumption, then Pop Goth is the return of that which has been repressed: it is a high-profile manifestation of the Goth/ic participation in the market and the recognition that Goth/ic cannot deny its ties to commodification and consumption. (Edwards and Monnet 2013, 3–4)

Or, as Catherine Spooner puts it: 'there is perhaps something inherently Gothic in the replication required by mass-marketing' (Spooner 2006, 29).

The notion of commercial imperatives is not new to Spain: as Aguilar observes, for example, Spanish horror of the 1960s respected censorship at home but competed with other European cinemas, and offered Spanish films at cheap prices (Aguilar 1999, 24). Yet it is a question that is particularly relevant for contemporary Spanish Gothic. One reason for the strong Gothic showing in recent Spanish cinema is the so-called commercial turn taken by many young Spanish directors from the mid 1990s onwards, making films that drew on the Hollywood genres they liked rather than art-house and allegorical films. One of these directors was the highly successful Amenábar, discussed in Chapter 5. The split between genre and art house is, of course, not as clear-cut as this but Spanish film critics frequently disparage Gothic and horror production simply for being imitative of Hollywood and thus, by implication, both shallow and commercial, on the assumption that commercial products must always be shallow. Yet commercial imperatives do not necessarily need to be reduced to one, Hollywood, common denominator. In his discussion of *El orfanato* cited above, Smith argues that 'The "Spielbergization" of Spanish film, which *Fotogramas* still claims to recognize in *El orfanato*, is no longer an attractive strategy for multinational studios. With the North American market "stabilized", they now attempt to tailor their product to fit the tastes of still growing international audiences' (Smith 2012, 68).

The question of commercialisation inevitably has an impact on that of circulation and exchange: commercially successful products in one country are more likely to circulate to another. It nonetheless offers clear and valuable evidence that the Spanish Gothic is part of a contemporary cultural exchange that sees Spanish texts arguably participating in a wider, debatably transnational Gothic as much as, if not more than, looking to specifically national cultural concerns. It argues, in effect, that the contemporary Spanish Gothic is one mode through which Spanish culture looks outwards as well as inwards. Ramos Alquezar (2011, 50) observes that 'le fantastique espagnol semble soumis, tout au long de son histoire, à une tension entre la volonté de rendre compte d'une identité nationale et la recherche d'une "déterritorialisation"' (Spanish fantasy, throughout its history, seems to have been subject to a tension between the desire to take national identity into account and the search for a 'deterritorialisation').

The tension identified by Ramos Alquezar is also to be found in the theories of cultural circulation of Tom O'Regan and Millie Buonanno. O'Regan's discussion of cultural exchange is based on the distribution and circulation of film, and film is a central concern of this book but I believe that his concepts apply to the exchange of cultural ideas and texts more widely. He states: 'By cultural exchange we mean the circulation – the giving, receiving, and redisposition – of cultural materials among differentiated socio-cultural formations' (O'Regan 2004, 263). I am interested in all three elements of circulation, the 'giving, receiving and redisposition' of O'Regan's definition, as regards the contemporary Spanish Gothic. A similar argument comes from Millie Buonanno, writing on television drama. She argues that 'television drama, with its variety of geographical locations and social environments, human and professional types, intimate and public situations and relationships, opens the door wide to innumerable experiences of dislocation' (Buonanno 2008, 79). Television drama is subject to circulation itself: successful television series, formats and franchises are sold to other countries. Paul Julian Smith, for instance, discusses the transport of the US series *Ugly Betty* to Spain and its reformatting into a local version, though he also reminds us that *Ugly Betty* itself came to the United States from Colombia (Smith, 2012, Ch. 9). Another format is the British amateur cookery show *The Great British Bake Off* that has successfully translated to other countries (see Cook, 2012 and 'The Great British Bake Off', 2015). It is not just a question of commercial trading in television products, however, but also cultural trading in ideas. Buonanno points out, however, that local cultures do not remain passive in the face of such dislocations. She refers to 'indigenization', 'the process through which forms and expressions of external cultures, elaborated by other societies, are appropriated, re-elaborated, and restored by diverse local societies in configurations that are consistent with their own home-grown systems of meaning' (88). This is not a phenomenon unique to a globalised era, however. Buonanno also notes: 'Probably no culture exists that has survived and developed without being modified and upset by its contacts and relations with alien forms and practices' (110). Thus, culture is always transcultural, where the giving, receiving and redispositioning posited by O'Regan are integral and always have been.

Buonanno's ideas clearly overlap to a great extent with those of O'Regan, suggesting that the concept of the travelling narrative extends beyond television to other media. She also observes, however, that such redisposition does not simply entail a straightforward embedding of a narrative into a new culture. The narrative is not simply dislocated but facilitates an 'imaginary deterritorialization' (108). Such deterritorialisation has been heightened by the global circulation that often overrides the sense of linear exchange between two cultures. There is, therefore, a sense of tension between a sense of place and its loss. Buonanno ultimately seems to weigh the resolution of such tension in favour of indigenisation as a flexible way round the fixity of imperialist structures of communication (90) but she does quote Anthony Giddens to argue that 'place – permeated by distant influences – becomes like a dream or phantom' (20).[1] Place becomes spectral, something that haunts a text without being fully present.

The reference to the phantom of course invokes the Gothic here. If earlier I talked about the Gothicisation of circulation, O'Regan makes an implicitly similar point: 'Cultural exchange is double-faced. It is part and parcel of the mechanisms that establish a sense of collective identity; and, equally importantly, it is part of disestablishing the same' (280). I should like to suggest here that the tension which arises from Buonanno's model of the travelling narrative, the double face of O'Regan's cultural exchange, is a Gothic one. When Buonanno ultimately comes down on the side of indigenisation, she offers some response to the fears of Warwick, Botting and Hogle but, for me, the Gothicisation of circulation is also interesting and, with the increase in circulation, its Gothicisation comes to the fore. It is a *mise en abyme* in which the Gothic circulates and its own circulation becomes Gothic, and so on to infinity. This can be a terrifying prospect, as the theories of Warwick, Botting and Hogle suggest.

In her discussion of Gothic circulation, Byron adopts a pattern that reflects Buonanno's dichotomy of deterritorialisation and indigenisation. She remarks: 'As Gothic begins to incorporate narratives, figures, and tropes from various different countries, awareness of historical and cultural specificities becomes increasingly important, and this may have some implications for critical readings of Global Gothic' (2012, 374). Byron goes on to say, however: 'As new figures from myth and folklore become internationally appropriated, however, a kind of cultural deterritorialization often seems to take place' (Byron 2012, 374). Taken together, these concepts do much to question the pessimistic sense of the Gothic as undifferentiated flow. Buonanno's dialectic of indigenisation and deterritorialisation implies some sort of locus whereby such processes can take place. A location, a specific culture or cultures, are clearly implied. O'Regan's giving, receiving and redisposition suggest something more specific than an endless circulation: they hint at a backwards and forwards, a reciprocity, and fixed points or people, even if fixed only momentarily, whereby giving and receiving can take place. Place may be simply a phantom, as Giddens suggests, but its very haunting quality indicates how much we learn for a sense of place even as we, our cultures, are troubled by it. Place is always already a trace, there to be read into a narrative, as I have argued elsewhere (Davies 2012). A sense of place, however spectral, oddly counteracts the sense of passiveness in the face of the undifferentiated Gothic flow posited by Warwick and Botting. Botting has explicitly acknowledged that his vision of contemporary Gothic includes a passive audience, or rather, a pacified audience.

> With postmodernity, terror becomes endemic and transgression is both limitless and exhausted, ceaselessly used up in playful circulations of aesthetic games. The unpresentable is little more than a resource to be capitalized upon, a space to be filled with so many different images, hyperactivating and passifying consumers at the same time as they leave them wanting more: all readers and spectators have, perhaps, become woman in the process. This woman, however, is only the global instantiation of hypercapitalism's subjectile. There may be other modes of becoming, an awomanly space in which unrecognizable, troubling, unpredictable, monstrous forms have yet to appear. (Botting 2007, 173)

(The gendered aspects of Botting's comments posit intriguing and worrying implications which I return to in Chapter 3.) In contrast, Buonanno and O'Regan's theories indicate that cultures, and the people who participate in them, are active rather than hyperactive. The processes of indigenisation and deterritorialisation offer an opportunity for active intervention, for the giving, receiving and redisposition of which O'Regan speaks. These processes are not, of course, confined to active intervention: we cannot automatically dismiss Botting's fears as far-fetched. Nonetheless, the prospects for contemporary Gothic are more varied than Botting suggests, and my intention in this book is to look at some examples of how Spanish Gothic operates, both intrinsically and extrinsically.

The models offered by Buonanno and O'Regan are dialectics, and we cannot separate out the deterritorialisation, or the giving, from the indigenisation or receiving and redisposition. The fact that contemporary Spanish Gothic works as a dialectic is something that causes great anxiety, one that is itself Gothic. We have already seen some of these concerns arising from its deterritorialisation, as critics wonder if Spanish Gothic is becoming too international, too Americanised. We shall encounter such fears again in this book. The claim to the national proves slippery, and Hispanic criticism runs the risk of losing its foothold. Yet we must embrace this dialectic in order to understand the purport of Spanish Gothic today and move beyond a cursory dismissal. As Dani Cavallaro argues: 'the Gothic vision foregrounds the need to face up to incompleteness as a condition which may not and must not be redeemed [. . .] plenitude is only ever a broken promise, while the gap is the precondition of creativity' (Cavallaro 2002, 63).

About this Book

To discuss how these processes occur, I shall present a series of case studies that illustrate different aspects of Spanish culture as a Gothicised nexus. Chapter 2 begins with the life and art of Francisco de Goya, a Gothic classic, to examine how these have been refigured in biopics to include a heritage aspect that stresses spectacle and a museum aesthetic over narrative. In such biopics the figure of Goya himself comes to encompass the concept of the biopic artist hypothesised by Griselda Pollock as both tragically feminised and exemplary of unfettered masculine sexuality but it also incorporates the sense of Gothic as fakery hypothesised by Hogle. The contemporary biopic also renders Goya as deterritorialised, a transnational figure that renders Spain itself as a spectral trace that nonetheless haunts the twenty-first-century Goya. The biopics concerned are: *Goya en Burdeos* (Goya in Bordeaux, Carlos Saura, 1999), *Volavérunt* (Bigas Luna 1999) and *Goya's Ghosts* (Miloš Forman 2006).

Chapter 3 moves away briefly from the emphasis on film to tackle the commercial circulation of the Gothic, taking as examples two of Spain's bestselling authors, Arturo Pérez-Reverte and Carlos Ruiz Zafón.

Focusing especially on the successful and widely translated novels *El club Dumas* (The Dumas Club) and *La sombra del viento* (The Shadow of the Wind), the chapter begins by looking at books and libraries as Gothic entities, liable to trickery, betrayal and fakery (Hogle's idea of counterfeiting seen in a new way). It then proceeds to draw on the theories of Fred Botting concerning Gothic as writing of excess and the post-industrial circulation of Gothic imagery to foreground contemporary circulation of the popular Gothic as simply a continuation of the older motif of the found Gothic manuscript. The materiality of the manuscript, while unreliable, nonetheless suggests a desire for the tangible artefact that implicitly questions the fear of ephemeral circulation posited by some critics.

Chapter 3 also briefly visits the question of the Gothic as a form of historical memory. As *La sombra del viento* is set primarily during the Spanish Civil War and the era of the Franco dictatorship, many Hispanists have claimed the novel as a form of recuperation of suppressed voices from history. I briefly interrogate that assumption in Chapter 3 but tackle it more fully in Chapter 4 which takes as its subject the traditional Gothic motif of the haunted house. Far from seeing the house as a symbol of the Spanish nation, I argue that the haunted house is unlocatable, a source of pleasure as well as horror, and ultimately a highly questionable way of recuperating repressed memories, and I call for more nuanced interpretations that take into account traumas and pleasures beyond the national. I compare the film *NO-DO* (The Haunting, Elio Quiroga, 2009), a film dealing with the Catholic Church under Franco, with Jaume Balagueró's transnational *Darkness* (2002), to demonstrate that both houses follow similar patterns that work against an automatic equation of haunting with national trauma.

Like Chapter 4, Chapter 5 suggests the difficulty of establishing the Gothic as specifically Spanish but also how the Spanish Gothic can infiltrate a Hollywood aesthetic in an apparently seamless trajectory. The focus here is the Gothic work of Spain's leading director of photography, Javier Aguirresarobe, whose roots lie in the Basque Country and whose career started in the vanguard of Basque film-making in the democratic era, a movement that aimed to establish a specifically Basque cinema as opposed to Spanish. Today, however, Aguirresarobe works primarily in Hollywood and has taken with him his particular approach to lighting, one that not simply emphasises the shadows and gloom, which we would expect from a Gothic film, but one that both pinpoints the Gothic secret at the heart of the film and occludes it. The chapter traces a trajectory from the Basque film *La madre muerta* (The Dead Mother, Bajo Ulloa, 1992), through *The Others* (Alejandro Amenábar, 2001), made in English by a Spanish director, to *The Twilight Saga: New Moon* (Chris Weitz, 2009), a controversial

Hollywood blockbuster. Aguirresarobe's work goes some way to countering the loss of authority, and thus meaning, that Botting in particular perceives. Nevertheless Aguirresarobe also interrogates the centrality of the Anglo-American to the Gothic mode, suggesting an excess of meaning to the Gothic but also a challenge to the authority of the Anglo-American Gothic canon.

The final chapter traces a reverse process to that of Chapter 5, the indigenisation rather than the deterritorialisation of the Gothic. The theme of this chapter is Gothic medicine and its simultaneous recognition and attempted repression of the problematic, diseased, disruptive or dead body. The body reintroduces the concept of materiality to a Gothic mode that is regularly perceived as being in danger of collapsing into nothing more than simulacra; yet the body itself is unstable, vulnerable to the control of Gothic medicine while eventually also able to elude it. If Aguirresarobe enables a Basque/Spanish Gothic style to pervade film elsewhere, then the films discussed in this chapter hide behind myriad intertextual references, from films around the world, to smuggle in the fact that efforts to control the body occur very close to home. This occurs through the cinematic work of personnel strongly identified with Spain. Firstly, Pedro Almodóvar's *La piel que habito* (The Skin I Live In, 2011) provides an example of how Gothic medicine creates an excess of meaning through the body, in opposition to such medicine's intentions. Secondly, the chapter considers the displaced body of the actress Belén Rueda who has become strongly associated with Spanish Gothic and horror film. The focus here is on two recent Rueda roles: the wandering eyes and sight of *Los ojos de Julia* (Julia's Eyes, Guillem Morales 2010) and the wandering body of *El cuerpo* (The Body, Oriol Paulo 2012). The example of Rueda shows how the demands made on both the actor and the character she plays – demands that may be contradictory – give rise to an excess of meaning in the need for the body to be both visible and invisible. The visibility and invisibility of the body function much in the way that Spain as nexus operates throughout this book, in which its contribution to the Gothic often goes unperceived but, at other times, is plain for all to see. As is the interaction of Spanish Gothic with the Gothics of elsewhere: Spain as part of a wider Gothic culture plays a significant role but, as we shall see, perception and point of view are unsurprisingly related.

Note

1. It is unclear from Buonanno's reference to which work of Giddens she is referring.

CHAPTER 2

Heritage Gothic:
Goya Biopics

In the previous chapter, Goya was mentioned in passing as a possible purveyor of the Gothic, recognised as such by scholars. Goya's work responded very much to the political and social situation in the Spain of his time but much of his work has resonated beyond its original context and he continues to fascinate today. A new exhibition in Britain of his portraits, for instance, drew strong and adulatory press interest (see, for example, Coomer 2015, Cumming 2015, Sooke 2015). Goya also appears in popular literature. The novel *After Goya* by Haarlson Phillipps (2011: complete with facsimile of Goya's signature) constructs a thriller narrative around two rediscovered minor pieces by Goya. *Memory of Bones* by Alex Connor (2012: with frontispiece self-portrait of Goya in top hat) is another thriller that builds on the real-life mystery surrounding the removal and disappearance of the dead Goya's head from his body, a fact that, on its own, would place Goya in any Gothic pantheon. Scott Mariani's *The Lost Relic* (2011) has its hero pursue the perpetrators of a robbery that included a Goya sketch. Even Dan Brown used the artist's name to label a ship heading for the Arctic Circle in *Deception Point* (2006). In these examples, Goya retains an association with the dark side, with crime, danger and monstrosity, in other words with the Gothic. Goya also becomes a free-floating signifier, a label that can be easily and superficially attached to any story. If, in the previous chapter, I spoke of the deterritorialisation and indigenisation involved in cultural exchange, it seems that, in Goya's case, he is easily deterritorialised and incorporated into any story that wants him; and yet his art derived from the very specific context of the weakness of the Bourbon monarchy at the end of the eighteenth century, the invasion and occupation by Napoleon's forces, and the restoration of an anti-liberal Bourbon monarchy that ensured Goya's flight into exile.

This chapter considers Goya as a form of heritage that demonstrates his life and work to be a nexus for contemporary Spanish Gothic, exemplifying both inward and outward stances that celebrate Spain's probably best-known Gothic artefacts while simultaneously deterritorialising them. This process occurs through the tendencies of heritage film to offer a form of museum aesthetic that opens up a gap between the artist and his work in their context and our own heritage gaze today. It also occurs through the genre of the biopic and artist biopics in particular. To describe the films I shall be discussing as biopics is perhaps stretching a point. Only one of the films concerned [*Goya en Burdeos* (Goya in Bordeaux), Carlos Saura, 1999] purports to tell us something of the artist Goya's actual life. Another (*Volavérunt*, Bigas Luna 1999) tells of a political mystery of which Goya might have been a witness: or, at any rate, he knew some of the characters involved. A third film (*Goya's Ghosts*, Miloš Forman, 2006) is a work of fiction that nonetheless draws on historical events and on Goya as a witness to them. All three films, however, portray Goya within his historical context as a critical witness to the political and social situation that he painted: as a historical character, Goya functions well for my argument as a focus of a biopic. These films testify to Goya as horrified witness and recorder of what he saw as the ills of humanity.

In addition, all three films offer a triangular relationship among artist, art and society that, in turn, is haunted by the spectres of Goya that remain with us today: his paintings. The Goya films considered here have a further link to wider Spanish history because, in all three, Goya bears witness to the political intrigue of the Spanish court as well as to the violence or suffering of ordinary Spaniards under the sociopolitical conditions of the time. This includes, in *Goya en Burdeos* and *Goya's Ghosts*, depiction of the invasion of Madrid in 1808 by Napoleon's troops. As the biopic may also do, however, these films draw us into speculation and downright fiction. The depictions of the relationship between Goya and the Duchess of Alba offer the clearest example: both *Goya en Burdeos* and *Volavérunt* assume a sexual relationship between the two but this has never been definitely proved, while the death of the duchess from poison is also speculation. Much of *Goya's Ghosts* is a fictional narrative that spins from the (real) portrait of Francisca Sabasa y García although real-life characters, such as the Spanish king and queen as well as Goya himself, are incorporated. The speculative nature of these biopics coincide with the pastiche and simulation of the heritage film.

Most Gothic texts are by definition heritage texts in that a common characteristic of them is the infiltration of the present by the past as encapsulated in the very term 'Gothic'. Catherine Spooner is one of many critics who would argue 'Gothic as a genre is profoundly concerned with the past, conveyed through both historical settings and narrative interruptions of the past into the present' (Spooner 2006, 9). Yet, as we saw in the previous chapter, the invocation of a Gothic past is also fake, as Hogle argues (Hogle 2001). Heritage cinema itself, however, provides a pastiche of the past. This confluence of two different kinds of fakery can be found with recent biopics that look back at the life of Goya, himself thought of as a precursor to the somewhat neglected Spanish Gothic. Spanish cinema does not have a strong reputation worldwide for heritage cinema. Indeed, as Paul Julian Smith points out, there is not even a precise term in Spanish for heritage cinema: *cine histórico* comes the closest but this simply refers to films that are set in the past. Smith argues that tradition and heritage, reception, and questions of possession and alienation do not come into the discussion of such films even though they are as pertinent for Spain as for Britain, the country perhaps best known for heritage cinema (Smith 2006, 102). Smith suggests that this arises from a double bind of a preference for the present and contemporary on the part of Spanish film scholars and critics, and because the Spanish Civil War and Francoism hang heavy over notions of recuperating history (103). It may also arise, in my view, from a preference for auteurist social realism that has been very pronounced within film scholarship and criticism until the last decade or so. There is a particular irony here in that Carlos Saura, an auteur noted previously for such social-realist films as *Los golfos* (The Delinquents, 1960), and *Deprisa deprisa* (Hurry, Hurry, 1981) as well as elliptical films such as *Cría cuervos* (Raise Ravens, 1975), has directed one of the heritage films I discuss here. Yet visiting heritage attractions is as popular in Spain as it is in Britain (102), and heritage films exist that have met with box-office success: Smith cites Vicente Aranda's *Juana la Loca* (Juana the Mad, 2001) as an example (106). We could also quote the surprise success of Pilar Miró's 1996 literary adaptation of Lope de Vega's *El perro del hortelano* (The Dog in the Manger) wherein a strong part of the pleasure of watching lies in the rich visuals of colourful costume and bucolic pastoral scenery. Arguably, recent films addressing the Spanish Civil War and its aftermath also indulge in heritage values to a degree, offering up costumes and music from the 1930s and 1940s, though success here has been mixed.

Heritage is reinforced by costume and *mise en scène*, conforming to Vincendeau's 'museum aesthetic' (Vincendeau 2001, xviii). Vincendeau further argues that 'the concern of heritage cinema is to depict the past, but by celebrating rather than investigating it' (2001, xviii). This coincides with the views of Belén Vidal who argues that much heritage cinema is concerned to reassure rather than to mourn:

> The emphasis on sedate pictorialism (*la belle image*) and individual stories, often set against the backdrop of turbulent times, gets associated with reactionary attempts to conjure up reassuring images of national identity in the face of seismic changes. (Vidal 2012, 56)

To some extent, Goya fits this template, yet his art, an example of the very pictorialism Vidal discusses, problematises this hypothesis because of the Gothic nature of much of his work. The nature of this work is hardly reassuring, drawing as it does on Gothic motifs of monstrosity, violence and torture, ghosts and shadows. Yet Goya is part of the museum aesthetic that Vincendeau posits because, today, museums are the repository for much of his work and, as I will go on to claim, Goya's recent biopics incorporate the museum aesthetic as part of their look and style. The museum aesthetic of Goya in these films is thus not far from Jerrold Hogle's contention that modern Gothic has, from the very beginning, been based on the idea of the fake (with the Gothic revival in architecture, such as Walpole's Strawberry Hill; Hogle 2001, 293). Hogle argues that, in the nineteenth century – and, I would argue, the two centuries that follow:

> the Gothic refaking of fakery becomes a major repository of the newest contradictions and anxieties in western life that most need to be abjected by those who face them so that middle-class westerners can keep constructing a distinct sense of identity. (Hogle 2001, 297)

Gothic fears are both conjured up and displaced to the past in a way that celebrates them (as the fine art of Goya) and petrifies them, confined to the museum and now to the heritage film. They become another element of the pastiche of heritage film. His images thus become detached from their 'real' moorings and hard historical truth so that, despite the insistence on rationality, his art can be, and in these films is, used both for the pastiche of the heritage biopic but also for the fakery of the Gothic.

Goya himself becomes a pivotal figure in this regard. Vidal quotes Thomas Elsaesser to argue that the 'biopic addresses an imaginary consensus through the focus on the exceptional individual "who is both within and outside given ideological discourses, who belongs to his age and in some sense transcends it"' (Vidal 2012, 111). Alternatively, Griselda Pollock posits:

> The artist, like the writer or musician, functions as the embodiment of an idea of creativity that renders the life significant. By making a narrative picture of this life, a biopic, the film promises to reveal to us the magical nature of genius. There is a long history of treating the artist or poet as a figure apart – melancholy, suicidal, mad, asocial. But in modern times – perhaps as a result of the increasing remoteness of artistic practice from the public in general – the artist has become paradigmatic of the pathology of creativity. Represented as a hysterical figure of difference and marginality, or tragically feminized (western society's sacrificial victim, a Christ figure), the artist can also embody a creativity born of masculine sexuality unfettered by the restraints of bourgeois ideology (Picasso) and become a heroic figure of resistance to social order like the unassimilable cowboy or wild man. (Pollock 2001, 34)

Or, we could say that the artist functions as the Gothic shadow of the society in which he (and it is usually he) lives. Goya becomes Pollock's 'heroic figure of resistance to social order' cited above, drawing attention to the society he lives in precisely as Gothic. Yet Goya himself proves to be an ambiguous figure: his Gothic and grotesque imagery functions partly to record the excesses and abuses of his age, partly to protest against them, but perhaps also to exorcise the fact that his life and work depend on the society he caricatures. Marina Warner comments: 'Goya's own position remains enigmatic, in spite of the furious, impatient captions he scrawled on the drawings; and in this Goya is the forerunner of twentieth-century instabilities about the sovereignty of reason'. And she goes on to observe:

> When Goya drew the *coco* and the terrifying booby, possibly observed from his own everyday world, he disclosed something of his future method, which would dissolve the distinction between observed material and dream work, and would stage the reality of nightmares, and of other, allegorical and mythic ogres and giants – the Colossus of war and the infanticidal Saturn. (Warner 2000, 40)

In Goya, rationality is not a neatly bounded entity but porous, nowhere more so perhaps than in his famous etching 'El sueño de la razón produce monstruos' (normally translated as The Sleep of Reason Produces Monsters) in his series of etchings, *Caprichos*. The Spanish word *sueño* is normally translated as 'sleep', suggesting that reason must be ever awake and vigilant to prevent the rise of the monstrous. But *sueño* also means 'dream', which offers up a very different interpretation, suggesting that monstrosity is the natural consequence of the dreams of rational people. Monleón, for one, notes the ambiguity of the word *sueño* and argues that Goya's picture 'suggests that there is indeed some continuity between the realism of reason and unreason, the latter being, in fact, a creation or product of the former' (Monleón 1990, 41). This deliberate strategy of ambiguity chimes with Warner's dissolution between the real and the dream, and also with Pollock's pathology of creativity. Goya comes to stand for a dark side of art in which his masculine creativity (often tied to sex, as we shall see) undercuts the feminine passivity and servility of his position in society. Goya himself becomes darkly ambiguous, wielding his own Gothic power. Yet this power, too, will be placed at a distance as the biopic Goyas of the three films here indulge us with their own museum aesthetic. The focus on Goya's life and art allows an indulgence in the Gothic that is nonetheless paradoxically detached.

To look at this process in more detail, let us first establish how our three films work to foreground the artist's life as Gothic.

The Artist as Ghost in *Goya en Burdeos*

Drawing on the work of Michael Meneghetti, Belén Vidal observes that 'Biography has been called the necrophiliac art, a "haunted" form of writing, imparting a textual afterlife to the dead': in film this is mitigated through dependence on the actual actor playing the role. Vidal interestingly draws on the idea of a medium for the role of the actor:

> on the one hand, the actor *is* the medium insofar as his/her body [. . .] connects the historical figure with the audience, making the spectator experience history vicariously. On the other, 'medium' suggests a practice with an altogether more troubling outcome – a form of communication with the dead, the *frisson* of bringing the dead back to life in an illusion that we know to be always temporary. The biopic is [. . .] a deeply uncanny form, a form of thanatography or *death* writing [. . .] as opposed to life writing. (Vidal 2014, 15)

This suggests that biography – and, by extension, the biopic – is a matter of ghosts.

The Goya of Saura's *Goya en Burdeos* is very much bound up with the close connections between death, memory and haunting. Santiago García Ochoa argues that, in Saura's filmography, 'El personaje-creador funciona siempre como un espejo que refleja al propio Saura' (The creative character always acts as a mirror that reflects Saura himself: García Ochoa 2005, 154). Thus, Saura himself becomes a ghost, a mirage. The film's dedication to his brother, the artist Antonio Saura, is also significant as Antonio died in 1998, a year before the film was released. Of the three films which feature in this chapter, this is the only one in which Goya actually dies (and in which he is born: immediately after his deathbed scene Saura cuts to another scene in which a child is being born. As the scene fades to white, Saura offers us a quotation from André Malraux, that modern art begins after Goya. Is it Goya being born, or modern art, or both? Saura does not tell us.) The film as a whole involves a series of flashbacks, the memories of the elderly and ailing painter, to Goya's burgeoning artistic career and relationship with his patron, the Duchess of Alba (Maribel Verdú). These flashback scenes are interspersed with scenes of the life of the older Goya now in exile in Bordeaux, with an emphasis on his relationship with his daughter Rosario (Dafné Fernández). The film is told from the point of view of the old and ailing Goya (Francisco Rabal): it is the people of his youth who haunt him, including his younger self (played by José Coronado) with whom he occasionally enters into dialogue. The people of his memories are his ghosts.

The elder Goya is frequently lit in white tones that match his white

Figure 2.1 José Coronado as the young Goya of *Goya en Burdeos*.

nightshirt in which he is often dressed, the recurrent motif of whiteness suggesting his own ghost-like nature as he hovers on the brink of death. As he walks through the passages of his home, the walls become transparent to follow him: when he does this in his white nightshirt (as in his first sequence, in particular) he again appears spectral. The stumbling Goya of old age is the one who will carry out his seminal Gothic work on the Black Paintings but he is also a far cry from the fairly sharp operator that is the young Goya, though the white-painted face of the latter when he appears on screen for the first time, offers a colour bridge to the ghostliness of the former. The white paint is a fashion statement for the society he is moving in, hinting strongly at its Gothic decadence. In another scene, the two Goyas, both in white, appear as ghosts to each other and to us as they appear to walk through blue backlit copies of the etchings from the *Caprichos*, commenting on them (and wondering what happened to the Duchess of Alba, his/their former muse). As the older Goya walks out of shot, the younger one stands behind the etching of 'The Sleep of Reason' and comments: 'La fantasía abandonada de la razón produce monstruos imposibles: unida a ella es madre de las artes y origen de las maravillas'. This means literally that reason's abandoned fantasy produces impossible monsters: but, united to reason, it is mother to the arts and the sources of wonders. The first of these two phrases repeats the ambiguity of the word 'sueño': has fantasy left all reason behind or is it the product of reason? A similar phrase is uttered in a new scene shortly afterwards by the older Goya as he tries to comprehend his daughter playing the piano (which he cannot hear): 'La fantasía unida a la razón es madre de las artes y origen de las maravillas' (Fantasy, allied to reason, is the mother of the arts and the source of wonders). The blurring of fantasy and reason immediately reminds us of Goya's deliberate Gothic strategy as discussed above. These ghostly copies of the *Caprichos*, however, a motif repeated elsewhere with some of Goya's other paintings, tap into a museum aesthetic by presenting them as relics, museum artefacts, ghosts in their own right as revenants from the past. In a later scene, the younger Goya appears to the older one in his bedroom and they talk about their artistic influences: in this case, the young Goya haunts the old one. The paintings themselves also celebrate ghosts, as in the painting of St Anthony performing a miracle to clear his own father of murder. The tomb of the victim is opened and the victim speaks from the grave to identify the murderer. Shadowy figures appear behind the young Goya as he recounts the story despite his voice-over stating that he wanted to reduce the superstition of the scene by combining it with elements of Madrid life. When we cut to such scenes, we discover Goya looking at the duchess, who appears very alive but is herself a ghost from the past, a ghost captured in Goya's paintings so that, for him (and for us), her ghost is never laid to rest.

The duchess often appears as a ghost haunting the elder Goya's memories, often lit in a cold blue. The old Goya's memory of the duchess as portrayed to us is a menacing one that points towards death, in contrast to the interaction of the younger Goya with the living duchess who is haughty but lively, flirting with Goya and eventually taking up a sexual relationship with him. The duchess as memory, however, is nearly always dark, heralded by threatening music, especially in the scene where the young Goya is critically ill and hallucinates that he sees her. Yet Goya is fascinated by the ghost of the duchess, following her down the corridors of his home. The duchess as ghost also suggests alienation, as when old Goya drifts in his nightshirt in a Bordeaux street, lost and confused, and thinks he sees the duchess walking past him. The reverie with accompanying music is abruptly cut short when he bumps into some French people who ask him if he needs help: because he does not understand their French, they dismiss him as mad. His memory isolates him from others, as do his Spanish language and experience, and the ghost comes to represent all this. Even the younger Goya, however, has a deathly hallucination of the duchess while he is very ill: she appears to emerge from a portrait and overwhelm him with her shadow while he looks at her in helpless horror. (This must be a ghost of the future as, at this point, the real duchess must still be alive but it also remains a ghost of the past because the young Goya is remembering his past just as the old Goya does). On this occasion, Goya recovers, though his illness renders him deaf, but the same motif, of the duchess covering the older Goya with her shadow as he lies in bed, will signal his death. Both Goyas comment on these events in voice-over, the older saying that he turned bitter and isolated, the younger saying that he began the series of etchings known as the *Caprichos* which we might consider the first clear entry of Goya into the Gothic.

At a later point, as the older Goya reviews his Black Paintings and the figures from the paintings come to life and surround him, there is a cut to a close-up of the duchess, lit in blue, who backs away from the camera through the room with paintings. As people begin to enter the room, she exits, backwards, and a white sheet descends, again shot with blue light, threatening to smother everyone beneath. From here we move to a scene where the younger Goya sketches a naked duchess. A warm gold light pervades the room but, by the end, as Goya and she start to make love, what is noticeable in terms of colour is the blue sofa she lies on and the blue wallpaper in the background. Soon after, the scene fades to the older Goya drawing her from memory and reminiscing about her, including her death. Goya blames the queen and then, ghost-like, his images of her appear on the wall behind him. The blue tones and the portrait of the queen, dominating the room and dressed in black, offer a Gothic association of these now dead women with colours of coldness and death.

The toing and froing between the timelines of the older and younger Goya confuse the rigid division that linear time gives between life and death, reflecting the way in which Goya's memory moves back and forth, creating his own timeline. Thus we witness the death throes of the duchess, only to see her alive again at a garden party a few sequences later. Even then, there are hints that point backwards to her mortality, such as the white dress and red sash that feature in one of Goya's portraits, the birds flying away in anticipation of winter, and the autumnal air of the scene. Santiago García Ochoa comments on the mobile timeline of Goya's story: 'Su secuenciación transmite una imagen bipolar de Goya, que oscila constantemente entre las luces y las sombras' (Its running order conveys a bipolar image of Goya who continually oscillates between light and shadow: García Ochoa 2005, 147). He also interprets the spiral Goya draws on a window as encapsulating the film's structure, the manifold – many folded – foldings of time and space in which Goya is lost, like a labyrinth, and which ends not with his death but with his birth, the final sequence of the film (150). But the collapse of linear time into a labyrinth suggests that we always run the risk of encountering ghosts as Goya does, so his obsession with the spiral implies a similar obsession with haunting.

The aesthetic of the film contributes to a Gothic sensibility from the opening credits which stress shadows and red tones that, in turn, allow objects to stand in sharp relief, such as the cow's carcass, the bowls of blood and the severed head. As the credits proceed, the carcass is dragged along the ground and then hung in the air without any apparent human intervention, nets draped in the background like cobwebs. And, as the credits end and the accompanying music comes to a climax, the camera zooms in on the interior of the carcass which dissolves and morphs in a waxy manner into the face of the elder Goya bathed in white light. Cinematographer Vittorio Storaro, renowned for his use of colour, insists on the symbolic use of red, blue, white and yellow. He adds strong contrasts, too: the white of the dead birds in Goya's kitchen is punctuated by the red mark on their breasts where they were shot, and they drip blood into a bowl. The vivid colours of the cinematography contribute to a heritage aesthetic in its deliberate stylisation, echoed in the set pieces in which Goya's paintings appear to come to life, from the garden frolics of young women to the animation of Goya's etchings *Los desastres de la guerra* or the disasters of war. Storaro's cinematography underscores the painterly nature of the film, echoing Andrew Higson's comments on heritage cinematography: 'the camera style is pictorialist, with all the connotations the term brings of art-photography, aesthetic refinement, and set-piece images' (Higson 2003, 39).

Goya both is and is not part of this heritage. In one sense, he is not part of it precisely because he records what others do, he is the horrified witness. But, on another level, he is also culpable because he creates the Gothic disorder as much as he records it. The older Goya tells Rosario:

> Con la imaginación, puedes cometer los mayores crímenes, que nadie te pedirá cuenta por ellos. Puedes subir al cielo, bajar a los infiernos, ser grande, infinitamente pequeño, ser un artista genial, el mejor de los estrategas, el más grande y poderoso de los políticos. Solo hay un peligro, niña. Tienes que detenerte a tiempo para no ser devorado por la oscuridad y la locura.
> (You can commit the greatest of crimes in your imagination, as no one will call you to account for them. You can rise to heaven, go down to hell, be very big or infinitely small, be a brilliant artist, a supreme strategist, the greatest and most powerful of politicians. There is just one danger, my dear. You have to be able to stop yourself before you are swallowed up by darkness and madness.)

This scene cross-cuts with the one in which Goya (still the older Goya) is painting the Black Paintings, with thunder and lightning and the hat crowned with candles to see by. The younger Rosarito (Ainhoa Suárez) has woken from a bad dream of being chased by a large dog, which she links to the picture of the dog in the Paintings on the walls: a connection, then, between nightmare and painting. As he leads her back to bed, Goya tells her that the greatest monster of all is Man who outdoes all other animals in ferocity. Animals act from instinct and are thus innocent but this is not true of humans. As he continues to paint, his head suddenly begins to hurt: he collapses to the table rather in the pose of the Sleep of Reason. The paintings seem to come to life as he looks at them: blood actively flows from the mouth of Saturn devouring his son, and the ghastly pilgrims from the Black Painting of the San Isidro pilgrimage cluster round him.

In this way, Goya becomes an example of Pollock's pathology of creativity, here feminised, helpless in the face of his own creations, and in great pain; and, apparently at least, far removed from Vidal's suggestion that heritage cinema ultimately aims to reassure. He also, however, reflects masculine creativity in his speech to Rosario: he himself is the one who has 'committed crimes' in his own imagination. Yet the stylised way in which the picture comes to life and the figures become animated (played by the theatre troupe La Fura dels Baus), make this scene more about spectacle than narration. This occurs similarly in the animations of the *Desastres* and the execution scene of *El 3 de mayo de 1808* (The Third of May 1808): they emphasise the Gothic nature of Goya's work but simultaneously distance us from the horrors he depicted by the spectacle. As with Saura and Storaro's aesthetic, the animations fit Higson's definition, as set pieces concerned as much with recreating Goya's art as with the spirit that lies behind it. Saura's old Goya himself becomes part of the set-piece approach, as he rests his head on his arms in the face of the animated figures from his black pilgrimage, in the manner of *El sueño de la razón*. The power of the pathology of creativity is compromised by the deadening and distancing hand of heritage.

The Gothic Double in *Volavérunt*

Bigas Luna's *Volavérunt* does not examine Goya's career as a whole but focuses on one element of it, his involvement with the Duchess of Alba and with political intrigue at the Spanish court. The title refers to one of the etchings in Goya's *Caprichos*, and depicts a beautiful woman appearing to fly over the heads of three decrepit figures: a butterfly or moth is attached to her head. The young woman closely resembles paintings and sketches Goya made of the duchess, and so some commentators have assumed that the woman in the etching must be the duchess, though there is no direct evidence for this. Indeed, the costume and stance of the female figure can also be linked to Goya's depiction of prostitutes ('Goya en el Prado: Volaverunt'). The word 'Volaverunt' has more than one meaning, including the phrase 'They flew'. This interpretation links the picture to witchcraft: the three figures below are thus witches, perhaps teaching a neophyte their trademark skill of flight. It is an interpretation which fits

Figure 2.2 Francisco de Goya, *Volavérunt.*

with other etchings in the series that suggest an uncomfortable complicity between young women and old crones.

The original picture thus suggests a Gothic juxtaposition of beauty with ugliness and with witchcraft that is typical of Goya's work. It is striking, then, that Bigas Luna has reinterpreted the notion of Volaverunt to refer to the Duchess of Alba's pubic hair. The duchess herself (Aitana Sánchez-Gijón) takes the term from Goya's picture and applies it in this way; and Bigas Luna foregrounds the importance of this idea through his title sequence in which the pubic area of the model in *La maja desnuda* (The Naked Maja) features prominently, eventually framed by the second V of the title. Wheeler (2014, 216), cites *Volavérunt* as an example of 'an ongoing fixation with eroticism' in Spanish heritage film; and Bigas Luna's filmography more generally has a strong element of bawdiness. In terms of the Gothic, however, this image of the pubic triangle in the credits sequence is noteworthy for the way in which it morphs into a matching shape of a glass, the glass that has contained the poison that kills the duchess. Indeed, we can hear the gasping sounds of a woman which will turn out to be the duchess's death throes though, at this point, it could equally be cries of sexual pleasure, a more obvious conclusion here given the preceding images. Bigas Luna clearly means this credit sequence to disorientate us (this, at least, seems to be the only reason why he might deliberately have included the sound of a telephone at the beginning of the opening credits) but, from the very beginning, he associates sex both with unnatural death and with the more Gothic side of Goya's art. The equation is repeated at the end with the same image of the pubic triangle and an accompanying voice-over that remarks that Goya is now considered as one of the best painters in the history of the world.

Goya's work and viewpoint therefore comprise a crucial element in the Gothicisation of this tale of political and sexual intrigue. Goya himself (Jorge Perugorría) is portrayed primarily as a passive bystander, a witness to events. His own significance comes in retrospect through his art which makes him a central figure for us now, though not for the main political players at the time. The emphasis on him as witness draws on his sub-sequent status as artist recording his perceptions of Spanish society: his facial expression of distaste at the indulgence in sex and drugs at the duchess's dinner party suggests him as a critical observer. He refuses the duchess's offer of 'polvillo de los Andes' (Andean powder, or cocaine): she takes some herself, however, and says that she would like to fly. This reference back to the etching separates Goya from what he observes as he records the desire to fly but has no desire to do so himself. Goya's role as witness is thus apparently of a piece with the real painter's image as recorder of a violent, corrupt and superstitious society headed by a deca-dent royal family and political leaders (epitomised here by the character of Godoy (Jordi Mollà), first minister of Spain and reputed lover of the queen). This quasifictional Goya, however, is implicated in events as far more than a bystander. As in *Goya en Burdeos*, he is the duchess's lover (though not often, as demonstrated by his surprise at her *petite mort* after orgasm, something with which her other lover, Godoy, is very familiar). More particularly, however, he sees himself as culpable in the duchess's death because his paints were used to poison her. He and Godoy conclude that she must have been murdered but, when Godoy asks him who could have been the murderer, Goya replies that he will not accuse anyone:

'simplemente le cuento lo que he visto', I am just telling you what I saw, a comment that underscores his role as a bystander and witness.

Goya is largely responsible for the creation of uncanny doubles in the duchess and Pepita (Penélope Cruz), another mistress of Godoy. The model for the pair of paintings *La maja vestida* (The Clothed Maja) and *La maja desnuda* has been a matter of some debate: in *Volavérunt* both the duchess and Pepita lay claim to the role. There are two parallel scenes in which Goya draws them and feels their bodies: though one result of this parallel is that women's bodies lose any individuality, becoming literally nothing but their sex (as the emphasis on the pubic triangle reminds us), the link of this parallel to Goya renders this doubling an uncanny one. The duchess and Pepita may both be Goya's models and Godoy's lovers but they are distorted parallels of each other, through class in particular. When the king (Carlos La Rosa) and queen (Stefania Sandrelli) arrive at the duchess's house, Pepita is present but hidden away in the crowd (and near her, even more obscured, is Goya in his customary role as witness). Pepita is snubbed repeatedly at the duchess's dinner party, and her elegant costume cannot but remind us of the first time we see her, dressed in peasant clothes and dancing round a fire. When it comes to dancing, however, the duchess lacks the stamina of her rival: the two dance together after dinner but the duchess collapses. Pepita appears to faint shortly afterwards but this will turn out to be a ruse. Above all, however, Pepita's role in the duchess's death is suspect, as she confesses to having stolen one of Goya's poisonous paints and added it to the duchess's wine, though she claims to have lost her nerve and poured the wine away later. It is a commonplace of doubles that one double means or does harm to the other; and, while responsibility remains opaque, it is certainly true that the duchess does not survive her encounter with Pepita.

Pepita's recourse to Goya's paints suggests the significance of control of paint and of colour. At her dinner party, the duchess addresses Goya, saying he can finish her off with his violets and greens. ('Tú tienes tus violetas y tus verdes para acabar conmigo.') She has learnt the lesson that Goya taught her earlier, that paint can kill because of the lethal substances it might contain. On the other hand, she also thanks Goya for his paintings because they will tell the world what she was like when alive, so paint becomes ambiguous in its capacity to preserve and to prolong life beyond the grave. Her comment prefigures her death but also hints at the heritage element of this film: her life and her death are of interest to us precisely because Goya painted her. Yet paint also becomes part of a power struggle over the question of who owns the paint: the duchess tries to buy the *maja* paintings because she says the body in the painting is hers. Goya never clarifies this, reflecting the uncertainty surrounding the paintings as we know them today. Bigas Luna offers scenes of both the duchess and Pepita posing in the same way as the *maja* paintings but, in fact, the model for the painting has never been confirmed. Who really owns this painting? The duchess claims ownership because she thinks she is the subject of the painting; Goya carried out the artistry but the painting is now in the possession of Godoy who refuses to sell. The duchess's attempt to buy is a failed effort to assert control over her self and her body, and her failure prefigures her death. As the artist, Goya is complicit in Godoy's power over the duchess, just as his paints are complicit in her death. This is reinforced when she asks Goya to apply paint to her face to cover up her ageing: he does indeed paint her face as if he were making up a corpse. As with *Goya en Burdeos*, this film uses colour to reflect the underlying Gothic theme, echoing the stylisation of Storaro but also underlining the link between paints/colours and dying. In the death scene, the duchess is dressed in red, and red saturates the *mise en scène*: she stumbles out of her room and clutches a table bearing red roses and red wine (the green of the poisonous paint absorbed into the wine's deadly colour, though Goya will later find its telltale residue). The dinner party immediately before her death is shot in tones of gold but the duchess is marked out in her red dress, while a few other red splashes – Godoy's waistcoat, some details of Pepita's dress, the cardinal's robe – serve to spotlight the main players in her death.

Volavérunt is thus shot through with the Gothic and, like *Goya en Burdeos*, reveals Spanish history itself to be Gothicised even if Bigas Luna, unlike Saura, confines himself to a small part of political and court intrigue. And, as with *Goya en Burdeos*, the heritage elements clearly deaden the atmosphere: the sumptuous costume, setting and props stiffen the action into a display just as Higson posited. Mercedes Águeda Villar takes the film *Volavérunt* to task for its display of the paintings *La maja vestida* and *desnuda*: she points out that they appear in frames that reproduce exactly the frames in which the pictures are currently displayed in the Prado Museum in Madrid. This is not how they would have been displayed in Goya's own time: they would have been hidden away as part of a private collection of pornographic art rather than displayed on the walls in the frames the Prado Museum is currently using (Águeda Villar 2001, 90). In a film which plays fast and loose with historical events, do we really care that Bigas Luna got it wrong about the frames? Those of us who have seen the originals, can we remember the frames they were in? Águeda Villar is an art historian concerned more with authenticity than the requirements of the heritage film: her point about the frames, however, underscores the need for settings, props and costumes to tally with our contemporary experience and imagination of the past, so that the presentation of the two pictures coincides with the idea of the museum. Authenticity is not the point but the past as a museum exhibit very much is.

Within this setting, Goya is not lost in a temporal labyrinth of his own making as Saura's old Goya was but he is clearly out of his depth in the milieu his painting talent has led him into and, as a result, is complicit with its corruption and violence. His painting and his paints give him a dark power that ultimately serves aristocratic political society. Yet they also render him susceptible once again to the deadening effect of the heritage gaze.

Goya's Ghosts: the Ghost and the Double

The duchess does not feature in *Goya's Ghosts* at all. Instead, Forman turned to Goya's portrait of Francisca Sabasa y García for his fictional story about Ines (Natalie Portman), a young woman who suffers torture at the hands of the Inquisition, and who is then raped and serially sexually abused by Father Lorenzo (Javier Bardem). Ines remains abandoned in prison until the overthrow of the royal family and the invasion by Napoleon in 1808 when she is released as part of a general amnesty. She is by now totally deranged. Her family is dead, her home is in ruins, and Lorenzo will shut her up again, this time in an asylum. By the end of the film, Ines is a spectre of the past, obsessed with her dead baby daughter by Lorenzo. (In fact, the daughter, Alicia, also played by Portman, is still alive and works as a prostitute.) At the end of the film she follows Lorenzo's dead body for burial, after he is executed (garrotted) for participating in Napoleon's regime and renouncing the Church. Goya (Stellan Skarsgård) is once again a witness to these events and, to some extent, is the primary mover of Ines's downfall as he has taken her as a muse for many of his paintings and thus brings her to Lorenzo's attention.

Ironically, given that *Goya's Ghosts* boasts the most international cast and crew of the three films discussed here, this film is the one that plays to the particularly Spanish strain of the grotesque and *esperpento*. *Goya's Ghosts* opens with Goya's sketches of violence and witchcraft, overlain with a menacing drumbeat and chords. This sequence then starts to cross-cut with shots of priests, including Lorenzo, looking at the pictures. The tone is thus set for a replay of Spain's Black Legend and the old Gothic association of Spain with superstition and religious backwardness. Chris Perriam (2011, 119) also notes the 'grotesque incongruities' of the 'opulent' dinner scene with the family of the tortured Ines, who make pleasant small talk over dinner with their daughter's torturer. These incongruities are only

Figure 2.3 Stellan Skarsgård as Goya in *Goya's Ghosts*.

heightened by the fact that the family subsequently strings up Lorenzo and torture him in their turn (in vain, as they never recover Ines, a further cruelty). There are also hints of grotesque humour or *esperpento* in the sequence in which Goya paints the queen's portrait while the king is out hunting. When the king returns and asks the queen which part of his kill she wants to eat, she requests a vulture.

Father Lorenzo is the focus of much of the grotesquerie, both as a priest of the Inquisition and as a revolutionary inspired by France: his message of severity, toeing the line and punishment never varies regardless of the side he appears to be on. His patronage casts a reflected grotesque light on Goya himself who becomes the record-keeper of Lorenzo's career of *grand guignol* throughout the film until the moment he follows Lorenzo's dead body, sketching it as it is wheeled away. Goya is horrified by Lorenzo's garrotting but he also sketches the event, producing drawings reminiscent of the real Goya's sketches of garrotted men. When, in the early sequences, one of the Inquisition members claims that Goya works for the dark powers, it is, of course, ironically true: Lorenzo has just commissioned Goya to paint his portrait. He argues that it is not Goya who should be punished but the evildoers depicted in his prints; but, in saying this, he leads to his main argument, a call for greater severity from the Inquisition, regretting that so few have been burned at the stake recently. He wants a return to the old ways and asks to be able to lead the battle against evil. Goya's deafness in this film is associated each time with Lorenzo's status: as Lorenzo is condemned in absentia for his confession to torture, and his portrait burnt, Goya hears bells ringing that hurt his ears, and again later, as Lorenzo accuses Goya of being venal enough to work for anyone who pays. The uncomfortable bind between the two characters in enhanced by the apparent contrast between the actors who play them. Much of the grotesqueness of the film derives from Bardem's performance as Lorenzo. Perriam says of Bardem that 'out-of-kilter intonation and word stress only sometimes contribute positively to the effect of alien wickedness attaching to the characterization [of Lorenzo]' (2011, 118, but sometimes is often enough). Bardem's heavily accented English contrasts with the urbane, measured tones of Skarsgård whose fair colouring also counters the black costume and heavy black eyebrows of Bardem's Lorenzo. Nonetheless, these men are yoked together by Lorenzo's patronage and Goya's record-keeping and, above all, by the shared secret of Ines. Marina Warner suggests that, with the images in his notebooks and etchings, of witches, giantesses and the like, 'Goya was mocking the credulous – the faithful, the accusers of witches, the witches themselves and the Inquisition, who conducted the trials' (Warner 2000, 39). Yet, in *Goya's Ghosts*, Goya himself becomes part of the grotesquerie he records: he may mock the credulous but he is tied to a man who gains power by exploiting that credulity. As Lorenzo's dead body disappears from view in the final scene, the last thing we see is Goya sketching: the scene then gives way to the closing credits over the Black Paintings. Finally Forman's Goya has overcome his patron and is now the master, only to become the author of some of the most Gothic pictures ever painted.

Yet, surely, the most grotesque thing in the film is the degradation of Ines and her daughter. Ines's father is a wealthy man but his granddaughter is a hardened prostitute who resists any efforts to save her. Ines becomes almost zombie-like, changed from the pretty young woman who graced Goya's portrait to a dirty, wizened and deranged obsessive, longing for the child she believes dead. Forman's Ines is a grotesque version, an uncanny double of Francisca Sabasa García, the original model. Alicia is a further example of grotesque doubling, as she looks uncannily like her mother (unsurprising as Portman plays both roles) but lacks her innocence. Yet, if these women act as doubles of each other, they also act in some way as ghosts. Alicia carries with her the haunting trace of her mother: her position as prostitute is rendered ironic and poignant precisely because of our awareness of her mother's history (a history she herself does not know). Ines herself carries the haunting imprint of Sabasa García's portrait. This haunting capacity for the women arises because of Goya's intervention, both in painting the original portrait of Ines and in consequently recognising the daughter of his muse. Goya acts as our witness to the doubling and haunting.

An early sequence links Ines to Gothic notions of ghosts and witchcraft but also to painting. Observing a portrait propped against the wall in Goya's studio, she sees that the face is painted out. She disagrees with Goya's explanation that it is a portrait of a ghost, and a discussion ensues about ghosts and witchcraft. Though Inés believes witches can be identified through a disgusting appearance and smell, Goya argues that the witch he knows is pretty and smells of jasmine, and he is painting her portrait now. Lorenzo will compliment Goya on this portrait later but, under much darker circumstances, when he and Goya are invited to dinner at the house of Ines's father who subsequently tortures and blackmails Lorenzo in exchange for her return. Thus, the portrait is imbued with a Gothic sensibility that, in turn, heightens Goya's status as a purveyor of the Gothic. The connection between the woman, the Gothic and art is replicated with Alicia. Goya recognises Alicia while sketching in the park: he spots her looking for clients. Just as Ines has returned to him from what he thought was the dead, so Alicia reminds him of the Ines he originally painted but now clearly in distorted form. Lorenzo arranges for Alicia to be sent away to an American whorehouse; British forces capture the cart in which she and the other whores are being transported and the next we see of Alicia is on a balcony with British officers, watching and laughing at her (unknown) father's execution. Forman here reproduces a painting attributed to Goya, *Majas al balcón* (Young Women on a Balcony) but the backstory he supplies for the painting renders it explicitly grotesque. In this sense, just as with *Goya en Burdeos* and *Volavérunt*, Goya's relationship with a woman – here both ghosted and doubled – is Gothicised through paint and through art.

The painting and sketching sequences once again show Goya's ambivalent position. His role as an ineffective bystander is demonstrated during the dinner-party torture of Lorenzo but also as Lorenzo later indulges in revolutionary demagoguery as he denounces the former Chief Inquisitor (Michael Lonsdale) when Goya is not only a bystander but dependent upon an interpreter to translate the words that he himself cannot hear. His one active intervention, the rescue of the deranged Ines, proves pointless as she never recovers her sanity. It is, however, Goya's painting of her that sets the whole plot in motion since Lorenzo sees the painting and desires the woman portrayed therein. When Goya paints the queen's portrait (with a wonderful cameo from Blanca Portillo as the queen), he insists she must sit for as long as he needs her while together they prevent the king (Randy Quaid) from watching Goya as he paints. As with *Volavérunt*, painting is associated with suffering. A montage of Goya etching one of his pictures of superstition, and getting it printed, includes a printing press reminiscent of the torture machinery used on Ines. Painting, then, confers a certain amount of power on the artist, even to the extent of power by association with inquisitorial instruments, a power Goya tries to use in his efforts to protect and then to rescue Ines.

Goya's Ghosts extends the emphasis on painting as something to be looked at in a museum style in similar ways to *Goya en Burdeos*. Philip French (2007) notes a touch of 'spot the painting' in his observation that: 'The portrait of Wellington (the one stolen from the National Gallery over which James Bond does a double-take when he sees it in Dr No's lair) figures in a wonderful montage behind the final credits'. In another scene, the new king, Joseph Bonaparte (Julian Wadham), looks at a collection of artworks including Velázquez's *Las meninas*, Bosch's *The Garden of Earthly Delights* and Goya's portrait of the previous royal family: the scene functions as a virtual mini-tour of Madrid's Prado Museum where all these paintings are, in fact, kept. And, when Lorenzo argues with Goya about the wisdom of reuniting Ines and Alicia, the centre of the frame is occupied by the half-finished Colossus of Goya's Black Paintings. Some critics commended the director of photography, Javier Aguirresarobe, as being 'painterly'. Perriam describes Aguirresarobe as an 'iconic' director of photography and notes that his 'efforts (and linked to them the painterly pretext of the bio-pictorial aspect of the film) lighten as well as dignify the convoluted and coagulated plot' (Perriam 2011, 119). Similarly, Roger Ebert comments: 'And the cinematography of Javier Aguirresarobe is, well, painterly; look at the compositions, the colors, and especially the shading', and adds:

> Milos Forman's 'Goya's Ghosts' is an extraordinarily beautiful film that plays almost like an excuse to generate its images. Like the Goya prints being examined by the good fathers of the Inquisition in the opening scene, the images stand on their own, resisting the pull toward narrative, yet adding up to a portrait of grotesque people debased by their society. (Ebert 2007)

Ebert's comment neatly captures the dead hand of heritage Gothic in which the grotesque becomes nothing more than a source of images from which we can be enchanted, horrified – and distant, just as in the Prado itself. (I shall say more about Aguirresarobe's work in Chapter 5.)

Goya's Ghosts received a bad press on its release, and much of the criticism contains a note of disdain for the heritage angle. Matt Zoller Seitz (2007) for the *New York Times* described it as 'an unwieldy mix of political satire and lavish period soap opera', while Kim Newman for *Empire* argued that:

> The plot has the cardboard complexity of a lesser 18th century novel, with messengers turning up every ten minutes with bad news about world events (another

guillotining, invasion or defeat) and characters scurrying around bumping into each other on lovely Spanish locations over decades. (Newman 2007)

The lovely Spanish locations hint at a heritage aesthetic that cannot quite redeem the poor plot: the Gothic was, of course, well endowed with 'lesser 18th century novels'. Academics tend to agree with Newman: Perriam cites the same quotation from Newman that I have, and speaks of the film in terms of:

> a TV drama-style over-determination of facial expression, costume, lighting, furnishings, and terms of reference which are much simplified, with a dependency on stock, if understandable, demonizations of the activities and practices of the Inquisition. (Perriam 2011, 119)

Vidal also dismisses the film as an echo of the Europudding film, with the confusion of languages (English and Spanish), clichés from Spanish history and a bad performance by Bardem (Vidal 2012, 70). Duncan Wheeler is kinder when he argues that 'the film was an attempt, however ill-conceived, to defy generic expectations by couching the visual delights associated with heritage cinema within a narrative that was far from anodyne' (Wheeler 2014, 222) but he feels that the attempt failed and the visual aesthetic did not rescue the film from flopping. Not everyone was scathing about the film (Ebert 2007, French 2007) but, for many critics, heritage proved to be a burden that the film seems unable to bear.

Heritage and the Gothic Artist

All this seems a far cry from the celebration and reassurance that Ginette Vincendeau and Belén Vidal claim for the heritage film. Yet, as the art historian Águeda Villar suggests, Spanish critics and film-makers have historically shown an ambivalent approach to Goya. On the one hand, there is a desire to separate Goya's life and art from the so-called 'romantic fantasy' of episodes such as those with the Duchess of Alba in order to emphasise Goya as eternally a great artist rather than a man living in a particular time. This is a desire to pluck Goya and his art out of history. On the other hand, there were attempts during the Franco era to rehash the rumours about Goya and the duchess, though such attempts often came to naught because of censorship difficulties (such as a ban on showing the picture *La maja desnuda* on screen: Águeda Villar 2001). In Goya's case, the sexual and Gothic aspects of his work are an essential part of his heritage: the films in this chapter play the odds by insisting on Goya as great artist, as a heritage to be celebrated, and by proffering the seamier sides of his art and life as part of that heritage. Águeda Villar's comments suggest that Goya as a heritage icon is ambiguous in Spanish culture: the desire to herald him as one of the world's greatest artists alongside a mixture of distaste, prurience and, more latterly, relish of the sexual side of his life and work, as the films by Saura and Bigas Luna attest. (Neither they nor Forman deal with Goya's wife or son as part of their stories: the most Goya's wife gets is a brief cameo in *Goya en Burdeos*.) Goya thus also belongs to a different form of heritage, one we touched on briefly at the very beginning of this chapter: Pollock's suggestion of the biopic artist as both tragically feminised and exemplary of unfettered masculine sexuality. Pollock's concept coincides with Hogle's notion of neo-Gothic as the ghost of an already spectral past, the abjection of contemporary anxieties. Yet he also becomes the ghost of the real, as biography and contextual history are themselves rendered as ultimately beyond our reach.

Julie Codell has spoken about such artists in her own work on artist biopics, her specific subjects being Caravaggio and Francis Bacon. She speaks of

> the posthumous idealizations of artists in cultural memory and their seemingly innate marginalized, dirty, immoral, and self-destructive abject selves. Biopics mask these contradictions by condemning society's conformism, treating creativity as a violent act [. . .] (160)

Goya's own complex reality and, in particular, the fact that he was a court painter, suggest that he was not himself an *enfant terrible*: his Gothic works are interspersed with a series of paintings of members of the Spanish royal family as well as sponsors, members of the aristocracy, and other eminent persons. The films do a good job of connecting the Gothic with the royal family, intermixing the paintings without much attention to chronology, or inserting royal family members into the action. For example, the queen appears in all three as a threatening presence, and portrayed as a likely poisoner of the Duchess of Alba in *Goya en Burdeos* and *Volavérunt*. Her most Gothic appearance is as a ghost in Goya's own living room, in *Goya en Burdeos*. An image of her as Goya originally painted her looms over the room as Goya talks to Rosario about the queen's dangerous power. Such motifs lend a Gothic tinge to *all* Goya's work, even to his more pastoral pictures. As someone who needed the money and favours of wealthy society, Goya is never completely separate from it, as all three films make clear: he moves in aristocratic or moneyed circles.

Yet he also observes these circles with a certain amount of alienation and distance that allow for heritage viewers themselves to remain at one remove from a total nostalgia to the past. One extra dimension that these films offer is Goya's disdainful gaze on aristocratic society. *Volavérunt* exemplifies this at the duchess's dinner party. Goya's facial expression of distaste at the indulgence in sex and drugs at the dinner party suggests him as a critical observer. He refuses the duchess's offer of cocaine: she takes some herself, however, and says that she would like to fly. This reference back to the real etching of *Volavérunt* separates Goya from what he observes: he records the duchess's desire to fly but has no desire to do so himself, and the etching in fact distances him from the notion. This mixture of disdain for and dependence on the aristocracy parallels Pollock's hysterical figure of difference and marginality, only able to express his difference through his art. His dependence means that he can observe the society he moves in only without intervening in it in any meaningful way. It is not without significance that the only time in these films in which Goya appears to act decisively is in *Goya's Ghosts*, the most fictionalised of the narratives that has only a tangential relationship at best to Goya's actual life. And even that effort to change things proves a failure, as we have seen. Nonetheless, Goya's disdain in the scene in *Volavérunt* described above implies a measure of power involved in judgement that counters the abjection of his feminised weakness. That disdain for those with power is, according to these three films, what fuels his art. Codell suggests that 'artist biopics made around 1990 radically revised the notion of abjection from a mark of denigration into a creative force' which casts new light on the artist as feminine abject (Codell 2014, 160).

The disdain does not, however, apply to sexual relations. Pollock speaks of the creativity, born of masculine sexuality at odds with society (2001, 34), as a contrast to the artist as feminised and abject. Codell suggests that: 'Melodramatic romance plots appear in male artists' biopics to underscore their abject natures: Van Gogh's abnormal sociality, or Toulouse-Lautrec's deformity' (163). To this we could perhaps add Goya's deafness. Certainly romance features in all three films. Saura and Bigas Luna play on the rumour of a sexual liaison between Goya and the duchess, with Saura, in particular, exploiting the status of the duchess as a muse that haunts the artist until the day he dies. Forman's film displaces the sexuality on to Lorenzo's abusive relationship with Ines but there is no denying Goya's own fascination with her, as suggested in his gentle flirtation while he paints her portrait. For this artist, sexuality simply draws him into the society he critiques and compromises him: he becomes part of the world of monstrosity and the grotesque that he portrays in his art. Codell observes that 'Artist biopics are melodramas, and male artists are figures of lack – without social acceptance or normative sexualities, even if heterosexual' (171), and continues, 'Only in death does the artist attain symbolization, or rather his art does. In life he is emasculated' (172). But, for all his abjection, Goya survives while his lovers do not (only in *Goya en Burdeos* do we see him die). His creativity ensures that they are remembered only through him. The women in these three films become indelibly associated with the Gothic and with death. Ines, the duchess and Pepita become ghosts or become doubles; they are the subjects of, and/or participate in, conspiracies; they are exploited by a patriarchal society; they are imprisoned, they are murdered, or they are victims. And in these films, in particular, they suffer the additional indignity of being fictionalised and of being turned into paint. Their stories are given a sexual spin – the assumption that Goya and the duchess had an affair, or Goya's obsession with the female subjects of his portraits, and, above all, Bigas Luna's fixation on the Duchess of Alba's pubic hair. They all become subordinate to his desire and to his art.

The Ghost, Fakery and Transnational Imagery

The three films under discussion recuperate interpretations of the past that are avowedly Spanish, and a past that is much safer to recuperate than the more controversial matter of the Spanish Civil War. Vicente J. Benet has noted that the War of Independence of 1808–13, and the resistance against Napoleon, have been used as a cohesive image of national unity in cinema as far back as the early Franco era (Benet 2012, 220): its comparative neutrality as a marker of national cohesion is still true today when more recent historical events continue to divide Spanish opinion. Yet the Goya films under discussion here also look beyond the national towards international viewers, as has become common for heritage films. Vidal has observed that heritage films 'fulfil the need for a type of mainstream popular film that mobilises a shared iconography recognisable across national borders while also capitalising on cultural difference as a commercial asset' (2012, 62) – and she specifically includes the artist's biopic in her observation. Vidal further argues that traumatic pasts are a vital ingredient in transnational heritage films: 'Alongside this shift towards transnational productions and forms of storytelling, an important trend in the European heritage film is the return to traumatic national pasts' (66–7). She also speaks of *Goya's Ghosts* as part of a line of 'European super-productions shot in a neutral variety of "international" English that seek to compete against the Hollywood blockbusters with literary and historical narratives enhanced by high-concept marketing', a post-national phase of heritage film that aims to compete internationally (70). *Goya en Burdeos* is not transnational to this extent, though it did gain an international release

Figure 2.4 Jorge Perugorría as Goya in *Volavérunt*.

in keeping with Saura's international art-house reputation: *Volavérunt's* release was largely confined to Europe. The character of Goya himself, however, also suggests national/transnational as a spectrum rather than as a simple either/or. Saura used two actors to play Goya, both Spanish: Francisco Rabal plays the older Goya looking back at his past career, while José Coronado plays his younger self in flashback. The oscillation between the two actors itself provides much of the Gothic atmosphere. *Volavérunt* has Cuban actor Jorge Perugorría as Goya: Perugorría has appeared in many films from Spain. The choice of an actor from Spain's last colony (which freed itself from Spanish control in 1898) offers a positioning for Goya of being semi-detached, observing Spain but not quite of it. *Goya's Ghosts* uses Stellan Skarsgård in the role of Goya, an unusual choice given the large number of Spanish nationals who acted in the film, including Javier Bardem above all. Indeed, when Bardem was contacted about the film, he thought it was in order to play the part of Goya rather than his actual role of Father Lorenzo. Bardem's Lorenzo is the figure of action while Goya watches what he does, often with horror or distaste, yet this observer of the ills of Spanish society is rendered further an outsider by the fact that he is played by a Swedish actor who is able to transfer readily to other film industries and other cultures.

With Cuban and Swedish actors playing the artist, there is an implication of an underlying and increasing detachment of the role from Spain. Forman's own international cast and crew for *Goya's Ghosts* unsurprisingly underscore this further. There is an irony in that this film, which is fictional, is the one that most strongly emphasises history, in particular the Napoleonic invasion and occupation which do not appear in *Volavérunt* and turn up belatedly in *Goya en Burdeos*. Commentators on *Goya's Ghosts* tie the Napoleonic invasion to heritage. Thus, Perriam links the heritage aspects of *Goya's Ghosts* with an intent to profit from the bicentenary of Spanish resistance to Napoleon in 1808 (Perriam 2011, 118). Vidal argues that, in *Goya's Ghosts*, 'the relationship between the painter and his mysterious model is the springboard for a story of intolerance and persecution that features the Spanish Inquisition and the Napoleonic invasion' (Vidal 2012, 71). Nonetheless, the very same film opens up Goya's history to deterritorialisation. The discussion of the Inquisition in the opening scene of *Goya's Ghosts* conveys how widespread across Spain Goya's prints are already: various Spanish cities north and south are mentioned (Toledo, Seville, Cadiz), as is Rome. One priest cries 'This is how the world sees us!' and, of course, he is right, as Goya's art has been material in the dissemination of an image of Spain as backward and superstitious. But Goya, his art and his stories also offer interpretations that have nothing to do with Spain at the turn of the eighteenth and nineteenth centuries and everything to do with local and contemporary concerns. Seitz, for instance, argues in a rather contradictory fashion:

> By recreating Inquisition brutality, 'Goya's Ghosts' aims to denounce the West's bludgeoning response to terrorism. But its rhetorical tactics are jejune; its comparison of 21st-century America and Inquisition-era Spain doesn't track; and its second half abandons satire for half-baked historical melodrama. (Seitz 2007)

If turn-of-the-century Spain does not map on to the concerns of America today, that might be because Forman was not attempting any such comparison. Forman denied the parallel with the invasion of Iraq in 2003 (see Dawson 2007) but did see the Inquisition as reminiscent of communism in Czechoslovakia (his home country) while Wheeler sees links with George Orwell's *Animal Farm* (Wheeler 2014, 222). Yet the Europudding tag that *Goya's Ghosts* carries must surely mean that we are not surprised at the ways in which the narrative can stretch to fit references some distance away. This coincides with the move within heritage film more widely towards deterritorialisation in the last couple of decades. Belén Vidal speaks of the denationalisation from the 1990s of the European heritage film. 'Since the mid-1990s the European heritage film has entered a post-national phase in which aesthetic and industrial choices are often conditioned by the input of Hollywood studios with the ultimate goal of international market penetration' (Vidal 2012, 72). The nature of contemporary heritage film thus increases the possibilities of detachment from a national context, and for very pragmatic reasons: as Vincendeau observes, 'heritage films have also made a significant impact at the international box-office, their exportability crucial to non-English speaking cinemas' (Vincendeau 2001, xxii).

In her discussion of artist biopics Pollock states: 'I want to suggest that the discourse on madness and art operates to sever art and artist from history and to render both unavailable to those without the specialised knowledge of its processes which art history claims for itself' (Pollock 1980, 65). The films do incorporate a certain amount of history, but Goya's Gothic discourse detaches his art to some degree, while the museum gaze gestures towards the specialist knowledge of art history. This is a process of deterritorialisation. Goya's particular grotesque style, and its incorporation of motifs of corruption, venality and witchcraft, are the products of the sleep (or dream) of reason: his biopics render his genius international, underlined by concluding references to his role as internationally recognised artist, the precursor of modern art. The focus on the artist as misunderstood genius is complemented by an emphasis in these films on art as product. Vidal observes that:

> when the painterly makes its entrance into a film sequence it can also provisionally suspend the spectator's engagement with the narrative. Its effect is one of (often) kitsch juxtaposition of two different regimes of viewing and two different value systems. 'Tableau' and 'portrait' shots introduce moments of stillness and contemplation into the textures of the filmic, and exploit the public image of historical figures as a commodity fetish, reassuring the audience of the authenticity of the spectacle at the cost of momentarily loosening narrative identification. (Vidal 2012, 42)

The camera films rather as Goya paints, both being part of this pictorialism, while *Goya's Ghosts* and *Volavérunt* have painting sequences that serve no other narrative purpose than to establish Goya is Goya. The camera, however, is depicting Goya himself in exactly the same way, so that the film Goya is both producer and product of the pastiche. This tendency is emphasised still further in the recurrent presentation of Goya's art as a form of gallery, most notably in *Goya en Burdeos* but present in the other two films as well. Pollock, writing of the Van Gogh biopic *Lust for Life* (Vincente Minnelli and George Cukor, 1956):

> the spectator is positioned as viewer of pictures produced by photographic representations through which Van Gogh is placed as a figure in his own landscape paintings. At the same time, these landscapes are offered as externalised, visualised images of the artist's 'inner' landscapes. (Pollock 1980, 95)

Goya is, above all, a viewer and critic of his own art, just as we are: he visits his own museum. As he tours his own galleries, he also opens up a Gothic gap between heritage cinema as pastiche and the past it is pastiching. In *Goya en Burdeos* the young and old Goyas even offer a dialogue with each other on the work they created together, like art critics. Pollock comments that: 'the notions of madness and art which produce the category "mad genius" have little to do with clinical pathology or definitions of sanity, but [. . .] concern those special and distinct modes of being which set the artist ineffably apart' (1980, 65). What Pollock emphasises here is the idea of the artist as separate from the rest of society. But, in this dialogue, the two Goyas offer us the chance to be separate, too, just as they are from the society they critique through their work. Their comments serve, in fact, to distance themselves, and us, from their own work: we all become art critics as they do.

Is Goya then an emblem of the already fake within the Gothic? Perhaps, in the sense that his works as seen in these three biopics are themselves reproductions, simulacra, that diminish the power of the Gothic. For us today, Goya's art is always already 'faked', reproduced through media, such as film, that have a more ready and immediate impact than the originals tucked away in art galleries. The particular art gallery of work offered to us in these films is a virtual one. Thus, Vidal (drawing on Fredric Jameson) suggests that style replaces 'real' history: 'These postmodern representations raise anxieties about the ways in which a new visual culture of pastiche and simulacra dominates our relationship with the past, displacing traditional forms of written culture, in particular literary culture' (Vidal 2012, 17). Goya's work in these biopics are simulacra that replace the real works of art.

These three biopics are shot through with the Gothic, not surprisingly given that Goya is a figure around which Gothic imagery coalesces. The Gothic arises not simply from a corrupt and cruel society depicted in all its monstrosity, one in which ghosts and doubles abound. It is also to be found in paint, in paintings and in the very act of painting. The biopic Goya is not quite the wild child discussed by Pollock and Codell but he clearly shares in the ambivalent position of the artist that they outline, abject through his complicity and powerlessness but simultaneously empowered through his artistic capacity to render Gothic all that he sees, demonstrating his ultimate mastery over his society, immortalised only through him. At one remove from the seat of political and social power, his Gothic vision is what we nonetheless know of the world he depicts. But, on another level, his gaze is reduced to one that we ourselves adopt, of the museum visitor surveying his work. His Gothic vision is reduced to 'a *simulacrum*, as a symbol repetitiously manufactured from a pattern or mould (which is itself a ghost of the counterfeit)' (Hogle 2001, 299). Hogle's counterfeit parallels heritage Gothic as spectacle and display so that the Gothic in Goya's art is reduced to an exhibit, distanced still further by the film form.

We do not simply have a reproduction of Goya's original work but a filmed version of a reproduction of an original work, and thus (as we saw in the previous chapter) we are 'haunted by the ghost of that already spectral past and hence by its refaking of what is already fake and already an emblem of the nearly empty and dead' (298). And, in this way, Goya's work detaches itself from its Spanish context to become a free-floating signifier.

Nonetheless Spain still exists as a trace across all three films. If Goya himself is increasingly played by foreign actors, Spanish ones infiltrate a transnational one such as *Goya's Ghosts* while *Goya en Burdeos* provided a swansong for Paco Rabal, one of Spain's greatest actors. In addition, the contribution Goya has made to a transnational Gothic stems from his own very specific context, the particular political figures and the political intrigue, the trauma of the Napoleonic invasion and occupation and the War of Independence. Spain acts as a nexus: its particular Gothic contribution is very much the territory from which Goya's images become deterritorialised, the latter term implying the land from which it is detached. Spanish history is also a ghost, and one that cannot be faked quite as easily as Hogle might think because of the concrete peculiarity of Spanish history (including its effect on Spain today). Spain itself is a ghost of this international Gothic, 'the ghost of that already spectral past', encapsulated in Saura's film in the gesture of the old Goya's spectral Spanish dance to a tune that only he and we can hear.

CHAPTER 3

The Gothic Bestseller:
The Circulation of Excess

One reason why the Gothic mode has been perennially concerned with the circulation of tales is because of the common device of the rediscovered manuscript that combines a mystery over origins, and thus authority and authenticity, with the undeniable tangibility of a document. Yet that tangibility itself may be fragile as documents crumble and perish or are lost. The fragility of the discovered manuscript is something that persists even in the two novels that are the subject of this chapter because the books which form the subject of each are subject to theft, forgery or fire. The lost-and-found nature of the discovered manuscript introduces doubt – how authentic is it? – but it also allows for tales of the past to be recirculated in new times for new generations. This motif occurred in that most seminal of Gothic novels, Walpole's *The Castle of Otranto*, and was repeated in many novels after that. This suggests the Gothic tale as a physical entity that, precisely because of its physicality, is able to endure across historical eras and thus functions as a form of cultural exchange across time as well as space. Even tales which appear to be transmitted orally need to be written down in order to be exchanged in this way. Yet these manuscripts may still prove fragile, as the decaying and partly illegible manuscript of *Melmoth the Wanderer* demonstrates.

My underlying premise of this chapter takes as its initial premise the Gothic interest in the circulation of tales in their physical form, with an emphasis on books as close cousins of the found manuscript. The Gothic interest in the book and its circulation persists today even though, or perhaps because, the equation of the book's text with its materiality is increasingly questioned with the rise of the e-book, the circulation of texts via the Internet, the efforts to preserve texts in digital form and the ability to read books on devices such as tablets and Kindles. Spooner (2014) has observed how the Gothic book is thriving in the digital age, partly through a stronger emphasis on graphics and a facilitation of interactivity on the part of the reader but also through a nostalgia for the book as physical artefact. She argues that the Gothic of the last two decades has seen a 'retreat into textuality in which books, readers and writers are routinely Gothicised' and goes on to remark:

> It cannot be a coincidence that this marks a moment in history at which the developed world's relationship with the book itself is undergoing an intense shift in the light of developing information technologies. In twenty-first-century Gothic, nostalgia for the book as object combines with fear concerning information itself [. . .] the Gothicisation of books engages with an underlying concern with the way that, in the twenty-first century, power is bound up with information. (Spooner 2014, 186)

There is a clear irony as to the Gothic book providing a form of retreat in the digital age, given that such books can disorientate and trap the reader and can themselves become bound up with issues of power. Whoever has the book, has the power. Nonetheless, Gothic publishing is booming, including in Spain. Many Spanish authors, such as Julia Navarro, Julián Sánchez and Javier Sierra, apparently inspired by the success of Dan Brown's *The Da Vinci Code*, have written contemporary thrillers in which the characters track down hidden artefacts that frequently symbolise a hybrid of Christian and occult beliefs. Others, such as Jerónimo Tristante, use models like Conan Doyle to create a mixture of Gothic atmosphere and detection, set in the past. The field even gives way at times to gentle parody, as in Matilde Asensi's *El salon de ámbar* (The Amber Room, 1999). Significant Spanish figures of real life are sometimes placed into fictional narratives as, for example, in *La Clave Gaudí* (The Gaudí Key, 2007) by Esteban Martín and Andreu Carranza, another (rather poor) Gothic thriller in the Dan Brown style. The most noted writer of Spanish Gothic today, however, is undoubtedly Carlos Ruiz Zafón whose novels have achieved international success, especially his breakthrough novel *La sombra del viento* (The Shadow of the Wind, 2001). The bestseller status of this novel ensured wide translation and distribution of the two novels that developed the story and characters of *La sombra* – *El juego del ángel* (The Angel's Game, 2008) and *El prisionero del cielo* (The Prisoner of Heaven, 2011) Ruiz Zafón's back catalogue was also reissued and translated, in particular his children's novels such as *El príncipe de la niebla* (The Prince of Mist, 1993). Ruiz Zafón's success as a Spanish author who sells well abroad is matched by only one other author, his predecessor Arturo Pérez-Reverte. Pérez-Reverte writes mysteries and historical novels, and is not primarily a Gothic author as Ruiz Zafón is. Some of his mysteries do, however, take on a Gothic atmosphere. While many Gothic writers produce work that clearly derives from anglophone models (though their derivative nature does not necessarily reduce their worth), Pérez-Reverte and Ruiz Zafón have ensured that the flow of the Gothic is not simply one way.

Perhaps the most Gothic of Pérez-Reverte's novels is *El club Dumas* (The Dumas Club, 1993; later filmed as *The Ninth Gate*, Roman Polanski, 1999). The novel has two storylines that intertwine and both are about the authentication of physical texts; one storyline features a manuscript that purports to be the original of a chapter from Dumas's *The Three Musketeers* (*Les Trois mousquetaires*, 1844) while the other features the search for an authentic copy of a book, *Las nueve puertas* (The Nine Doors), that holds the key to summoning the Devil. The central character of both plotlines is a book dealer, Lucas Corso, and all the principal supporting characters profess an interest in books. The passion for books, and in particular for books as physical entities, is shared by the plot of Ruiz Zafón's *La sombra del viento*. This book is about another book with the same title, and about the efforts of the central character to preserve it against the wishes of its author who wants to destroy it. Robert Richmond Ellis suggests *El club Dumas* as the 'obvious precursor' of *La sombra*: both are popular novels about books and reading (Ellis 2006a, 847–8). Clearly, both novels draw on the persistent Gothic fascination with physical texts and with the circulation, preservation and inheritance of older Gothic stories and, as such, they form the basis of my discussion in this chapter.

I begin by looking at books and libraries as Gothic artefacts, repositories of Gothic knowledge and purveyors of evil. I then return to Hogle's concept of fakery from the previous chapter in order to approach it in a new way: the challenge to authenticity of the lost manuscript. Following this discussion, I shall return to the question of the post-industrial circulation of Gothic imagery to foreground contemporary circulation of the popular Gothic as predominant over the haunting power of stored knowledge from the past. Within this circulation, the novels of Pérez-Reverte and Ruiz Zafón are themselves included, as well as the books that feature within the novels, thus suggesting this circulation as *mise en abyme*. This circulation will, of course, bring us back to the question of Spain as Gothic nexus.

El club Dumas

As regards *El club Dumas*, most academic writing focuses on the Dumas manuscript plotline. My own interest, however, centres primarily on the *Las nueve puertas* plotline although, given the intertwining of the two plots, the Dumas plotline cannot be totally forgotten. I find the continual preference in academic writing for the Dumas plot and the comparative neglect of *Las nueve puertas* to be intriguing, especially since the Dumas plotline is wound up before the final chapter. If the preference arises from the canonisation of Dumas as opposed to a taste for occult plots which hints uncomfortably at trashy, lowbrow writing, then the irony is obvious, given Dumas's own mass popularity.

El club Dumas is a book about books and the evil that books can do. Spooner argues that 'The arcane, cursed or dangerous book has always been a recurring feature of Gothic fiction, but in the twenty-first century it has become an increasingly dominant motif' (2014, 186). This remark certainly applies to *La sombra*, as we shall see, but, in this respect, *El club Dumas* is a clear precursor: its books and libraries (and their dangers) were in turn anticipated by Eco and Borges (Perona 2000, 372). *El club Dumas* is a quest for an authentic Gothic manuscript that turns out to be fake – a point I shall return to below – but it is equally a book about authentic Gothic readers and their obsessive relationship with Gothic books. The obsession of Pérez-Reverte's characters with the secrets held by Gothic books, the preservation of the books along with their secrets, the discovery of those secrets – this obsession is itself Gothic, and even spills over into the Dumas plotline. *The Three Musketeers* is not in itself a Gothic book but its readers certainly act in a Gothic way. Botting, in speaking of the Gothic as a writing of excess, castigates contemporary Gothic for its emptiness, as we saw in the Introduction; but a novel such as *El club Dumas* suggests an active fixation that proves far more sinister and dangerous than pleasurable passivity. Gothic books become a pursuit in both senses of the word. Both *Las nueve puertas* and the Dumas manuscript drive their owners or pursuers to obsessive or irrational behaviour, behaviour redolent of the Gothic. In the case of *Las nueve puertas*, its association with evil is readily apparent in that it holds a secret ritual to summon the Devil but its effect on the characters concerned with it suggests its power to pervert reason and sanity. There are three copies of the book (or, as Corso's investigations uncover, one book with the key to the ritual distributed among the three copies): the owners of each copy demonstrate worrying behaviour. Fargas is obsessed with his library to the point of madness while Baroness Ungern is tainted by her Nazi past. Varo Borja, who sets Corso on his mission to locate the authentic copy of the book, shares both characteristics: he murders in order to obtain the copies belong to Fargas and the baroness but his murderous tendencies stem from his monomania about the Devil.

Corso, the sympathetic protagonist, shares the obsession with books: despite his ostensibly mercenary and thus pragmatic motives, his knowledge of books arises from his passion for them. He pursues *Las nueve puertas* until the end of the novel and, as a result, is compromised by the violent acts his sponsor commits as well as by his presence at Varo Borja's ultimately botched ritual to summon the Devil. He enjoys the risk involved in his pursuit: when he accepts his commission from Varo Borja, he recognises that he is playing a dangerous game but he likes playing (Pérez-Reverte 1998, 88). If this is not enough to taint Corso's obsession, he also has the protection of the Devil masquerading as a girl calling herself Irene Adler in an explicit reference to Conan Doyle's Sherlock Holmes story, 'The Adventure of a Scandal in Bohemia'. Nonetheless, the association with the Devil shows the risk of being obsessed by books. By the end of the novel, Corso discovers he has lost his shadow (492), implying that he is now aligned with the Devil (who is waiting for him when he leaves Varo Borja's house for the last time). The narrative ends with his recognition that books cannot ultimately be trusted:

> Reía entre dientes, como un lobo cruel, cuando inclinó la cabeza para encender el último cigarillo. Los libros gastan ese tipo de bromas, se dijo. Y cada cual tiene el diablo que merece. (493)
> (He laughed through his teeth, like a cruel wolf, as he bent his head to light his last cigarette. Books play that sort of trick, he said to himself. And everyone gets the devil they deserve.)

Corso is often laughing cynically to himself (to the extent that I grew weary of this constantly repeated feature): the comparison to the wolf's teeth as a final image nevertheless suggests that he has moved beyond cynicism. There is a hint in his final attitude of malevolence. It is not a coincidence that the final chapter is called 'Un recurso de novela gótica' (A Recourse to the Gothic Novel), given that this last scene ties the central character to the Devil so firmly; and the chapter title simply confirms the Gothic thread that has run throughout the novel. For, in fact, Corso was earlier marked by the Devil with her own blood: Irene traces four lines of blood across his face (357). And, as he enters Varo Borja's house as a prelude to the final climactic scene, '[l]o cierto es que fue su imagen real la que vio por última vez en la placa de metal bruñido atornillada en la puerta' (what is certain is that he saw his own true image for the last time, in the polished name plate screwed to the door: 472): this implies that his reflection subsequently disappears, always a sign of evil. Of all the characters, Corso is the one closely aligned with the Devil (despite the aspirations of Varo Borja and the baroness) and is thus tainted. Ellis (2006b, 29–30) argues that Corso is aligned with the Devil partly because he reads, reinforcing the close link between reading and evil. It is not surprising then that Corso is the one to crack the code of the three copies of *Las nueve puertas*, through his love of books and his peripatetic approach to them, a profile that coincides with that of Irene Adler, as we shall see.

Corso's comment that books play tricks reinforces the idea posited throughout the novel that books are treacherous. Varo Borja notes of his copy of *Las nueve puertas* 'Hay algo en él que no suena como debe' (There is something in it that doesn't sound right, Pérez-Reverte 1998, 80), suggesting his copy as an uncanny version that differs from his idea of an ideal version (a version that, we subsequently discover, does not exist). The cryptic Latin abbreviations of the book, which we see at the bottom of the illustrations, add to the sense of a secret code which only initiates can read – those who know about dangerous books. The Dumas plotline echoes the idea of books as treacherous, given the uncertainty about the authorship and authenticity of the manuscript in Corso's possession. Yet their danger does not detract from the pleasure of possession. Spooner cites *El club Dumas* as one example of a 'fascination with dangerous books' in the later twentieth century (Spooner 2014, 188), and comments that 'The sinister threat of the book as artefact goes hand in hand with the pleasure of the book as object' (2014, 205). *Las nueve puertas* is a newer version of an older book, the *Delomelanicon* (Pérez-Reverte 1988, 81–4), suggesting the constant fascination with the dark arts that indeed sustains a publishing industry then and now, for our own pleasure in reading books like *El club Dumas* derives in part from a similar fascination at one remove.

And, just as books are treacherous, so are the people who possess them or pursue them. The Dumas manuscript is the key to membership of a secret Dumas society (in the film version, which omits the Dumas plotline, this secret society is dedicated to the occult and devil worship). When Corso discovers the existence of the society, he finds he has to rethink what he had thought he knew about Boris Balkan and Liana Taillefer, the central characters of the Dumas plotline: Liana, in particular, reveals herself to be not so much a sex siren (as Corso initially thinks) as someone who uses sex as a means to an end, the possession of the Dumas manuscript. Corso and the book dealer La Ponte have their own secret society based on their love of Melville's *Moby Dick*: el Club de Arponeros de Nantucket (the Harpooners' Club of Nantucket). They came to know each other through their shared interest, a mercenary interest, in books. Books bring them together and also divide them: their brotherhood dissolves with La Ponte's betrayal of Corso over the Dumas manuscript. Corso betrays and cheats as well: for instance, deceiving Varo Borja about a mythical Swiss customer for a book (Pérez-Reverte 1998, 720). Balkan describes Rochefort in *The Three Musketeers* as a symbol of dark forces, and describes the character's plot against d'Artagnan as diabolical (130). The Dumas plotline therefore reinforces the notion that books are untrustworthy and lead to danger, betrayal, evil and the dark arts.

Both plotlines also suggest secrecy, another key element of the Gothic: books and people both hold secrets. The secret society of initiates can also be found in the *Las nueve puertas* plotline, if not so prominently. Thus, Corso and Fargas toast each other as 'dos miembros de una cofradía secreta tras establecer los signos de reconocimiento' (two members of a secret society, having established the signs of recognition; 189); while Corso and the baroness trade occult references as demonstrations of their arcane and unusual learning. The Devil's mission seems to be to keep herself a secret: as with many Gothic ideas, the secret is brought to light only to be buried again. (We shall encounter this idea in more detail in Chapter 5.) Similarly, the Devil comes in an unexpected guise but the clues are there for those who know how to read them. It is not clear how far Corso can read the signs, which is ironic given his expertise in books and his study of *Las nueve puertas*, but the final line, which I quoted earlier, suggests he has at last recognised the Devil. For all the book learning of Varo Borja, he cannot summon the Devil but, instead, is cast into flame (like the baroness). Earlier in the novel, Corso notes an expression of disdain on Irene's face when he asks her if she knows Varo Borja (388). Corso's encounter with the Devil – but also his commercial knowledge – alerts him to the trickery of the book and what exactly is wrong with it. If Irene is the Devil, she is therefore the author of the pictures in *Las nueve puertas* that give the clue to finding her. She seems more impressed by the fact that Corso has worked out how the books work together than by Borjas's efforts to summon the Devil; in other words, Corso knows the secret of the book.

At the end of his discussion with Varo Borja on the *Delomelanicon*, Corso observes that it is easy to make a book say what you want, especially if it is old and written ambiguously (84). Varo Borja implicitly agrees: he believes that his collection of books on the Devil '[r]eflejan preocupaciones, misterios, deseos, vidas, muertes . . . Son materia viva: hay que saber darles alimento, protección . . .' (reflect our worries, our mysteries and desires, our lives and our deaths. They are alive: you have to know how to nourish and protect them . . .; 85, ellipsis in original). Yet, if readers make the book, the reverse is also true. Balkan tells Corso that there are no more innocent readers as we are what we have read: 'Ante un texto, cada uno aplica su propia perversidad' (Everyone applies their own perversity to a text). As a result, 'el exceso de referencias puede haberle fabricado a usted un adversario equivocado, o irreal' (for you the excess of references could have created a false or fake adversary). In this way, Corso constructed his own story and his difficulties arise because, above all, he knows too many literary references (457). Within this intricate relationship between readers and books, in which the latter speak to but also shape the desires of the former, there is, as Alberto Montaner Frutos observes (2000, 218), a lack of the authentic object, the true copy of *Las nueve puertas* which Varo Borja asks Corso to find. The result is the never-ending circulation of readers and books in search of an ideal that can never be found. But it is also true that readers and books are locked together in a vicious or virtuous circle (depending on your point of view) in which the books make the reader but cannot exist without him or her.

While *Las nueve puertas* performs a similar function to that of the traditional Gothic manuscript, and the investigation of it incorporates the study of the past and of Roman Catholic reactions to occult worship, the Gothic effect is concentrated on the present. This might suggest that, in contrast to Botting's concerns about the postmodern era, 'past images and forms [. . .] worn too thin to veil the gaping hole of objectless anxiety' (Botting 2002, 298), the obsession with the Gothic has endured as long as the Gothic has, and present-day obsessives have merely inherited their tastes from a long line of predecessors. Rather than a lack of potency of today's Gothic, the Gothic of the past has the power to affect the present, as is traditional with Gothic texts. As Spooner, for example, observes, 'Gothic as a genre is profoundly concerned with the past, conveyed through both historical settings and narrative interruptions of the past into the present' (Spooner 2006, 9). Simultaneously, the present allows us to reread the past. Varo Borja's final ceremony goes wrong because of action in the present, the forgery by the Ceniza brothers of one of the illustrations (which across the three copies contain the secret of how to summon the Devil). Varo Borja and the baroness study the Devil of the past, and trade quotes with Corso from old books, but the Devil of *El club Dumas* acts in the present. The Devil appears in contemporary form, a young woman in jeans and a duffel coat, first noticed by Boris Balkan at his *tertulia* because she behaves in a different way from the others:

> Vi cómo una de las estudiantes sonreía; mas no pude adivinar si el gesto, absorto y algo burlón, era consecuencia de mis palabras o de secretas reflexiones ajenas a la tertulia. Me sorprendió, pues ya he dicho que los estudiantes suelen escucharme con el respeto que mostraría un redactor de *L'Osservatore Romano* al recibir en exclusiva el texto de una encíclica pontificia. Eso hizo que me fijase en ella con interés; aunque al principio, cuando se unió a nosotros con una trenca azul y un montón de libros bajo el brazo, ya había llamado mi atención a causa de sus inquietantes ojos verdes y el cabello castaño muy corto, como el de un chico (Pérez-Reverte 1998, 131).
> (I saw how one of the students smiled but I couldn't work out if the gesture, absorbed and rather sardonic, was because of what I was saying or secret thoughts that had nothing to do with the *tertulia*. I was surprised because, as I've already said, students

usually listen to me with the sort of respect that an editor of *L'Osservatore Romano* would show on receipt of a papal encyclical. So I looked at her with interest though, when she joined us, in a blue duffel coat and with a pile of books under her arm, she had already attracted my attention because of her startling green eyes and chestnut hair cut very short like a boy's.)

Irene's smile appears to be in response to Balkan's description of the character Rochefort as a symbol of dark forces. When Corso comments on Balkan's use of the word 'diabolical' to refer to Cardinal Richelieu and asks if Richelieu was interested in the dark arts, the girl turns to look at him (while Balkan adds that Richelieu was a bibliophile and collector of books, including many referring to the occult; 139–40). Though at this stage her identity as the Devil is unclear, Pérez-Reverte provides sufficient mysterious hints to suggest that this unnamed character will have some significance. With hindsight, her green eyes and contained amusement underscore the later clues to the Devil's identity, along with her occasional air of age-old experience, her awareness of Fargas's death without apparently having been on the scene, and the fact that the shadow of a cross on a church steeple, moving closer to her feet as she sits in a café, never actually touches her (394). Throughout the novel, Irene remains self-contained yet a dogged follower of Corso's doings so that her constant company contains a nod towards that highly Gothic text, James Hogg's *Confessions of a Justified Sinner* (1824), though Corso is no Robert Wringhim. She also reveals surprising strength as she fights off Corso's attacker. Jorge Zamora notes that Irene is constantly in shadow, often surrounded by cold air or a suggestion of mist (Zamora 2008, 163). And, towards the end, Pérez-Reverte refers to the Devil's rebellion and fall from grace when Irene admits that she is free, 'como si ya hubiera pagado por su derecho a decir aquello' (as if she had already paid the price for her right to say that; 464).

Yet what is also clear from the very first encounter with Irene is her affiliation with books and, in particular, books related to the occult. One of the first things Balkan notices about her is that she is carrying a pile of books and that she smiles at the implicit influence of the occult on the plot of *The Three Musketeers*. The fact that she deliberately takes her name from a book character, and a femme fatale at that, suggests her affinity. Corso's simultaneous attraction to, and distrust of, the latter-day Irene Adler resemble the attitude of Sherlock Holmes to the original. But the reincarnation of Irene is also frequently to be found reading a book and has a strong knowledge of literature. She is reading Maturin's *Melmoth the Wanderer* when Corso encounters her in the hotel in Sintra (Pérez-Reverte 1998, 228–9): when Corso asks her if she likes reading Gothic novels, she replies that she likes to read, pure and simple, and always travels with a few books. She gives Corso a copy of Jacques Cazotte's *Le Diable amoureux* (The Devil in Love, 1772) as a present (273). Though she professes a disinterest in the Dumas manuscript, she assists Corso in tracking it down when it is stolen from him as well as protecting him in a previous aborted attempt at robbery. (She clarifies that she did this because the manuscript was in the same bag as *Las nueve puertas* and thus stolen at the same time.) And she is to be found reading *The Three Musketeers* while waiting for Corso during his dealings with the baroness (300): Carolyn Durham observes that Irene is the only one actually to read the novel throughout *El club Dumas* (Durham 2001, 473). In this sense, then, the Devil echoes Corso's links to the two separate plots: indeed, these two characters are the only two primary links and this suggests they are also linked to each other.

Like Corso, Irene has a specific affinity with books that are old: twentieth-century writings figure little, if at all. This coincides with Corso's impression that she is old beyond her apparent years. There is, too, a sense that she is trying to recapture some lost memory, as when she looks in the windows of antique shops in Paris:

> Parecía buscar huellas de sí misma en los objetos antiguos; como si, en algún lugar de su memoria, el pasado convergiese con el de aquellos pocos supervivientes traídos hasta allí por la deriva, tras cada naufragio inexorable de la Historia. (259)
> (She seemed to be looking for traces of herself in the old objects as if, somewhere in her memory, the past converged with that of those few survivors brought there by chance after each inevitable shipwreck of history.)

In turn, Corso's knowledge of the Devil is closely linked to literature, 'Mis referencias sobre lo que el diablo ama o desprecia son exclusivamente literarias' (My references for what the Devil loves or hates are purely literary), and mentions *Paradise Lost*, *The Divine Comedy*, *Faust* and *The Brothers Karamazov* as references (287–8). He immediately follows this remark with a discussion as to which of these devils he prefers: it turns out to be that of Milton so that it cannot be a coincidence that Irene refers to the Devil's fight with God and fall from grace, a central element in *Paradise Lost*.

The ultimate clue to the mystery of *Las nueve puertas* is Corso's realisation that Varo Borja's ritual cannot work because the Ceniza brothers forged the final illustration which was previously missing from his copy. Durham observes that *El club Dumas* questions the whole idea of what is an original novel. This is true for the Dumas manuscript: Balkan shares out the chapters in order to disguise the fact that Dumas's collaborator, Maquet, was materially involved in writing *The Three Musketeers* – thus, the original Dumas manuscript is a fake (Durham 2001, 475). The same applies to *Las nueve puertas*, partly because the 'original' text crosses the three different copies. Durham's other reason comes initially from an error when she says that all three versions have a forged engraving: in fact, only one of them does. Even with just the one forgery, however, she is right to say that there is no longer an original copy of *Las nueve puertas* (ibid.). I would add to this the putative manuscript of Taillefer, the original owner of the Dumas, who commits suicide at the very beginning of *El club Dumas*. Taillefer tried to write his own popular novel but Boris Balkan claims he plagiarised and wrote badly, lifting his tale almost wholesale from an earlier, obscure novel: being found out led him to commit suicide (Pérez Reverte 449 and 451–2).

Hogle has identified fakery as essential to the Gothic: clearly he did not have in mind the sort of activity indulged in by the Cenizas but, as we have seen previously, he posits that modern Gothic has always been based on the idea of the fake from the very beginning. *El club Dumas*, therefore, offers a new form of fakery that differs from the heritage pastiche we encountered in the previous chapter but within which Hogle's argument, 'the Gothic refaking of fakery becomes a major repository of the newest contradictions and anxieties in western life that most need to be abjected by those who face them' (Hogle 2001, 297), equally applies. *El club Dumas* suggests that such contradictions and anxieties include the difficulty of telling the authentic from the real: such contradictions and anxieties are exacerbated precisely because there is no real – these Gothic manuscripts are all ultimately fakes. Who can tell whether it is the authentic copy in circulation? This applies even to *El club Dumas* itself. Durham observes that the French translation differs from the English one in significant respects, with important alterations in the epigraphs used (Durham 2001, 476–7) but she goes further than this to point out an apparent error in the English one. A pronoun in an epigraph from Agatha Christie's *The Murder of Roger Ackroyd* (1926), a notoriously first-person novel, has been mistakenly changed to the third person. But, as Durham points out, what exactly is the original text now being misquoted? Who introduced the error – the English translator? Pérez-Reverte himself? A mistranslation of Pérez-Reverte's source? (477–8).

We return to a *mise en abyme* of fakes, each one echoed by the previous one, in which any thought of authenticity disappears into infinity. The manuscripts themselves become abject, associated with evil and dark rituals but, like most abject things, they also give rise to multiple pleasures and, indeed, multiple obsessions. The abject fixation of the characters with their manuscripts becomes a frenzied search for the 'real thing': even the cynical Corso, who is still demanding payment for his services at the denouement, is not exempt. Haunting is, of course, integral to the Gothic: indeed, the discovered manuscript with which we started this chapter itself contains the ghosts of the past. For Fargas, books are like ghosts: he stays in his ruined home because '[e]ntre sus muros vagan las sombras de mis libros perdidos' (the ghosts of my lost books wander between its walls; Pérez-Reverte 1998, 200). He later plays the violin to conjure up their spirits (225). Corso himself is haunted by the ghost of his former lover Nikon: after lying in bed and thinking of her, 'Se levantó despacio de la cama para no despertar al fantasma que dormía a su lado' (He got up slowly from the bed so as not to awaken the ghost that slept by his side; 65). Gothic love resembles the passion for dangerous books. Thus, Nikon tells Corso that he is as dead as his books while Corso perceives himself as 'montando guardia entre fantasmas de papel y cuero' (standing guard among ghosts of paper and leather, 66). The motif of haunting and ghosts links naturally to the obsession with books, as all the central characters are haunted by some book or other. Both Botting and Hogle might fear this as we have previously seen. If obsession equals excess, then *El club Dumas* suggests the dangers of excessive circulation. The physical book, which might offer some semblance of material reality to oppose the haunting, simply becomes the object of Gothic obsession and, once again, reveals the uncertainty of the Gothic manuscript.

La sombra del viento

Just as with *El club Dumas*, *La sombra* is also about the circulation of books that cause havoc among those who have any interest in them. Glennis Byron observes that *La sombra* is a book about books, part of 'a well-established Hispanic tradition of books about books, a tradition moving from Cervantes through Borges to Pérez-Reverte' (Byron 2013b, 77). Ruiz Zafón's *La sombra* is about a book by Julián Carax, also called *La sombra del viento*. Ruiz Zafón, however, is also writing about the movement of books over time and space and, indeed, the trade in books. The novel's protagonist, Daniel, the son of a bookseller, assumes guardianship of Carax's novel after a visit to the Cementerio de Libros Olvidados (the Cemetery of Forgotten Books), a vast archive of books that have been forgotten and await adoption. Daniel's book is the gateway to the story of its author and of the bourgeois society of Barcelona, itself rendered Gothic through the doomed love of Julián and Penélope, the daughter of Julián's benefactor, Aldaya. It is also the start of a circle of initiates who read the novel and become obsessed with it while Daniel is haunted by a mysterious, Devil-ish figure who turns out to be Carax himself.

As in the case of *El club Dumas*, critique of *La sombra* has a pronounced critical trend, in this case towards seeing the story in terms of Spanish history (for example, Ellis 2006a, Meddick 2010, Ramblado 2008, Ryan 2009); and I should like to pause briefly to discuss this trend as it has a resonance for Spanish Gothic texts that will also feature in Chapter 4. Given the fact that the main action of the book takes place during the Franco era, it is not surprising that commentators have foregrounded the historical context. Ruiz Zafón makes reference to some of the features of the dictatorship, such as Inspector Fumero's heavy-handed and corrupt policing, and Daniel's sidekick Fermín Romero de Torres's previous time in prison (covered in the third part of the trilogy, *El prisionero del cielo*, which references the Franco era more overtly). The sense of clandestine activity surrounding the book and the mystery of the Aldaya dynasty chime with a sense of Spanish history as well. The insistence on Spanish history causes some anomalies, however. Judith Meddick, for instance, equates Julián Carax, with the dead and disappeared of the Spanish Civil War and, indeed, his disappearance and exile in Paris might provoke such associations for those who are aware of the historical implications. Yet Carax's exile is for personal, rather than political, reasons while Nuria lies about his death and burial (Meddick 2010, 250–2). Thus, Carax's association with the Civil War is more tenuous than Meddick admits: it can be read just as easily in terms of a Gothic romance harking back to the Golden Age of Gothic in the eighteenth century. In a similar vein to Meddick, Cinta Ramblado argues that, because Carax vanishes in 1936, the year the Civil War started, his disappearance must be connected with politics and his story must be politically tinged (Ramblado 2008, 73). Certainly, 1936 will trigger associations with the specifically Spanish past for those aware of it but the various ill-fated romances and the circulation of the book at the centre of the novel are narratives of personal relations on which, ultimately, politics has no effect. If anything, the opposite is true, at least as far as Fumero is concerned, the only character who explicitly claims any political motive: his commitment to the Francoist cause stems from his rejection by Julián's circle. Given the international success of *La sombra*, we should also bear in mind that many of the book's readers will not make these associations.

We should further remember Ken Gelder's comment on popular fiction (of which *La sombra* is certainly an example): 'Popular fiction is, essentially, genre fiction' (Gelder, 2004, 1). While this might appear a sweeping statement, Gelder's comment nonetheless reminds us of the value of genre as a framework for the study of popular fiction such as this novel. Glennis and Gordon Byron suggest that, though many scholars have viewed the novel as a memory text which recuperates a lost Spanish past, this is not how many readers and reviewers have understood it because it is also a self-consciously Gothic novel. Though Glennis Byron has pointed out elsewhere that Ruiz Zafón only belatedly acknowledged *La sombra* as a Gothic novel (Byron 2012, 371), Byron and Byron argue that the novel became an international bestseller 'not just by openly embracing the gothic, but by flaunting it, appropriating its tropes and its traditions in a highly self-conscious and even flamboyant manner'. They quote Stephen King who said "'If you thought the true gothic novel died with the nineteenth century, this will change your mind. *Shadow* is the real deal, a novel full of cheesy splendor and creaking trapdoors, a novel where even the subplots have subplots'" (quoted in Byron and Byron 2012, 73). The Gothic elements therefore provide a more immediate impact than the historical background and tie in more readily with Gothic motifs such as those acknowledged by King. Other commentators have also noticed the Gothic mode. Maria Sergia Steen (2008) cites the traditional, large bourgeois houses, Daniel's curiosity, Nuria's final explanation, the frightening figure of Carax, and Fumero's jealousy as examples, while Eduardo Ruiz Tosaus (2008) describes the novel's structure as labyrinthine, recalling another Gothic motif.

It all depends, perhaps, on how one interprets the past. Ruiz Tosaus, commenting on Ruiz Zafón's *oeuvre* as a whole, argues that many characters are rooted in the past, trapped by their memories:

> presos de sus recuerdos, que deciden dirigirlos hacia presencias fantasmales o espectrales que vuelven una y otra vez sobre los pasos que ya dieron en busca de una redención muchas veces inútil (Ruiz Tosaus, 2009)
> (prisoners of their memories, who decide to direct them towards ghostly or spectral presences that retrace over and over the steps they took earlier in search of a redemption that is often useless)

He later argues that 'Los personajes de *La sombra* [. . .] son herederos de un pasado que no les ha tocado vivir pero sí padecer, entre el pasado y el presente se produce un efecto de espejo inevitable' (The characters of *La sombra* have inherited a past which they suffer rather than live; between the past and the present an inevitable mirage is created; ibid.). And he quotes the image of Russian dolls in *La sombra*, the suggestion that each narrative contains another one:

> Paso a paso, la narración se descomponía en mil historias, como si el relato hubiese penetrado en una galería de espejos y su identidad se escindiera en docenas de reflejos diferentes y al tiempo uno solo. (Ruiz Zafón 2008, 19)

(Step by step, the story was collapsing into a thousand stories, as if the tale had entered into a hall of mirrors and its identity split into dozens of different reflections while, at the same time, remaining one single reflection.)

With the hall of mirrors and the Russian dolls, we gain a sense of *mise en abyme*. Such images suggest story and history as multifaceted so that it is not wrong to read *La sombra* through the prism of Spanish history but that history means other things as well. Yet the past which is uncovered throughout the novel has little to do with Franco or the Civil War. Byron and Byron tell us that:

> it is only on this level of personal relationships that there are secrets to be dis-
> covered: the incestuous relationship, the death of Penélope, Daniel's repressed
> memories of his mother crying from her coffin. These personal traumas have only
> indirect connections, if any, to the wider social and political events. (Byron and
> Byron 2012, 81)

This point I believe to be crucial, though the question then arises as to why Ruiz Zafón set the plot in this precise era: the references to Spanish history are still there to be picked up on. Spanish history itself becomes Gothicised, with repressive patriarchal fathers and warped progeny, imprisonment, violence, and the struggle between old ways and new. The Franco era was, in itself, Gothic just as the Napoleonic occupation was for Goya but history becomes subordinate to the Gothic mode and merges into the imaginary settings and Gothic ambience of Ruiz Zafón's Barcelona. As I shall discuss below, however, even Glennis Byron will ultimately be unable to resist trying to place the novel's setting very much in the real Spain in preference to *La sombra*'s popularity.

For my purposes, this is a personal story about the circulation and preservation of books, just as in *El club Dumas*, and on this level, too, the Spanish past impinges only indirectly on the narrative. Placing this novel in the Franco era fixes the narrative in historical time, yet the novel is equally about the circulation of Gothic texts across time (a far shorter timespan than in *El club Dumas*) and space. While the timespan fits within the Franco era, the circulation of Ruiz Zafón's *La sombra* in the present day breaks that boundary so that the various tales within his novel circulate beyond those for whom the Franco era has a particular resonance. A case could be made for saying that the movements of Carax's novel parallel those of Carax himself through history but Byron and Byron's point about the personal suggests Spanish history as only tangential. The romantic tale of star-crossed lovers repeats itself (Julián and Penélope, Daniel and Bea) so that Daniel is haunted by personal memories rather than by the ghosts of the Spanish past. This duality of interpretation coincides with Lee Six's own response to Byron and Byron's ideas:

> Glennis and Gordon Byron allude to a mysterious kind of deceit when they empha-size the importance of the fact that that the books in *La sombra del viento* are inten-tionally misfiled in the library where they are kept. The implication is that it suits someone (read hegemonic Spanish culture?) for certain books (read stories from the past) not to be easy to find. Here, perhaps, lies the resolution of the contradiction between memory text and gothic readings of the novel: the past, emblematized in the books, is not buried and so needing to be dug up, the memory text idea; but neither is it omnipresent, the gothic haunting concept. If it is unburied but mis-shelved, perhaps this can be read as meaning that it resides in liminal territory, a kind of limbo between oblivion and ever-present haunting, thus enabling the two readings of the novel to co-exist. (Lee Six 2012, 6)

One could also argue that it is the popular Gothic, just as much as Spanish history, that lies in this luminal territory, misfiled and in a kind of limbo because unrecognised or dismissed. I shall discuss below how this liminal territory is precisely that of circulation.

In contrast to *El club Dumas*, books do not inspire evil (the only evil character in *La sombra* does not like books) but they are nonetheless Gothicised through haunting. Tiffany Gagliardi Trotman suggests that Carax's *La sombra* functions as the ghost of a past generation, and perhaps the ghost of Carax himself: 'The book represents the narrative trace of Carax's past, but the presence of the book also constitutes a cover, as it were, for the absence of its author' (Trotman 2007, 250). Byron (2013b, 77) observes that the *La sombra* of Carax functions as a ghost in another way: it haunts the *La sombra* of Ruiz Zafón. Ellis observes this as well: 'Julián's text never appears within the Ruiz Zafón text, but instead haunts it as an ever-possible displacement of meaning and disintegration of unity'. Indeed, Ellis goes on to suggest that the two novels are in opposi-tion to each other in regard to who has the final mastery of language and discourse, that is, which discourse is the authentic one: 'This phantom text, a sign of the fluidity of discourse and the instability of identity, is nevertheless held at bay by the overarching Ruiz Zafón text, which strives to reaffirm discourse as a system of fixed signs and a means of achieving a fixed self' (Ellis 2006a, 844). The Cementerio de Libros Olvidados, the library to which Lee Six refers and where Daniel first finds Carax's novel, is a repository of books that want to be found and recognised, reclaimed from the past, refusing to be laid to rest (and, in that way, contradicting the ostensible purpose of a cemetery).

In a manner reminiscent of Corso in *El club Dumas*, Daniel undertakes a quest that involves both the discovery and circulation of books. Though

Daniel's entry into the Cementerio marks him from the very beginning of
the novel as a bibliophile and initiate in the mysteries of books, his attitude
to his chosen book and his circulation of it go counter to the symbolism
of the Cementerio as a bibliographic burial ground. The cemetery is, of
course, a symbol of death, giving an additional Gothic air to this book
repository. It smells of death and has a doorknocker shaped like a devil
(Ruiz Zafón 2008, 81) while Daniel observes that Isaac, the guardian of
the Cementerio, looks like the knocker (82). Catherine d'Humières (2007,
344), speaks of the Cementerio and its books in terms of ghosts:

> un cimetière étant en effet l'endroit où l'on ressent la presence de l'absence, con-
> formément à la croyance que veut que les morts tout comme les livres, d'après les
> habitués de l'immense bibliothèque – continuent à vivre tant que quelqu'un pense
> à eux.
> (a cemetery being, in fact, the place where one feels the presence of absence in line
> with the belief, according to the habitués of the immense library, that wishes that the
> dead, like books, continue to live as long as someone is thinking of them.)

D'Humières's remarks suggest Carax's La sombra del viento is itself a ghost
which haunts Daniel and Carax and, indeed, Ruiz Zafón's own novel.
Barcelona is rendered Gothic through its own resemblance to a cemetery:
Padre Fernando, the childhood friend of Carax, Aldaya and Miquel,
describes 'una suma de ruinas' (nothing more than ruins) in which the
palaces and monuments are simply the corpses of a dead civilisation (242).
In that sense, Barcelona is the appropriate setting for a narrative in which
books come to represent the dead and the lost, allowing the dead and the
lost to haunt the living.

Both novels circulate the stories of the past to new readers and, in the
case of Carax's version, these new readers in turn uncover new stories of
people haunted by the past. One example is Daniel's acquaintance with
Nuria, herself haunted by her lover Miquel Moliner and by Carax. Nuria
has her own part to play in the circulation of books through keeping a copy
of each of Carax's novels (and, in this way, ensuring the stories are preserved when other copies perish in a warehouse fire). She is the one who
hides La sombra in the Cementerio where Daniel will find it. Yet those who
read and circulate the book are to some extent complicit in keeping the
spirit of the books alive, as Daniel's father observes (Ruiz Zafón 2008, 16):
both they and the original author conjure up the book as ghost. The
readers become spirits or ghosts in their turn through reading the book:
'los libros que se han perdido en el tiempo, viven para siempre, esperando
llegar algún día a las manos de un nuevo lector, de un nuevo espíritu' (the
books that have been lost in time live on for ever, waiting for the day that

they fall into the hands of a new reader, a new spirit'; 16–17). These spirits are Gothic ones, however, and the books are rendered as Gothic artefacts: as his father takes Daniel to the Cementerio for the first time, he tells him that some things can be seen only in the shadows (14), implicitly associating the books with darkness. Daniel tells Bea that he has taken refuge in Carax's novel 'como quien escapa a través de las páginas de una novela porque aquellos a quien necesita amar son solo sombras que viven en el alma de un extraño' (like someone who escapes through the pages of a novel because those people he must love are only shadows who live in the soul of a stranger; 214).

But, if books are not evil, as they are in *El club Dumas*, they nonetheless give rise to secrecy, trickery and betrayal. The authorship of Daniel's book entails a level of mystery highly reminiscent of *Las nueve puertas*. Carax has disappeared, and no one is sure what has happened to him while, on the other hand, somebody is going about burning copies of his books, a person using the name of a character in Carax's *La sombra*: as with *Las nueve puertas*, knowledge and narration are not to be readily available but open only to a few initiates. Though there is no doubt that Carax is the original author (unlike the double plots of *El club Dumas*), the origin of his *La sombra* is unclear. The book dealer Barceló tells Daniel that the novel was first published in Paris but has never heard of the publisher (Ruiz Zafón 2008, 22). Books are also faked, as in Barceló's copy of Lope de Vega's *Fuenteovejuna*, apparently signed by the author in ball-point pen (43), a writing implement unavailable to Lope when he wrote the play in the seventeenth century: the pen claimed to have been used to write Victor Hugo's *Les misérables* hints at fakery too (44). (The latter nonetheless tempts Daniel to try his own hand at writing novels; 47). Books allow other forms of deceit: the supposed body of Carax (actually the body of his friend Miquel) carries one of Carax's books, tricking Fumero into thinking Carax is dead, and thus Carax himself is able to escape Fumero and survive (395). The bibliophilia of many of the characters leads them to read the secrets of *La sombra* according to their own interests. Echoing the discussions of Corso, Varo Borja and Boris Balkan in *El club Dumas*, Julián says that 'Los libros son espejos: solo se ve en ellos lo que uno ya lleva dentro' (Books are like mirrors: you only see in them what you yourself carry inside you; 250). When Daniel later goes to this house and explores, he is influenced by his knowledge of Victorian (that is, British) literature to start his search in the basement, underscoring the importance of literary references already mentioned in *El club Dumas* (360).

Carax's flat in Paris contains books and very little else (432), suggesting his own obsession; and such an obsession is again associated with the

Devil. Carax, like the Devil of *El club Dumas* has some claim to author-ship, and it is Carax's authorship that is at the heart of the mystery of his novel. Just as Irene Adler haunts Corso in *El club Dumas*, so Carax begins to haunt Daniel: early in the novel Daniel looks out of the window to see a figure looking at him before limping off into the mist and, in response, Daniel breaks out in a cold sweat. He remembers that an identical scene occurred in Carax's *La sombra* and, while Daniel himself cannot make out the face of the figure, he recalls that in Carax's novel this stranger was the Devil (52). Carax smells of burned paper and resembles a character from a book: Daniel does not say which book but it is not incidental that Carax adopts the name he gave to the Devil in his own *La sombra* (Laín Coubert) so, to that extent, he has escaped from his own novel and the link between fiction and reality is blurred in the way that the two versions of *La sombra* echo each other (99). In Carax's final confrontation with Fumero, Daniel believes that Carax disappears to be replaced by Laín Coubert (548). Shortly before turning thirteen, the young Julián Carax declares he wants to be Robert Louis Stevenson, having succumbed to the vice of reading (it is presumably Molins, who has care of Carax's old home and who is talking to Daniel about Julián's past, who labels reading as a vice; 156). As a child, Julián liked fantasy stories and developed the habit of drawing angels with teeth like wolves; he filled his exercise books with pictures of monsters, snakes and houses that could eat you alive (155). Writing books clearly draws the author into some sort of devilish compromise. It is just as well, then, that Daniel fails in his efforts to write because Padre Fernando thinks that Daniel resembles the young Julián while Fermín claims Daniel as Carax's unacknowledged son. According to Fermín, Daniel is looking for 'un progenitor perdido en las nieblas de la memoria' (a father lost in the mists of memory; 241). Writing becomes a Gothic activity that comple-ments the obsession of the readers: production and consumption become a seamless whole as books and stories are circulated down the generations. The desire to create, like the desire to possess, has demonic qualities.

Unlike *El club Dumas*, the plot of Ruiz Zafón's *La sombra* takes place over a short period of time but, nonetheless, the plot begins and ends with a sense of legacy, a heritage passed on. Daniel takes his own son Julián to the Cementerio de Libros Olvidados for the first time when Julián is ten (as Daniel was in his turn: 569). The love of books is something that was passed to Daniel by his father and is now passed down to a new gen-eration. The sense of legacy also revivifies the older generation. Daniel receives a new novel called *El ángel de brumas* (The Angel of Mists): Carax has started writing again. In that copy, Carax has written a dedication to Daniel that says Daniel has given him back his voice and his pen (567).

When Isaac dies, Fermín replaces him as the custodian of the Cementerio de Libros Olvidados (546). The stress Ruiz Zafón places on legacy at the end of his *La sombra* parallels the common Gothic motif of the past haunting the present but it also strongly implies a chronology that disturbs the sense of an ever-present, but exhausted, ephemeral flow that Botting posited (2002, 298). These books are tangible objects preserved and passed down; they do not simply haunt the present but materially interact with it. This is an element *La sombra* shares with *El club Dumas* where books are not simply circulated but passed on (we remember that the baroness is aware of who previously owned her own copy of *Las nueve puertas*). Here, too, the manuscripts of the past are material objects with a material effect on the present.

Popular Culture and Cultural Flow

There is an ironic contrast between the original *La sombra del viento*, mired in obscurity and the subject of a vendetta by its author, and Ruiz Zafón's book that brings it back to life. Of course, Ruiz Zafón could not know at the time he wrote his novel that it would become an international bestseller, though he might well have hoped so, but the contrast between the two versions of *La sombra* is striking in terms of circulation. While the original book was lost for years and then circulated only between a few devoted readers, protected from the destructive wishes of Carax, Ruiz Zafón's *La sombra* is easily available from almost anywhere in the world. And, on the back of this success, his other works have been reissued internationally, and the following two volumes of the *La sombra* trilogy have also achieved international success. (Over the years, I have regularly found copies of Ruiz Zafón's novels for sale at my local supermarket). Ruiz Zafón's example tells us that Gothic sells. Though she reminds us that Ruiz Zafón adopted the Gothic label only belatedly, Byron suggests that Gothic is now an aspirational brand marketable by international publishing companies. *La sombra* has been translated into over forty languages (Byron 2012, 370). Ruiz Zafón has since become an authority on Gothic, asked to pronounce on the best Gothic novels of the twentieth century (371). His earlier children's novels have also been republished and fit in with what Spooner describes as crossover Gothic novels that suit both (older) children and adults, blurring age demarcations for Gothic literature (Spooner 2014, 199) and that therefore increase the potential readership and circulation.

Pérez-Reverte has been longer established, first as a journalist and then as a writer of detective and crime fiction, as well as the series of Golden

Age adventures featuring the fictional character Captain Alatriste. As journalist and writer, he has been well known for many years in Spain but it is the last career that has made him famous worldwide, and the film *The Ninth Gate*, while a flawed work, has nonetheless circulated his name and his story further. For Pérez-Reverte, popularity, and thus wide circulation, is a key literary value: the Dumas plot in *El club Dumas* celebrates *The Three Musketeers* as a successful and attractive novel that has drawn many readers to it since its serial publication in 1844. Replinger, the Paris bookseller in the novel, connects the question of book circulation to Dumas, noting not only the great success of the latter's work in France but also further afield:

> Durante medio siglo Europa no juró sino por su boca. Las dos Américas enviaban barcos con el exclusivo fin de transportar sus novelas, que se leían lo mismo en El Cairo, Moscú, Estambul y Chandernagor. (Pérez-Reverte 1998, 268)
> (For half a century Europe swore by him alone. The Americas sent ships for the sole purpose of transporting his novels which were read in Cairo just as much as in Moscow, Istanbul and Chandernagor.)

Dumas was an international bestseller and, for Pérez-Reverte, an example of the traditional style of narrative that he prefers over literary developments in the twentieth century. Pérez-Reverte decries 'el imperio del esnobismo y la gilipollez y la vacuidad elevada a teoría literaria, a obra maestra imprescindible y a pequeña miniatura imperecedera' (the realm of snobbery and pomposity and superficiality elevated to literary theory, to essential masterpieces and immortal miniatures) that has brought the novel to the point of decease (Pérez-Reverte 2000, 366). This implies the popular novel as some sort of ghost, neglected and forgotten but still haunting the literati. He welcomes a return to 'traditional' language and structures:

> al género policíaco como sostén de la trama, a la historia como memoria y clave del presente, al paisaje cultural común iberoamericano, [. . .] contar novelas como siempre se contaron. Novelas que pretenden abarcar una parte del mundo narrando una historia con planteamiento, nudo, desenlace y con los puntos y las comas en su sitio. (367)
> (to the detective novel as a mainstay of plot, to history as memory and as a key to the present, to the shared Iberian–American cultural landscape [. . .] to write novels as they have always been written. Novels that claim to embrace a part of the world by telling a story with a conflict, a crisis point and resolution, and with commas and full stops in their proper place.)

Pérez-Reverte cites authors such as Eduardo Mendoza, Juan Marsé and Gonzalo Torrente Ballester as people who have resisted elitist literary values, preferring to write 'la novela de toda la vida, la escrita como Dios manda' (the novel of life, written as God wills it; ibid.). A key component of his literary standpoint is nonetheless wide circulation: Pérez-Reverte associates his preferred style of novel with popular and commercial success:

> Libros de éxito [. . .] Todos en las librerías, y bendita sea la época en que cada lector puede escoger lo que cuadra con su gusto y no verse obligado, como en otro tiempo lo estuvimos, a exiliarse en novelas extranjeras o en los clásicos, renunciando al presente o sintiéndose miserable porque se aburre con *Herrumbrosas lanzas*. (367)
> (Bestsellers . . . all in the bookshops, and blessed be the era in which every reader can choose what suits their taste and not be obliged, as we formerly were, to retreat to the classics or foreign novels, rejecting the present or feeling miserable because *Herrumbrosas lanzas* [novel by Juan Benet] bores them.)

Pérez-Reverte has, of course, borne out his own principles through his own success, to the extent that Nicholas Lezard, literary critic for Britain's *Guardian* newspaper, argued that 'Spain, like many Catholic countries, if you will forgive the gross generalisation, is not exactly a land of literature', at least before the advent of Pérez-Reverte (Lezard 2002, 28). Though it is hard to prove whether or not Pérez-Reverte has outsold Cervantes's *Don Quixote* (though I don't think it likely) and, despite Lezard's sweeping and inaccurate generalisation, the latter's underlying point, Pérez-Reverte's pre-eminence in Spanish literature at that time, is undeniable. Pérez-Reverte was highly successful both at home and abroad and stood out against other Spanish authors, past and present, precisely because of his success. *El club Dumas* confirms popular narratives as an elite secret, as the members of the secret society gather, including a professor of semiotics from Bologna, a clear reference to Umberto Eco (who with *The Name of The Rose* preceded Pérez-Reverte in combining mystery and the Gothic to form a bestselling novel: Pérez-Reverte 1998, 442). Pérez-Reverte's stance is also echoed by Ruiz Zafón who was not interested in 'producing work in tune with Spanish literary fashion' (Page 2004, 24). For both authors, popular culture is a secret kept from the literary elites and (according to Pérez-Reverte) even kept out of the bookshops but it is also the secret of their success. Bestsellers are not, however, written by the innocent. Baroness Ungern, for example, has used her occult research to write profitable books that sell internationally (Spain and Italy as well as France; 295). She freely admits that her primary interest in these books is commercial (311). As for Dumas, Boris Balkan argues that Dumas's collaborator, Maquet, was the real author of *The Three Musketeers*, something Balkan is determined to cover up 'en estos tiempos de mediocridad y falta de imaginación' (in these times of mediocrity and lack of imagination; 440).

When Boris Balkan first talks to Corso about Dumas's writing, he compares the power of Dumas's serial novels to that of soap operas: the novels catered well for 'una burguesía ávida de sorpresas y entretenimiento, poco exigente en cuanto a la calidad formal o buen gusto' (Pérez-Reverte 1998, 23). Balkan goes on to admit that he himself is a Dumas addict, one of an enduring line. His comments place him firmly on the side of popular literature and, in this, he echoes the views of his author (perhaps this is why Balkan is the only character presented in the first person). He tells Corso:

> Mas todos tenemos un guiño de complicidad al referirnos a ciertos autores y libros mágicos, que nos hicieron descubrir la literatura sin atarnos a dogmas ni enseñarnos lecciones equivocadas. Ésa es nuestra auténtica patria común: relatos fieles no a lo que los hombres ven, sino lo que los hombres sueñan. (445)
>
> (But we all give a complicit nod when we refer to certain magical authors and books through which we discovered literature without committing ourselves to dogma or learning the wrong lessons. That is our true common ground: stories that are faithful not to what men see but to what men dream about.)

And Balkan goes on to point out that even film and television are involved in the circulation of these stories. '¿qué es el serial televisivo sino una modalidad actualizada de la tragedia clásica, el gran drama romántico o la novela alejandrina . . . ?' (what is the television series but a contemporary version of classical tragedy, romantic drama or the Alexandrine novel?; 446).

Balkan is, of course, circulating such stories himself: his first-person position as the teller of *El club Dumas* is in itself indicative of this. Ellis observes: 'Yet if Balkan is the narrator, he is not a creator of fictions but instead a translator, editor, critic, and teacher [. . .] and in this sense a recycler of texts much like Corso himself.' He continues: 'By telling Corso [. . .] Balkan himself divulges the secret – that there are no individual creators and no original texts' (Ellis 2006b, 35). Durham observes that the characters Corso and Balkan travel themselves (Durham 2001, 466); indeed, they also ensure that the books circulate. Circulation is prevalent in *La sombra* as well. Nuria, for example, works as a translator from French and Italian (Ruiz Zafón 2008, 91), thus playing her part in the circulation of texts across borders and cultural flow. Daniel is not the only person interested in Carax's novels: his predecessor was Clara's teacher, Monsieur Roquefort, who came across an earlier Carax work by chance at a second-hand bookstall in Paris (34). Having read *La casa roja* (The Red House), Roquefort hunts for other novels over the next ten years, only to be thwarted. Nonetheless, the novels appear to function like ghosts as people claim to have heard of other novels or, indeed, in the case of one bookseller, handled them. This suggests their circulation. *La sombra*, in particular, proves to be of interest to more people than Daniel. Not only is Carax pursuing it but Barceló and his niece also take an interest: Barceló makes Daniel an offer for the book the first time they meet. The person searching for copies of Carax's novels is Laín Coubert, the name used by the Devil in Carax's *La sombra*, as previously mentioned, suggesting the circulation of characters as well as narratives. Yet it is precisely as Roquefort mounts his quest to find Carax's novels that he hears that somebody is acquiring copies only to destroy them (40).

Commerce and the Fear of Consumption

Roquefort passes his obsession on to Clara who reads *La casa roja* and later tells Daniel that 'Jamás me había sentido atrapada, seducida y envuelta por una historia como la que narraba aquel libro. (Never have I been captivated, seduced and absorbed by a story like the one that book told; 39). The references to seduction take us back to Botting's idea of Gothic readers and audiences as both passive and insatiable. Having previously discussed the positive power of the Gothic heroine and the female Gothic writer, he goes on to say (in a passage we have encountered before):

> The unpresentable is little more than a resource to be capitalized upon, a space to be filled with so many different images, hyperactivating and passifying consumers at the same time as they leave them wanting more: all readers and spectators have, perhaps, become woman in the process. This woman, however, is only the global instantiation of hypercapitalism's subjectile. (Botting 2007, 173)

Botting's comment reinforces the commerciality of the contemporary Gothic process, and its retreat from positive power back to older stereotypes. The contemporary Gothic readers are just as impressionable as the readers of Ann Radcliffe were supposed to be: not so far removed from the wide-eyed credulity of Catherine Morland in Jane Austen's *Northanger Abbey* (1817). Botting is here contrasting contemporary Gothic consumers with the feisty Gothic heroines of the eighteenth century but his use of the term 'woman' to describe passive consumers brings with it some very negative implications. Nonetheless, in the case of these two novels, it is not a question of Botting's 'so many' because scarcity and rarity are crucial elements of the discovered manuscript and, as we have seen, it is the circulation of the scarce that is valued here. In *La sombra*, when the publisher Cabestany refuses to sell his stocks of Carax's novel, the publishing house burns down one night (88) so hoarding, as in *El club Dumas*, brings trouble. On the other hand, a sign of Carax's recovery is when he starts to write again, initiating a new round of circulation. Circulation is healthy.

Book dealing as commerce is an integral part of *El club Dumas*. Pinto, Corso's friend in the Portuguese police, tells Corso (as justification for his own involvement in the secret circulation of books) that 'Los productos deben circular. Son las leyes del mercado; las leyes de la vida. No vender tendría que estar prohibido: es casi un crimen.' (Products need to circulate. It's the law of the market, the law of life. It should be forbidden not to sell: it's virtually a crime; Pérez-Reverte 1998, 233). Similarly, Achille Replinger, the Parisian book dealer, tells Corso that 'La gente viene a comprar y vender, y todo termina pasando varias veces por las mismas manos.' (People come to buy and sell, and everything eventually passes several times through the same hands; 262). The baroness knows how her own copy of *Las nueve puertas* circulated: at one point it passed through the hands of Cazotte, author of *Le Diable amoureux* (311–12). Aristide Torchia also travelled and acquired his occult knowledge from Prague, a city with an interest in magic and occult practices (304). Thus, Torchia, in his turn, also circulated clandestine knowledge to other countries: the original *Las nueve puertas* was published in Venice. The bridge between the past and the present involves both the circulation of books (so that Varo Borja, for instance, has only just come into possession of his copy of *Las nueve puertas*) and the storage of them in libraries, archives and collections. The three libraries that hold *Las nueve puertas* function in a similar way to the cemetery of lost books in *La sombra* and, in each case, the authentic book and the true intentions of the author (in one case the Devil, in the other an author who seems immortal and is often thought of as a devil) prove ultimately elusive and, in the case of *Las nueve puertas*, easily faked.

In contrast, Fargas describes himself as a 'bibliopath' (190). He inherited his books on the occult from his grandfather, 'aficionado a las artes herméticas, astrólogo aficionado y masón' (a devotee of the hermetic arts, a fan of astrology and a mason; 203). He would like to know the secret of *Las nueve puertas* as he would be willing to sell his soul to the Devil (204). Fargas says this precisely because he wants to hang on to his inheritance, preventing the circulation of books, so the notion of a bibliopath takes on a new resonance. Varo Borja destroys and steals books rather than circulating them, while the baroness hoards them in her archive. It is significant that all those who collect and hoard books tend to come to a bad end (Fargas, the baroness, Varo Borja, Taillefer) though communal hoarding seems to save Balkan's secret society. Yvette Sánchez (2000, 431), observes that bibliophiles in Pérez Reverte's novels also show a passion for collecting other things; so Enrique Taillefer (the person who sets the Dumas manuscript in circulation) collects porcelain, art and oriental rugs; Fargas collects art and furniture; and the baroness collects rare plants. There is a strong suggestion here that the obsession with books leads to hoarding. Circulation of books appears to be the key to survival; hence Corso, the arch circulator of books, is both the hero of the novel and the survivor.

Books as commerce also feature in *La sombra*. Daniel, like Corso, works for a bookseller. Ruiz Zafón takes the opportunity to make ironic comments on the publishing industry, given his own slightly belated success. The publisher Cabestany, Carax's Spanish publisher, is the subject of a few mild jibes as someone who likes cheap deals. Isaac tells Daniel: 'El idioma favorito de Cabestany era el de la peseta.' (Money was Cabestany's favourite language), and Cabestany bought the rights to Carax's work in the hope that Carax would be a commercial success in the Spanish market (Ruiz Zafón 2008, 85). Instead, Cabestany loses all his stock when his business burns down. Nonetheless, Cabestany still profits: Miquel subsidises the publishing of Carax's books (428) and so the publishing house earns money even though the books went straight into storage (429). There is also an ambivalent sense of the extent to which books circulate and are profitable that is missing in *El club Dumas*. Daniel's sense in the Cementerio of being surrounded by millions of pages of abandoned books suggests the risks of circulation (95). The reappearance of *La sombra* and Barceló's interest in it result in enquiries from Berlin, Paris and Rome at the end of the novel (522). Collectors are interested in it. This is related to the author's earlier flight from Paris after a duel with Jorge Aldaya and presumed death in the Spanish Civil War which raised the price of the books. It seems that Carax's books are collectors' items but it is a small circle of initiates, as in *El club Dumas*, for, even when republished, these books are not huge bestsellers. Barceló sets up a publishing house dedicated to republishing Carax's novels. The first volume, containing three novels, sells only 342 copies (565). In both novels, circulation and commerce are vital and healthy but the 'manuscripts' that are circulated, bought and sold are another Gothic secret.

Glennis Byron has written on the matter of circulation in *La sombra*, and argues that its gothicisation is ultimately a matter of marketing. She argues that:

> In recognising that gothic sells, and therefore focusing in their marketing strategies on the book as a gothic fiction, it is the publisher in collaboration with the media that constructs, categorizes and in a sense even comes to define what is understood by the gothic in contemporary culture. (Byron 2013b, 77)

This is of some concern for Byron who notes that 'Academics are increasingly not in control of the categories' (74) but I wonder if we ever were. That publishers have a significant role to play in defining what is contemporary Gothic cannot be doubted. *La sombra* itself attests to this, as Byron says, but, while circulation can occur without commerce, commerce still has a crucial role to play in circulation taken as a whole.

One of the elements that appears to frighten Byron most is the loss of a sense of place. She observes how the novel has given rise to a sightseeing industry around Barcelona, to the extent that the city becomes 'trapped by the writing, by fictions, as by anything else'. In her view, Barcelona comes to resemble nothing as much as Victorian London (78) but, for her, this does not mean that such a portrait conveys the authentic Barcelona (79). Dwelling on the walking tour set up on Ruiz Zafón's website, she argues:

> the walking tour he constructs does as much as possible to foreground a fabricated imported tradition of Victorian gothic and to marginalise what Barcelona is best known for: to repress and occlude rather than show off the city's true architectural inheritance, Gaudí and art nouveau architecture. (ibid.)

She goes on to poke holes in the authenticity of the walking tour, and then observes (I have to think, rather belatedly), 'Fakery has of course been endemic to gothic from the start' (80). Ruiz Zafón's Barcelona is an imported fake just as the Aldaya mansion of the novel is (81). Byron makes clear but debatable assumptions as to what the authentic Barcelona is, assumptions that surely simply fit older tourist trails (that continue to operate today) and have their own role to play in 'selling' Barcelona. How far, for instance, is Gaudí's Sagrada Família the authentic Barcelona, given that it is still not finished, the building work stalled for lack of funding at an early stage, and that other people have had to complete the architect's plans? As Joan Ramon Resina observes:

> the Sagrada Família has become an emblem of urban division. No one knows how the building would have looked if Gaudí had completed it. He left no comprehensive blueprints behind, and his models, sketches, and calculations were destroyed during the anarchist revolution in 1936. But construction proceeds on the basis of educated (and not-so-educated) guesses, much to the chagrin of many architects, artists, and intellectuals who see in every step toward completion a betrayal of Gaudí's genius [. . .] post-Franco sponsorship (much of it due to Japanese enthusiasm for Gaudí) has made people aware of the ever-wider departure from an imaginary 'original,' which existed only in Gaudí's mind. Indeed, construction is turning the Sagrada Família into a bad copy of itself. (Resina 2008, 155)

Of course, the Sagrada Família is an extreme example but the fact that investment in Gaudí is aimed at a tourist market rather than a local one, and that not everybody has the same understanding or even appreciation of his authenticity (as demonstrated by the anarchists), suggests that the authentic Barcelona is not to be so easily defined. This difficulty over authenticity seems to cause anxiety in academics as well. Byron is hardly alone in critiquing contemporary Gothic in this way, as we have seen previously. Gothic tourism appears to render the Gothic as toothless, and Byron's tone concerning the deceit of the walking tour echoes Botting's fears of passive consumers unable to distinguish the false Barcelona from the true one, the one stamped authentic because it lays claim to high culture. Tourism, however, is also a sign of the successful circulation of *La sombra* to the extent that the actual Barcelona, as well as its textual counterpart, become a nexus for Gothic circulation. As Ellis observes, Ruiz Zafón's own vision of Barcelona is clearly one of Gothic circulation. El Cementerio de los Libros Olvidados comes to symbolise Barcelona which thus becomes 'the nexus of all discourse' (Ellis 2006a, 854). Tourism, part of the life and the circulation of the narrative beyond the book itself, is therefore true to Ruiz Zafón's concept of Barcelona.

It is not clear in any case why an accurate understanding of Barcelona should matter as these novels demonstrate a clear flexibility with regard to location. Though *El club Dumas* starts in Madrid and ends near Toledo, the settings, via Portugal and Paris, are immaterial so that, in the film *The Ninth Gate*, there is no real problem in basing Corso in the United States. The film adaptation is itself part of the cultural flow. *La sombra* moves between Barcelona and Paris. Even old books move about and are part of a cultural flow. Neither key book in the two novels depends on a Spanish context, even if the context in which Daniel reads his book is steeped in the atmosphere of the Franco era. It is, though, intriguing that the ultimate trickery in *El club Dumas* is committed by Spaniards. In this sense, the Gothic is not in itself a local event though it can have impact locally. Carax gets his inspiration from both Barcelona – the scene with a Gothic house – and Paris, though his Gothic product nonetheless has a local impact on Daniel. Alternatively, the desire, condemned by Byron, to draw on British culture is not unique to *La sombra*. The series of novels by Tristante, mentioned at the beginning, model the central character Víctor Ros on Conan Doyle's Sherlock Holmes (though Ros is happily married). The novels feature apparently supernatural events that Ros explains away through reason, and this resembles many of the Holmes stories. Spanish steampunk has got in on the act as well. Félix J. Palma, for instance, sets his *El mapa del tiempo* (The Map of Time, 2008) in Victorian London and with British characters (including Jack the Ripper). Far from rendering Spanish culture inauthentic, these examples show Spain as a nexus, importing stories and motifs from other countries – and exporting them, as some of these novels are translated into other languages. Spanish culture selects which local and which foreign elements to use and profit from – like the walking tour of Barcelona.

The circulation of Gothic ideas in Spanish culture appears in microcosm in ideas of circulation of books through and across Spain within the two novels. *El club Dumas* is a Gothic text about the pursuit of another Gothic text, *Las nueve puertas*. Similarly, *La sombra* is a book about the pursuit of a novel also called *La sombra del viento*. The circulation of the Gothic in this way forms a *mise en abyme* that is reminiscent of Botting's suggestion of the endless recycling of Gothic ideas. Corso's role as a mercenary of books and Daniel's work in his father's bookshop link to Botting's sense of the Gothic as a capitalist, commercial consumerist flow. Botting's viewpoint is pessimistic, suggesting that the Gothic no longer has the potency it once did to reassure us that our fears will dissolve away. Indirectly, however, his argument goes against the emphasis on the Gothic book as physical object. As Spooner observes, 'Gothic writing is increasingly preoccupied with the book as artefact' (Spooner 2014, 193). Ellis similarly observes, with specific reference to the two novels of this chapter: the 'cult of the book as a discrete object, represented in *La sombra del viento* and even more fetishistically in Pérez-Reverte's *El club Dumas*' (Ellis 2006a, 840).

El club Dumas exemplifies this with the reproduction of the crucial illustrations from *Las nueve puertas*. If Varo Borja aims to destroy the book, the pictures at least are preserved and are circulated more widely, going against the idea of a small group of initiates. (I am sure I am not alone in peering closely at the illustrations, trying to decipher a putative code within.) Yet there is the matter of fakery that brings the book as physical object into question: its materiality is unreliable. Hence the illustrations of *Las nueve puertas* in the end hold no code and are a cheat. They are, in any case, fictional, part of Pérez-Reverte's narrative and not of the mysteries of *Las nueve puertas*. Of *La sombra*, Ellis argues that Daniel seeks to give life to the book but 'precisely because the book is boundless (not as a space of unlimited reader self-fulfilment but because textual signs continuously refer to other signs of signification and therefore can never be fully contained), it will elude him' (842). Perhaps the return of the book as physical artefact suggests not simply a nostalgia but a desire for meaning that will nonetheless prove elusive, as books may be material but they are not fixed. The Cemetery of Books is both a method of preserving books and of losing them. The books and manuscripts of *El club Dumas* are prized but are also mislaid or destroyed; and Corso, of course, is materially involved in their circulation. The materiality of the author is also a slippery concern in both books. Who is Carax? Who wrote *The Three Musketeers*? Who is really responsible for *Las nueve puertas*? Hogle is perhaps right, then, in seeing fakery as simulacrum, 'a symbol repetitiously manufactured from a pattern or mould (which is itself a ghost of the counterfeit' (2001, 299). The obsession with the contemporary version of the discovered manuscript perpetuates itself while the books themselves repeat the same Gothic pattern of mystery and devilry.

Nonetheless, when Hogle argues that eventually the Gothic will 'dissolve itself into sheer *simulation*, [. . .] a hyperreality of signs referring to other signs that cannot root itself even in quasi-industrial moulds' (300), I think his idea of the quasi-industrial is not realised here. And, with this comment, I should like to return to the concept of Spain as Gothic nexus. Both Pérez Reverte and Ruiz Zafón have distinctive approaches to their novels, and their success seems to have induced an assembly line of Gothic novels in the Spanish publishing industry. Nonetheless, I cannot equate this with the quasi-industrial moulds that Hogle speaks of, precisely because this is the *Spanish* publishing industry. *Pace* the commentators who read the Civil War into *La sombra*, both authors demonstrate a semi-detached approach to Spain in their narratives: the Gothic is, to my mind, stronger in both than the Spanish context in which the narratives are set. In both narratives borders are crossed, and both incorporate ideas, references and characters from other countries. With these novels, however, both authors demonstrate Spain as an active producer of the Gothic novel rather than as a victim of them.

CHAPTER 4

The Gothic House:
Problematising the National Space

The haunted house is a common motif of Gothic texts. As Kim Newman observes, 'The old dark house was the focus of the Gothic imagination well before the invention of the cinema' (Newman 2013, 96). Anthony Vidler observes of the nineteenth-century Gothic that

> The house provides an especially favored site for uncanny disturbances: its apparent domesticity, its residue of family history and nostalgia, its role as the last and most intimate shelter of private comfort sharpened by contrast the terror of invasion by alien spirits. (Vidler, 1992, 17)

Jack Morgan remarks: 'In the gothic context, there tends to be much ado about [. . .] real-estate matters, a reflection of the genre's notorious spatialization of fear' (Morgan 2002, 179). Peter Hutchings refers to the horror genre more widely but notes the importance of the house for figuring issues to do with the past: 'a recurrent feature of the horror genre is the house that contains secrets from the past, with the characters in these films often discovering that a familiar domestic setting is not so familiar after all' (Hutchings 2004, 74). This chapter studies the use of haunted houses in contemporary Spanish films to consider the varied uses made of houses and the ghosts that haunt them. Following on from the discussion of the role of the past in the Gothic novel of the previous chapter, this chapter starts by considering the valuable conceptualisation of Spanish historical memory of the Civil War and Francoism in terms of hauntology (as hypothesised in Labanyi 2001). It also considers the problems and contradictions that nonetheless arise from it, not least the fact that Gothic horror tales deliberately evoke ghosts and other monsters so that the repressed anxieties which are called forth by ghosts may arise as much from the demands of genre as of history. The chapter concludes by considering the house as part of an unstable cultural flow of Gothic, underscoring the ironic lack of fixity of the house that prefigures parallel arguments for the lack of fixity of the Gothic body in Chapter 6.

The focus of my consideration will be the film *NO-DO* (The Haunting, Elio Quiroga, 2009), an example of a haunted house that invokes a specifically Spanish past, in conjunction with the work of Jaume Balagueró, particularly his film *Darkness* (2002). My purpose in considering these two films in tandem is to problematise an equation that is frequently and, I would argue, too readily made between haunting and an explicitly Spanish hauntology. *NO-DO*'s title refers to the Noticias Documentales (usually abbreviated to NO-DO) or state newsreels made under the Franco regime: the title thus alludes to a specifically Spanish trauma, the country's suffering under Franco. (I say a Spanish trauma but not everybody found the dictatorship traumatic, thus immediately posing the problem of what a national trauma is; but an in-depth exploration of this matter is outside the scope of this chapter). *Darkness* does not even have a Spanish title, and the majority of the characters are not Spanish, though the traumatic events of the past which inform the action in the present do, indeed, take place in Spain during the Franco era. What these films have in common are the haunted houses and the child abuse that went on within them, abuse motivated by religious or satanic beliefs. I argue here for the Spanish Gothic house as demonstrating the sliding locations and porous spaces noted by David Punter and Glennis Byron (2004) that serve to problematise the insistence of many scholars within Spanish studies on a default meaning of ghosts as repressed war memories, and recuperate the idea of Gothic horror as pleasure, as posited by Robert Mighall (1999), whose ideas I apply below.

In arguing for this, I am not by any means dismissing the validity of interpretations that draw on Spanish national history and, indeed, I have carried out such interpretations myself (Davies 2012, Ch. 2). Nor do I wish to ignore the possibility that films such as the ones under discussion can, by their invocation of notions of ghosts and haunting, prompt memories and awareness of a troublesome past that needs to be dealt with in some degree. I do, however, argue against the supposition of a convenient and neat fit between the Gothic and the Spanish past. I believe it is crucial in this matter to tease out the complexities with which genre and mood frame the recuperation of the past through ghosts. It is, after all, not simply national history that can supply trauma. The two films that I focus on here and, indeed, some of the others that I mention in passing, address the question of the abuse and ill-treatment of children that has no clear political motivation. There is something troubling in the potential for seeing traumas such as child abuse as simply symbolic of national trauma rather than deeply scarring in and of themselves. I believe it is not only possible but also important to recognise that the recuperation of national trauma does not preclude the recuperation and exorcism of other traumas. The ghost is by definition historical, a revenant from the past, but its history is not necessarily national. Nicholas Mirzoeff argues: 'there is no possibility of visual culture's hauntology of visual media being anything other than historical. The question is whose history, told in what way and at what time?' (Mirzoeff 2002, 249). This is a question that those of us working on contemporary Spanish culture need to address with greater nuance.

In questioning the neat fit between haunting and Spanish twentieth-century history, I am not alone. Paul Julian Smith, for instance, comments of *El orfanato* (The Orphanage, J. A. Bayona, 2007):

> While a British critic like María Delgado reads *El orfanato* within the metaphorical context of the ghosts of the Civil War and the exhumation of collective graves (uncited in the film itself), it could be argued that the heightened contemporary awareness of the actual plight of missing, dead, or displaced children, abroad as in Spain, is an equally relevant and resonant context for the premise of *El orfanato*. (Smith 2012, 71)

Fernando Savater writes of Víctor Erice's Gothic film *El espíritu de la colmena* (The Spirit of the Beehive, 1973) that 'La colmena en la que se debate el espíritu de Erice es indudablemente España.' (The beehive in which Erice's spirit is explored is Spain without a doubt), and this concurs with the majority of interpretations of that film, interpretations that treat it in terms of the national past and less so in terms of modes and genres such as the Gothic. But Savater goes on to say:

> Pero el problema de la colmena, de lo uno y lo vario, de lo igual y lo distinto, del control, de la producción, de la sujeción a lo necesario, de la muerte, de la imposible fraternidad, de la maldad y la desdicha, los problemas que acongojan y rebelan al monstruo trascienden la siempre meritoria lucha contra el estilo totalitario. Recordar aquellos sin olvidar esta parece lo más digno de la vocación libertaria de la España actual. (2003a, 169)
> (But the problem of the beehive, of the one and the many, of the same and the different, of control, of production, of subjection to what is necessary, of death, of impossible brotherhood, of evil and misfortune – these problems which rebel against and distress the monster transcend the nonetheless valuable fight against totalitarianism. Remembering one without forgetting the other seems the most worthwhile thing in Spain's current liberatory vocation.)

According to Savater, then, it is no disservice to the memory of the Civil War dead to recognise that not all trauma, and thus not all haunting, can be mapped directly on to the framework of the War and Francoism.

Savater's reading nonetheless does not take into account the matter of the enjoyment of Gothic narrative, perhaps surprisingly given his fondness for both good and bad horror films. He is not alone, however, in stressing trauma at the expense of pleasure. Recent scholarship on the horror film has explicitly addressed the links between horror film and national traumas (Blake 2008; Lowenstein 2005). Linnie Blake argues that such traumas can be recovered and healed

> by focusing on the sites where ideologically dominant models of individual and group identity are sequentially formed, dismantled by trauma, but a willingness also to undertake a fundamental questioning of those ideologically dominant models of individual, collective and national identity that can be seen to be deployed across post-traumatic cultures, as a means of binding (hence isolating and concealing) the wounds of the past in a manner directly antithetical to their healing. (Blake 2008, 2–3)

This coincides with the argument within Spanish studies that film (and also novels) were early sites for the recuperation of memories of the Spanish Civil War and the dictatorship after the *pacto de olvido*.[1]

When Blake argues, however, that 'an escalating public interest in horror films' tells us of 'a public will to understand the experience of traumatic events while self-reflexively exploring the function of mass cultural representations of such trauma' (4), I am not so sure. Horror film – and Gothic texts more generally, my concern here – *can* do that, I have no doubt. I am less convinced that an escalating interest in horror (which Blake does not actually demonstrate) automatically implies a general will to understand past national traumas. It is unclear at what point such an impulse to analysis might come into play, in particular whether it comes into play in the decision of individual audience members to watch the film in the first place, and in their subsequent perception and interpretation of the cinematic narrative.

Thus, when José Colmeiro argues:

> We can see that Spain's historical trauma is the originating cause of these narratives populated by ghosts [. . .] It seems evident that the reappearance of ghosts in Spanish post-Franco culture has almost everything to do with the repression of the past, as an enforced prohibition during the dictatorship, and as a political taboo derived from the "pact of forgetting" during the political transition. (Colmeiro 2011, 31)

I have to admit that I do not find it evident at all. There might indeed be an impulse on the part of producers, directors and scriptwriters to explore these traumas through the motif of the ghost but, in the case of horror and Gothic film, it is just as likely (perhaps more so) that they prefer horror to history. The directors of the two films I have chosen to study in depth exemplify both possibilities: Quiroga, the director of *NO-DO*, deliberately selected a backstory set in the Franco era, but Balagueró does not talk of *Darkness* in historical terms at all. Furthermore, there is simply no guarantee that those who watch these films will inevitably interpret them in terms of the Spanish past. Andrew Smith argues as regards Gothic literature: 'the danger [. . .] is that such texts can merely be seen as doing history by other means and it is important that due acknowledgement is made of the literary histories which they also drew upon and which played a role in shaping a Gothic aesthetic' (Smith 2013, 7). What I am arguing for, then, is precisely a consideration of ghost films in Spain as part of a Gothic mode, a mode that is just as significant for the understanding of the film as national history is, if not more so.

One reason why Hispanists have seized on this equation between ghosts and history with alacrity is the influence of the seminal theorisation of hauntology and the Civil War by Jo Labanyi. Drawing on Derrida's concept of hauntology, she applies his ideas to the texts of the Civil War and the Dictatorship. Labanyi argues that there are 'many kinds of ghosts' and 'various ways of dealing with them', and goes on to suggest a tripartite model of ignoring the ghosts of history, obsessing about them, and exorcising them (Labanyi, 2001). I am suggesting here that there are other ways of dealing with ghosts, of which genre and mode are two, ways that provide a different narrative framework. Labanyi observes:

> In a country that has emerged from forty years of cultural repression, the task of making reparation to the ghosts of the past – that is, to those relegated to the status of living dead, denied voice and memory – is considerable. Derrida's notion that history occupies in the present a 'virtual space of spectrality' abolishes the supposed opposition between postmodernism and history, for history is always a 'virtual' rather than 'empirical' reality. The fact that Spain returned to democracy at the height of the postmodern vogue for 'virtual reality' should not necessarily be bemoaned as having prevented an engagement with the past. Perhaps instead we should consider the ways in which postmodernism, by breaking with empiricist concepts of mimesis, allows us to recognize the existence and importance of ghosts. (Labanyi, 2001)

Labanyi's point about the need to acknowledge such ghosts is an important point and, while I am suggesting a more nuanced approach to Spanish films with ghosts in them, I do not by any means wish to denigrate the desire to acknowledge ghosts of the past. I do, however, dispute the recurring interpretations that have by now reached a stage of conveyor-belt academic production, fitting Labanyi's template to a film and packaging it up neatly without much, if any, consideration of the other discourses – and, as Savater reminds us, other traumas – that frame a specific narrative. I cannot help feeling that some Hispanists take the obsessive approach to the ghosts of the past that Labanyi posits, unable to read any text except through the prism of that specific trauma, though Labanyi's threefold structure suggests that she is well aware of alternative positions for the reader or viewer. Labanyi's invocation of postmodernism, however, suggests not only a breaking with mimesis but with coherent narratives and underlying meaning. The ghosts of Spanish film and literature become part of a Gothic bricolage, possibly the circulation of empty images feared by Botting (2002, 298). They also form part of a postmodern instability that ensures that a ghost is, as a very minimum, semi-detached from its location. David Punter observes:

> What I suggest we particularly find in the numerous conjunctions of Gothic and the postmodern is a certain sliding of location, a series of transfers and translocations from one place and another, so that our sense of the stability of the map is forever under further siege. (Punter 2005, 170)

I shall return to the concept of instability below: at this point in my argument, I simply wish to indicate the challenges to currently prevailing interpretations that neglect some of the implications of Labanyi's many ghosts and many ways of dealing with them. There are other interpretative frameworks, of which genre is a significant one, that can open up the study of ghost texts to other insights. John Frow argues that it is vital 'to stress the open-endedness of genres and the irreducibility of texts to a single interpretive framework' (Frow 2015, 30), and one of my aims here is to help in opening up texts to other interpretations and approaches such as the ones I discuss in this chapter. Frow mentions how genre restricts meaning but also how genre is central to the making of meaning (10); this suggests that introducing the matter of genre to the Spanish hauntology debate carries its own risk but it also indicates that arguably we could not think of hauntology without also thinking about the genres that give rise to it.

I mentioned above that one neglected aspect of the horror film, with regard to its relation to national history, is that of pleasure, and it is this consideration I wish to turn to now before exploring the intricate connections of pleasure, genre and history in that ghostly location, the haunted house. One of the key sets of theoretical ideas I shall be using comes from Robert Mighall's book *A Geography of Victorian Gothic Fiction: Mapping History's Nightmares*. Many of the ideas Mighall offers from the outset fit uncomfortably with what I aim to do here: to understand the Gothic house as an unstable space that problematises the recuperation of the trauma of national history. For example, from the outset, Mighall declares that 'The "Gothic" by definition is about history and geography' (1999, xiv), an argument which I am attempting to challenge. Where I am in sympathy with Mighall, however, is in his questioning of the assumptions in Gothic and horror criticism that any relation of Gothic and horror to national history must involve the bringing to light and exorcism of trauma. He asks 'But is it the "business" of Gothic fiction to "articulate" or "negoti-ate" anxieties?' (167). (Though Mighall puts the concept of business in quotation marks, the commercial practice of producing and circulating Gothic film and literature for some sort of profit has its own impact on the questions I am raising here. I discussed the implications of Gothic as a commercial practice in the previous chapter.) Even more cogently, Mighall states that: 'Horror, because of its generic obligation to *evoke* or *produce* fear is not the most reliable guide for indicating supposedly "wide-spread" anxieties' (167, italics in original). This suggests that another way of considering the matter is through genre or mode as much as history, as the desire to recuperate memory is not always a convenient match with the demands of the horror genre to inspire pleasure through fear, that is, that we actively seek to experience fear in Gothic texts.

Various scholars have recognised the pleasures of the horror film (Carroll 1990, Hanich 2010, Hills 2005, Tudor 2002, Twitchell 1985) though they give different explanations for why this is so. Matt Hills, reviewing many of these theories, notes an oppositional binary between thought and pleasure when it comes to horror films, and argues that this is 'part of a cultural system of values that marks down "pleasures" as easy and counter-positions "theories" as difficult, demanding, and requiring labour' (Hills 2005, 8). The theories Hills speaks of are those that dismiss pleasure in horror as an aberration; for our purposes 'theories' stands for those discourses that deny pleasure in favour of the serious traumas of the past (which trump any value put on pleasure by their very seriousness). Pleasure is an element absent from most discussions of the ghost and memory within Spanish cultural studies although writings on Spanish horror film readily acknowledge fan activity, fanzines and magazines, film festivals and so on that clearly indicate horror as a source of pleasure (see, for example Aguilar 2005, Lázaro-Reboll 2012). The recuperation of memory through the Gothic is far from simply cathartic, in any case, because, as we shall discover, the ultimate response of most protagonists to the problem of the haunted house is simply to flee, leaving many traumas unresolved. The suggestion of pleasure disrupts and displaces national specificities, however. In the case of the films analysed here, the haunted house provokes its own expected fears which offer a morbid pleasure in both the uncovering of secrets and also their perpetuation in other haunted-house films. This serves to destabilise the link between location and history. Matt Hills notes that 'horror can immerse its audiences in an "anticipatory" mood or ambience that endures across the text, and which is not overwritten by specific narrative events or "occurrent" emotions' (Hills 2005, 25). By 'occurrent' Hills refers to emotional responses to specific moments in a horror film. Arguably, we could push this definition further to refer to emotional responses to a theme specific to a particular film or cluster of films. Such emotions, such as those responding to a past national trauma, exist alongside a general expectation of what a horror film will do; and, as the title of Hills's book (*The Pleasures of Horror*) strongly suggests, that expectation will include a substantial element of pleasure.

In considering the matter of pleasure, I would return to Labanyi's discussion, which includes an analysis of *El espíritu de la colmena*, the focus of Savater's comments mentioned above. The Gothic quality of that film has been noted by various commentators in passing, and in more detail by Robin Fiddian (2013) and myself (Davies, 2015a). In *El espíritu*, the central character, a little girl named Ana (Ana Torrent) forms part of a cinema audience watching James Whale's quintessentially Gothic film *Frankenstein* (1931). Labanyi points to Erice's insistence on 'shots of the cinema audience watching the shadows on the screen, showing how ghosts are given embodiment in the collective memory which, after the show is over, can continue to tell their story'. And she adds: 'Erice's representation of Frankenstein's monster likewise makes the point that ghosts, while they require remembrance in human consciousness, have an objective existence as the embodiment of the past in the present' (Labanyi 2001). The spectral quality of film, which makes characters and actors endure regardless of time and space, does, indeed, evoke the notion of the ghost. Ana and the audience, however, have gathered to watch *Frankenstein* not to remember the ghosts of the past but for pleasure, emphasised by Ana's particular fascination with the monster which the camera captured so serendipitously. It is Ana's pleasurable absorption in the film that sets her on her subsequent quest to find the monster in her own Spanish landscape. Pleasure forms a part of a Gothic circulation of *Frankenstein* that *El espíritu* takes up, refashions, and circulates again.

Having outlined some of the tensions embedded in interpretations of horror and ghosts in terms of national history, I shall now consider the haunted house in more detail as a motif that gives particular trouble when it comes to recuperating the ghosts of Spain's past.

The Unstable Pleasures of the Gothic House

If we are talking about Gothic houses, however, questions of space clearly matter here. If the haunted house is a familiar staple of the Gothic mode, then it nonetheless remains surprisingly unlocatable, devoid of specific geographical references. As a result, it becomes a slippery motif, subject to cultural exchange and even movement (such as Dracula's castle suddenly appearing in a small Californian town in the opening of the fifth season of *Buffy the Vampire Slayer*). Newman suggests that such houses 'are hard to find on a map but impossible to avoid in a storm' (2013, 96). David Punter and Glennis Byron also draw on the link between the map and a sense of fixity when they argue:

> What we find in the numerous conjunctions of Gothic and the postmodern is a certain sliding of location, a series of transfers and translocations from one place to another, so that our sense of stability of the map is – as indeed it has been since the first fantasy of a Gothic castle – forever under siege, guaranteed to us only by manuscripts whose own provenance and completeness are deeply uncertain. (Punter and Byron 2004, 51)

This quotation repeats almost verbatim Punter's comments on the postmodern Gothic that I quoted above. Here, however, Punter and Byron are applying these ideas specifically to the idea of a dwelling, a castle in their case, in reference to the classic Gothic of the eighteenth century, but a house for our purposes here. They propose that the Gothic dwelling recovers some stability through its link to the past: 'the traditional Gothic castle could be seen as embodying a past that goes back behind – or beneath – the "moment" of the subject, that asserts a different kind of continuity, even if it is one that can be known only under the sign of the secret, only in the "shadows" of the darkened study [. . .] (51)'. Yet the haunted dwelling – ironically, given its apparent symbolism of both time (the past) and space (the house itself but also its geographical location) – uncouples the link between haunting and national history. The haunted house is usually isolated, the nearest settlement an unnamed village (though there are exceptions such as the Barcelona houses of Ruiz Zafón's novels). Gothic houses tend to lie in the middle of the countryside or woods, or perch high on a hill or mountain (and, in this, they resemble Punter and Byron's castles). Morgan considers the house in terms of its separation from the rest of the community. 'The familiar gothic pattern situates an aristocratic dwelling high above the vulgar village, radically exclusive, cut off from scrutiny and normal moral conventions, and immune to the ordinary reach of law' (Morgan 2002, 181). In this sense, the Gothic house implies detachment from the outset: the generic settings go against the notion of fixity, the ability to identity a particular house as a result of its specific and recognisable place.

There are potential counterarguments that support a link between the

Gothic house and national history. Not all critics, for example, divorce the house so readily from its surroundings. Hutchings, writing of the American film *Halloween* (John Carpenter, 1978), makes the pertinent observation that the house is a mark of a terrible past event, the details of which are no longer known, but that the house remains in the community and the monster it contains is, indeed, created by that community (Hutchings 2004, 74–5). Similarly, Punter and Byron argue:

> Rather than being established as the demonic other to mainstream society, the monster is explicitly identified as that society's logical and inevitable product: society, rather than the individual, becomes a primary site of horror. (Punter and Byron 2004, 266)

The house as symbol is also associated with the family and domesticity; and, indeed, the frequent isolation of house from the rest of the local population coincides with a specifically family focus, the family as a form of entrapment. Dani Cavallaro argues that 'in the realm of gothicity, the family and its dwelling are often coterminous' (2002, 146) and argues further, 'Familial sins, passions and sorrows are projected onto the body of the house' (147). The sense of separation from the wider community may certainly remind us of Spain during the Franco era, particularly the early days of the regime when a policy of autarky was explicitly avowed. It is also not a big step to read the family in terms of a particular nation, and it is certainly a step that has been taken in connection with twentieth-century Spanish history. The old and decaying family home in *La sombra del viento* has, like the rest of the novel, been frequently read in terms of the recuperation of Civil War and Francoist histories but we also saw that such a reading was not inevitable. How far this may apply to other Gothic houses in Spanish texts is similarly debateable.

For example, Ernesto Acevedo–Muñoz (2008) and Colmeiro (2011) interpret the ghosts of *The Others* in terms of Spanish history but a case can equally be made for a more domestic reading, that the house in the film comes to stand for dysfunctional family lives in which violence and child abuse lie ready to hand. The Jersey setting in its liminality functions well as a more transnational site, diluting the link with Spanish history while being at a tangent to British national identity despite Grace's mannered English accent. (I discuss *The Others* in more detail in Chapter 5.) While the ghosts themselves might easily be interpreted as the monstrousness of the past come back to trouble living people who struggle to come to terms with the discomforts of history, the buildings they occupy do not fit this pattern so well. Despite the apparently neat fit of ghosts with the recuperation of Spanish historical memories, I think it would be reductive simply to think of the house as standing in for Spain, as the houses themselves appear never to stand any chance of recuperation. In many cases, including the films central to my discussion here, the living flee the house or, at least, attempt to do so. Consider, for instance, the house in *The Others* where the living family flee the house occupied by the ghostly Grace and her children whose final words in the film are 'This house is ours'. Similarly, the haunted house of *El orfanato* is occupied by dead children rather than living ones, despite the efforts of the heroine Laura (Belén Rueda) to makeover the house into a home for handicapped girls and boys. We could also consider the house in *El espinazo del diablo* (The Devil's Backbone, Guillermo del Toro 2001), a film that lends itself readily to Labanyi's hauntology framework, with the ghost Santi representing the forgotten victims of the Civil War; though, given Santi's position as a figure of horror, this reading is not unproblematic (Davies 2015b). The children's home which is the setting for the plot arguably acts as a microcosm of Civil War Spain, with the children caught in the middle of the fighting, and those associated with the Republicans dead or forced to flee. *El espinazo* indicates that suggesting the house or home as a private, 'family' sphere does not presume an unbridgeable binary between public and private; after all, affairs in the home may well be affected by what has gone on outside. Again, however, the house is abandoned to the ghosts, as the living survivors of the violent events within leave it in search of an uncertain future elsewhere.

It is this sense of abandonment (a term which can also indicate pleasure) that, for me, goes against the concept of the house as motif for the recuperation of national history. The Gothic house instead becomes abject, a repository not so much of secrets that we want brought into the light of day but of disgust, and of fascination with disgusting objects. The impulse to recuperate and clean away those secrets and fears resembles an act of what Morgan refers to as housekeeping:

> Housekeeping, in its deepest implications, is a primal imperative, part of our warding off of abjection – of decay, rot, squalidness. Healthy, civilized communities and individuals evidence an aesthetic interest and care, an engagement with themselves and their environment, that goes beyond the bare minimum to the dimension of a critical practice, an art. Places that evidence the lack of this critical endeavour bespeak incursions of morbidity into the communal body. (Morgan 2002, 186)

From this we could argue that the cleansing of the house is an example of housekeeping for the nation, unearthing the ghosts of the past in order to exorcise them. Examples such as *The Others*, *El orfanato* and *El espinazo*, however, suggest that the house is never clean as the ghosts remain in possession and the living are driven out. Thus, the house remains abject, as Chris Baldick observes: the Gothic house 'is not just an old and sinister building; it is a house of degeneration, even of decomposition, its living-space darkening and contracting into the dying-space of the mortuary and the tomb' (Baldick 1993, xx).

The house's abjection suggests an instability that ironically counters its apparent status as a fixed point of reference for the family. It also suggests pleasure. Julia Kristeva's study of the pleasures to be found in horror and the abject is now well known (Kristeva, 1982). If, as Morgan says, the Gothic house is a site of morbidity, nonetheless morbidity itself contains pleasure. The house incubates dark secrets which the protagonists take pains to expose (even when they discover that they themselves are the dark secret at the heart of the house, as with Grace in *The Others*). We take pleasure in both the process of uncovering the secret and the dwelling on the secret in morbid fascination (and, indeed, the sense of *dwelling* reinforces the specific role of the house in preserving morbid secrets). The pleasures of the Gothic house derive at least in part from the expectations of genre or mode: we know in advance what such a house should be like and what function it performs. Therefore, there is no easy fit between the haunted house and the recuperative quality of hauntology because, as Mighall suggests, the house is there to evoke fear and to dwell on it. Far from wishing to clear away the traces of the abject, we take pleasure in their preservation. This is, after all, why haunted houses are such a common feature of Gothic texts. To examine these considerations in more depth, I shall now explore in detail how the house in *NO-DO* and *Darkness* destabilises the link between the ghost and history.

NO-DO

In *NO-DO*, a young couple, Francesca (Ana Torrent) and Pedro (Francisco Boira), move to a house in the country with their new baby son. Francesca, a paediatrician, demonstrates an obsession with dead babies: the move to the house is undertaken in an attempt for her to recover from the birth of her son but also from an unspecified trauma from which her obsession arises. As Francesca goes about the house, she is accompanied by her daughter Rosa (Miriam Cepa). In fact, Rosa died when she was ten: as a ghost which haunts Francesca, she is able to make contact with the ghosts that haunt the house and to act as go-between. Francesca's own love for Rosa makes her amenable to Rosa's ghostly presence and thus more open to the other spirits in the house. Francesca's increasing insistence that the house is haunted is denied by Pedro who takes the baby away from her. Francesca is right, however: the house was once used for occult experiments with children on the part of the Roman Catholic Church. The ghosts are those of the children who died in these experiments. A priest, Father Miguel (Hector Colomé), helps Francesca and Pedro to confront not only the ghosts of the children but the elemental that has been occupying the house for many centuries and that is the root cause of the evil within it. Father Miguel dies in the ensuing exorcism: the house burns to the ground. Francesca and Pedro flee, and move to a new home in the suburbs.

If we wanted to read *NO-DO* in terms of Spanish history, we have plenty of licence to do so, as the director himself says in the DVD 'Making Of' feature that he wanted to make a film about the recent Spanish past. Sarah Wright argues that this film, along with *El orfanato*, 'conceives of Spain as an uncanny gothic mansion' and reflects 'the mood to investigate the past so long after the demise of General Franco' (Wright 2014, 158). The appearance of Franco in actual NO-DO footage within the film underscores the point still further. A crucial plot point in *NO-DO* is the making of clandestine documentary footage that recorded the occult experiments: the finding of snippets of film and then entire reels of footage propels the investigation. In one sense, Quiroga's version of the NO-DO is documenting the darker side of Francoism that the propaganda news-reels would never show. The treatment of the children of the losers under Franco has recently come under intense scrutiny, including accounts of ill-treatment, forcible removal from family, illegal adoption, and discrimina-tion. The Roman Catholic Church has been seen as complicit and culpable (see the final chapter of Graham 2012). The efforts to film the unfilmable, however (the NO-DO cameraman had invented a new form of film stock that could record ectoplasmic movement), has its own morbid fascination that is arguably echoed by Quiroga himself, dwelling on the horror of the house (he was also the scriptwriter). Indeed, in using the motif of found footage, Quiroga is drawing on a Gothic characteristic that goes back to the eighteenth century. As Spooner observes, found footage 'is rather like the discovered manuscripts of earlier Gothic fiction' (Spooner 2014, 191). It is also worth remembering that the past evoked in the film is not simply that of national history but part of a wider history of abuse and maltreat-ment of children, specifically at the hands of the Catholic Church, a past that has resonance in many countries today as historical instances of child abuse and ill treatment are uncovered (as mentioned by Paul Julian Smith, above). It should remind us of Savater's point that the War and the Dictatorship are not the only hidden traumas of Spanish Gothic.

Wright notes the significance of actor Ana Torrent in the role of the central character Francesca. As a child actor, Torrent rapidly became an icon of a cinema of resistance towards the prevailing Francoist ideology, particularly in her performance in *El espíritu de la colmena*. Wright suggests that 'Torrent embodies a temporal distinction between then and now a "present past": she is a work of memory' (155). Eric Thau argues in a similar vein that 'it is Ana Torrent's role as the iconic image of the Spanish conscience which sets her apart' from other child stars in Spanish cinema: Torrent as a child was explicitly associated with oppositional cinema (Thau 2011, 136). It is intriguing that hauntology comes to envelop the adult Torrent in these critiques. Wright talks of the adult Torrent as an uncanny doubling with Torrent the child (2014, 153), while Thau notes that 'Ana Torrent has been haunted throughout her career by this incessant discussion of her eyes, and of her magnetic impact on Spanish cinema' (Thau 2011, 132). I believe that this sense of haunting pertains at the level of mode as well as history, as Torrent in films such as *El espíritu* and *Tesis* (Thesis, Alejandro Amenábar, 1996) – and *NO-DO* – clearly functions as a Gothic heroine or Final Girl (Davies 2015a), in all cases inquisitive enough to question what is going on beneath the superficial appearance of reality. Torrent's acting roles as an adult have yet to overwrite her iconic roles as a child [*El espíritu*, also Carlos Saura's *Cría cuervos* (Raise Ravens) of 1975] but they are more varied than the fascination with *El espíritu* might suggest, and they certainly include a fairly strong association with genre film. Her role as Ángela in *Tesis* saw Torrent investigating violent crimes recorded on film, much as she does in *NO-DO*. This role, in particular, has given her a different iconic image, as the highly successful *Tesis* was one of the seminal films that kick-started a move towards an emphasis on commercial genre cinema in the mid 1990s. Torrent's persona therefore does not have the same resonance everywhere for everyone.

For Spanish film critics at the time of *NO-DO*'s release, the link to national history was the film's only redeeming feature. Ernesto Pérez Morán offers a dismissive view of the film in which the only notable element is the historical referent to the NO-DOs:

> Pero cuando el espectador cree que le han tomado el pelo, que la cosa va de terror patrio convencional y ramplón, y que no hay ningún trasfondo, emerge el entramado histórico de forma temible'. (Pérez Morán 2009, 262)
> (But just when the viewer thinks he's being taken for a ride, that it's a matter of the usual vulgar Spanish horror film, without any subtext, there emerges the historical framework in a fearful form.)

Pérez Morán denigrates the film for its commercial motivation, noting in passing the links to other films, specifically *The Sixth Sense*

Figure 4.1 The 'Spanish' haunted house of *NO-DO*.

(M. Night Shyamalan 1999), *Ringu* (Hideo Nakata 1998) and *Angels and Demons* (Ron Howard 2009). Andrés Rubín de Celis also notes the commercial impulse behind the film and quotes Quiroga himself who did not want to be simply a maker of cult films. Rubín de Celis also cites international references (George Romero, Tobe Hooper, Wes Craven and Sam Rami) as well as local ones (J. A. Bayona, Iker Jiménez) though he believes that Quiroga has lacked the sense of irony of John Carpenter or Guillermo del Toro (Rubín de Celis 2009, 42). These two critics perceive the film as formulaic, and the only highlight comes from the historical storyline observed by Pérez Morán. Formulaic Gothic is easily dismissed for its vulgarity and commercial motivation (particularly if it takes itself too seriously and lacks a sense of irony): only the references back to the Franco era offer any possibility of redemption for the film. The critics' attitude imply a disdain for the Gothic mode but it is their insistence that *only* the references to national history can redeem it that I wish to challenge. This insistence on national history neglects the pleasures of popular culture and the ways in which that culture undermines a fixed link between cultural text and the nation it derives from, as we saw in the previous chapter.

At the heart of *NO-DO* lies the Gothic house that is the subject of this chapter. In the 'Making Of' documentary on the DVD, Quiroga observes that the house used for filming had its own legend of executions and graves during the Civil War. The film crew claimed to see odd things during the shoot, suggesting that the actual location was haunted. These observations explicitly tie the house to Spanish history. The house as symbolic of Spain is therefore of a piece with the director's aims and the wider critique that reads the film in terms of Spanish history. The existence of elementals in the house predates the Franco era by some centuries, however. While the Church covers up the paranormal experiments conducted during Franco's time, drawing on an ideological authority fostered by the regime, it also hides away any earlier evidence of elementals. Father Miguel's superior shows him a painting, hidden since Franco's time, of an elemental visitation in Toledo centuries earlier. The picture is full of grotesque imagery, and the face of the Virgin in the painting has disappeared, replaced by a dark hole and two spots of red light. The evil of the house therefore points to monstrosity and haunting as inherent conditions of the house rather than something arising from specific historical conditions. Furthermore, the idea that the house symbolises Spain becomes extremely worrying in the light of what finally happens. The house itself is not restored but destroyed by fire, and that only after Father Miguel sacrifices himself to the elemental in an attempt to cleanse the house, a move clearly reminiscent of *The Exorcist* (William Friedkin 1973). Francesca does not cleanse the house or reclaim it: the end of the film sees her and Pedro transferred to a more modern suburb. The link of the house to Francoist history is thus problematic at best: the NO-DO crew and the Catholic Church are no more than a brief incident in the house's past, just as Francesca and her family are.

The house, meant to be a haven wherein Francesca recovers, in fact exacerbates her problems. Francesca is already and unsurprisingly obsessed with dead children, given the fact that her daughter Rosa died. This explanation of her motivation is kept half hidden for much of the film, however, and Francesca is initially presented as mentally unstable, needing the advice of a consultant, baptising dead babies in the hospital where she works and overly worried about her newborn son. The fact that her husband is a doctor, who does not always appear sympathetic, hints at his secondary function as her keeper, reminiscent of Charlotte Perkins Gilman's *The Yellow Wallpaper* (1892), as is the fact that Pedro removes the baby from Francesca's care, saying she is not currently well enough to look after him. The house Francesca and Pedro move into already has its ghosts from the past: the exploited victims, the majority of them children, used in the occult experiments. Yet Francesca also brings her own ghost with her, that of Rosa who keeps her company in the house and who functions as a conduit between Francesca and the other ghosts. Being in the Gothic house thus proves far from therapeutic for Francesca whose concern for dead children is simply exacerbated. Francesca will turn out to be right, of course, but the effect of uncovering the Gothic mystery at the heart of the house is not so much to heal her trauma as to aggravate it. Though an early sequence of the film shows Francesca and Pedro putting the house to rights and redecorating, the house wilfully reverts to horror iconography, such as the writing in blood on the wall that says 'La señora es mala' (the lady is bad), swirls of mist and religious statues on the upper floor, and footprints going up the wallpaper. Rosa also tells Francesca of the children hidden in the walls. The destruction of the house, far from suggesting cleansing, means that it can never be recuperated. As Wright notes, at the end of the film 'the haunting sense of the loss of childhood, enacted through its star, remains as a spectral presence' (Wright 2013, 118). From this we can deduce that both character and star evoke horror in the way that Mighall proposed, though I would suggest that Torrent's adult role as the central character in *Tesis* provides a more obvious comparison. It also provides an anticipation of Torrent's role in *NO-DO* for anyone who has seen *Tesis*. At any event, Torrent creates an expectation of the Gothic that matches the morbid fascination of Francesca which, in turn, aims to provoke similar feelings in the viewer.

The discussion thus far suggests that reading the haunted house in terms of the Civil War and Franco is far from straightforward. Genre and mode can account for the haunted house as much as, if not more than, historical memory. As we have seen, setting, plot, star image and inter-textuality in *NO-DO* have a strong Gothic resonance that should not be neglected. A comparison with *Darkness* further reveals the importance of the Gothic as an interpretative framework, so I shall go on to introduce *Darkness* and its haunted house before effecting a comparison of the two houses concerned.

Jaume Balagueró and *Darkness*

With the international cast (particularly in terms of the leading players),[2] use of English and Miramax partnership, *Darkness* was very much trans-national in scope (Lázaro-Reboll 2012, 251). Indeed, Balagueró's habit has been to film in English: all his films, apart from the *[REC]* films, have been in English, and there have recently been rumours that he will be filming in English again ('Balagueró, pesadilla en inglés', 2014)'. Balagueró has formed a crucial part of The Fantastic Factory, a Spanish production company whose policy was to make both low-budget and auteurist films in a bid for commercial fantasy and horror (Navarro 2005, 222). His influences tend nonetheless to lie far from Spain: Olivares Merino (2011, 44) observes the inspiration of Lynch, Cronenberg, Vincent Gallo and Christopher Nolan while Balagueró himself acknowledges *The Amityville Horror* (Stuart Rosenberg 1979) and *The Shining* (Stanley Kubrick 1980) as inspirations for *Darkness* (Navarro 2002a, 33). Lázaro-Reboll notes his long service in the Spanish horror film scene, starting with his fanzine *Zineshock* (Lázaro-Reboll 2012, 245). Balagueró's career is thus fully grounded in the horror genre: his work is the production and fostering of horror and Gothic narratives and lies far from any efforts to recuperate memories of national trauma.

Many of the critics commenting on Balaguero's films note the danger of his falling into repetition and cliché. Navarro (2002b), for example, notes that Balaguero shows skill at the level of visuals but not of narrative which is overly formulaic: the 'retórica filmica es un fin en sí misma y no una manera sólida, incluso poética, de contar una historia' (the cinematic rhetoric is an end in itself and not a solid or even poetic way to tell a story; 31). Later, however, he does claim Balaguero as part of the Fantastic Factory's auteurist strand (Navarro 2005, 222), implying that the director has a unique vision evident in the crafting of his narratives and thus contradicting his earlier point about an over-reliance on formula and cliché. In writing of *[REC]²* (2009), which Balaguero co-directed with Paco Plaza, Eulàlia Iglesias notes the tendency of Spanish horror to repeat well-known international formulas (41) though she argues that *[REC]²* manages to avoid simply repeating the formula of the first film (Iglesias 2009, 41). Such critique aims to undercut Balaguero's films at the level of genre, in a similar manner to *NO-DO*, of which the historical subtext is the only thing that appears to redeem it for the critics. It is only fair to note, however, that negative critique was not confined to Spain: Lázaro-Reboll (2012, 252) summarises negative reactions from American reviews from publication such as *The Hollywood Reporter*, *Village Voice* and *Entertainment Weekly*. Balaguero's stock has risen as a result of the *[REC]* series but early critique of films such as *Darkness* suggest the director as primarily another peddler of rehashed horror.

Balaguero's work reveals a fixation with haunted buildings: they feature not only in *Darkness* but also in *Los sin nombre* (The Nameless, 1999), *Frágiles* (Fragile, 2005), the first two *[REC]* films (2007, 2009), and even in the short film *Para entrar a vivir* (To Let, 2006), part of the Fantastic Factory's suite of films, *Películas para no dormir* (Films to Keep You Awake), by well-known horror directors. Olivares Merino (2011, 56) notes the emphasis in Balaguero's films on interior spaces rendered uncanny. Lázaro-Reboll (2012, 250–1) remarks on the publicity campaign that stressed *Darkness* as part of the horror genre, 'economically inserting the film into the haunted house subgenre. The publicity campaign in Spain and abroad conveyed the traditional promises and frights of horror promotion' (250). Lázaro-Reboll goes on to say (251) 'the house is home to an all-pervading darkness and the site of an abominable secret from the past'. The house motif risks becoming another of the formulas critiqued above. This does, however, raise the question of the haunted house in *NO-DO* as

Figure 4.2 The international haunted house of *Darkness*.

cliché, returning us to the dismissal of genre on the part of the critics and the role of genre as opposed to history in analysis of Quiroga's film.

The plot of *Darkness* centres on an American family who come to live in a slightly dilapidated house in Spain. It soon transpires that there is something wrong with both the house, which is haunted, and with the family. The father, Mark (Iain Glen), soon shows signs of mental illness while his son Paul (Stephan Enquist) is frequently disturbed by the activities of the ghostly children who inhabit the house and starts to suffer bruising. The mother, Maria (Lena Olin), pretends that nothing is amiss. It is left to the daughter, Regina (Anna Paquin), with the help of her boyfriend Carlos (Fele Martinez), to deal with the problems caused by the house. Regina often sees a mysterious man standing outside the house: this is the house's architect, Villalobos (Fermi Reixach) who later tells Regina and Carlos that the house was designed for occult purposes. Villalobos will later be killed as he is engulfed by darkness. The secret of the house is that it was built for an uncompleted occult ritual in which Mark's father and Regina's grandfather Albert (Giancarlo Giannini) attempted to sacrifice Mark as part of the ceremony. The ceremony involves slitting the throats of children, and is completed when Maria pierces Mark's throat when he is choking. Evil takes over the house, and Mark and Maria die. Carlos drives Regina and Paul away but, as their car enters a dark tunnel, he says that there is no escape. The film ends at this point as darkness engulfs the car.

Darkness posits the importance of the house from the very beginning, in the unknown child's voice-over dialogue, 'The house . . . they took us to a house', interspersed with flash shots of somebody in silhouette walking towards us down long passages. The subsequent images, brief shots of blood, upraised hands and a child running, and the voice-over suggesting that other children came to harm, immediately associate the house with violence towards children. The first full and stable shot in the film is of a house, indeed *the* house, plus the caption 'Spain, 40 years later'. The house will be occupied once more but this time by an American family who will become the conduit for the ghosts still dwelling in the house, the manifestations of the past secrets of children as victims of occult practices. The house is further marked as a site of conflict through the central character Regina rejecting it as a home within the first ten minutes and insisting on a return to the United States. As in *NO-DO*, the house is bound up with a past secret involving children as occult victims, a secret to be uncovered by the Gothic heroine. The time frame is also similar: though it is never explicitly stated, the original violence in *Darkness* must have been going on during the Franco era, if we assume that the film is set in the present (that is, circa 2002). There are, however, no references to Spain beyond the initial caption and, while Mark turns out to be the only surviving child of the original occult event, he is now American and based within an anglophone context. When Regina asks Carlos for help in investigating the house, he can find no documentation for it, suggesting the house as outside time and space.

Regina attributes all the ills of the film to the house, especially the strange behaviours of both her father and her brother, while she herself functions as the Gothic heroine (and her mother as the ineffectual and compromised older woman who often features in traditional Gothic narratives). Mark, who has Huntington's disease, is the primary locus of Gothic dysfunction and degeneration as he collapses mentally, leading in turn to physical self-harm. Much of Mark's mental collapse focuses on the house, as he breaks into a hidden room under the stairs, and then takes an axe to the floor to uncover evidence of the occult rituals held within its walls. Mark seems to take on the function of 'housekeeping' by bringing secrets into the light of day: for instance, hanging on the wall a picture of three mysterious old women. (Villalobos later sees an apparition of the old women on an underground train: they are a sign that he is shortly to die.) Mark rips up the flooring in one room to uncover a large circular carving in the shape of a dragon, an occult symbol. He rapidly loses the rationality that Regina possesses, however, so that, rather than exorcising the mystery, he is engulfed by it. If Mark uncovers the dragon circle under the floor, Regina carries out the research to identify the circle as a symbol of darkness but even this does not cleanse the house of its evil. Her action only facilitates the completion of the original ritual that scarred Mark in the first place. Mark's housekeeping thus contradicts Morgan's argument cited above, as it is a sign of madness rather than of health. It underscores, rather than diminishes, the morbidity of the house.

There is another meaning to the idea of the house – the family line running through generations. In terms of the Gothic, such an idea incorporates the concept of the family as decadent and corrupt, as Cavallaro argues above. The decay of the family and the building can be coterminous, as in Edgar Allan Poe's 'The Fall of the House of Usher' (1839). A parallel phenomenon pertains in *Darkness*, as the increasing evidence of evil in the house is reflected in the increasing dysfunction of the male family line. Regina notes that Mark's problems began when his son Paul was born and it is also noteworthy that his first mental attack on screen occurs while taking Paul in the car to school. The cross-cutting of this sequence with flashbacks to the earlier scenes in the house makes the connection clear that Mark's health has also suffered because of his past trauma: thus Paul becomes imbricated in this trauma, too. Paul has his own troubles: he is the prime focus of attention for the ghostly children, Mark's companions in the home forty years before who fell victim to the ritual. Paul can see the children and witnesses the mysterious movement of objects associated with children, such as colouring pencils and a toy merry-go-round. His body also becomes traumatically marked with unexplained bruises while his drawings of children show throats with red lines across them. It will transpire that cutting the throats of children is key to the ritual which is finally completed when Mark's throat is pierced in a failed attempt to stop him choking. Albert, an apparently benign presence in the family's life, turns out to be the source of the problems visited on his son and grandson as he formed part of the original ritual to kill the seven children. He failed originally to kill Mark but tells Regina that the ritual would have failed anyway because the victim has to be a loved child and he did not love Mark. (This appears to give rise to an anomaly in that Mark's death seems to complete the ritual but he is still an unloved child.) Albert recalls the figure of the mad scientist (which I discuss in Chapter 6) wielding a syringe to paralyse Carlos and threaten Regina. These traumas persist and repeat themselves from generation to generation and thus become undifferentiated, obliterating the distinction between past and present.

The Similarities of the Haunted House

NO-DO overtly draws on Francoist history while *Darkness* does not. The commonalities of the films, however, may help us to rethink the former in terms of the Gothic mode rather than in terms of hauntology. The houses have in common their haunting by the malevolent ghosts of children who were victims of occult rituals. The living families who come to occupy the houses carry a secret of past trauma involving children: the loss of a daughter in the case of *NO-DO* and a father who suffered as a child in *Darkness*. In both cases the relationships between family members are also troubled. Pedro takes the baby away from Francesca and does not believe her story: he also talks with her consultant behind her back. Mark's family learns to fear him: Regina cannot get her mother to look at Paul's bruises. Father–son relationships are particularly disturbing. Albert attempts to sacrifice Mark; Mark chases Paul with an axe. None of these elements necessarily entails a reading in terms of historical trauma. A comparison of *NO-DO* with a film by a director fully immersed in the horror genre and with a penchant for haunted houses suggests a very different interpretation for the former.

It is important, I feel, to emphasise the efforts of the families concerned to refurbish and thus, in a sense, to clean and refresh the haunted houses they hope to live in. (This also occurs in *El orfanato*.) Refurbishment exemplifies Morgan's concept of housekeeping cited above but, as we have seen, the house always reverts back to its old ways and its old inhabitants. Kim Newman remarks:

> Electric light and a coat of paint, some throw-rugs and scatter-cushions . . . they won't change anything, for the old dark house is more than a melodramatic convenience, it is a Gothic necessity. (Newman 2013, 102; ellipsis in original)

Indeed, the scenes in which the families carry out their refurbishment are perfunctory. There is a brief montage in *NO-DO* of stepladders in the background and Pedro and Francesca looking at wallpaper, and brief scenes of painting and failed lighting repairs in *Darkness* but much more time is taken up by the protagonists dwelling on the spooky spaces, moving slowly through them, lingering as they listen for noises. Thinking of the house in Gothic terms, then, indicates that there can be no recuperation, so the efforts of both families to makeover the houses are doomed from the very start, and, what is more, we know that to be the case. Gothic houses do not want to be made over: their purpose is to harbour and produce terror, as Mighall posits, and past traumas are not laid to rest.

The house produces terror in its living occupants as long as they inhabit it and, in *Darkness* at least, it is a terror that the occupants do not escape. The house remains standing but given over in its entirety to evil. In *NO-DO* the house burns to the ground, having consumed Father Miguel, who previously informed his superior that the elemental in the house could not be dislodged despite many previous exorcisms. This proves to be the exact opposite of Morgan's housekeeping on two levels: in one sense there is residual detritus that cannot be cleaned away, and the destruction of the house cannot be considered a form of maintenance or house*keeping*.

Francesca and Pedro's move to a modern, sunlit suburb is flight rather than victory and leaves a sense of anticlimax that I believe to be a weakness of the film. Evil has not been conquered and we are left with a consciousness of retreat rather than recovery. This failure of housekeeping is underscored in another sense by the fact that we have no clear indication that Francesca has moved on from her obsession with dead children; though it was her initial obsession that marked her out as of interest, so that the disappearance of this storyline at the end renders her uninteresting. Newman notes that the triumph of the dead over the living is a recurring feature of the haunted house, and argues this in a way that is highly suggestive of the two endings of *NO-DO* and *Darkness*:

> The best inhabitants can hope for is a last-reel conflagration, with the stones falling into a tarn or the grounds sewn with salt. The worst is that the house is still standing come the morning, and another night is only a sunset away. (Newman 2013, 96)

The Free-floating Gothic House

My intention in the discussion above has been to question the easy assumption that haunting in Spanish Gothic film must inevitably be understood in terms of national trauma and to argue for an understanding of the Gothic mode as an essential analytical tool. The similarities of the two films go against an automatic and inevitable reading of *NO-DO* in solely historical terms. One of the factors I explored in this discussion was the relation of the house to national space, and I should like to return to the question of space here to argue for the importance of the Gothic mode in another sense, that of contemporary Gothic as cultural exchange and circulation. The haunted house is a staple of the Gothic mode yet, in another sense, it suggests instability in that the haunted house cannot be reliably positioned in Spain and incorporated into its history. Spain is briefly referred to as the location in *Darkness* and implied by language and by historical referents in *NO-DO* but we have nothing more specific than that and, indeed, *Darkness* has an American family at the centre of its narrative. The child abuse, which is the secret of both houses, maps on to concerns about the Francoist past, as we have seen, but it maps far more readily on to characteristics of the Gothic mode. Intertextual references and parallels, easily recognised by fans, readily connect both films to other haunted-house films beyond Spain. *NO-DO* was released in the United States and Canada as *The Haunting* (also the title of the British DVD release): the English title clearly evokes Robert Wise's 1963 classic haunted-house film of the same name (and possibly Jan de Bont's 1999 remake). As has been mentioned, Father Miguel's self-sacrifice clearly suggests similar priestly actions in *The Exorcist*. Balagueró's international influences have already been referred to: in the DVD director's commentary, he cites the three old ladies in the photograph that Mark recuperates as a reference to Dario Argento's Three Mothers trilogy. He also cites *The Shining* as an influence, visible in particular in the scene where a crazed Mark tries to batter down a door with an axe.

Nevertheless, I do not want to argue for the circulation of Gothic simply through intertextual references, intriguing as they can be. I should like to suggest the narrative of the haunted house as another travelling narrative. The narrative of the haunted house is one that has been retold in many times and many places: it can be located, and relocated, anywhere to the extent that the link to a specific locale and history becomes slippery and, at times, highly tenuous. This does not mean that a specific history cannot be registered as a trace across the narrative based on the house, as *NO-DO* illustrates. The houses of films such as *NO-DO* and *Darkness* form part of a wider Gothic mode, however, that has become pronounced in the contemporary Spanish film industry but which has its antecedents elsewhere (see Davies 2015a) and which tap into memories and reflections of traumas that are unconfined by national boundaries: traumas which, as Savater rightly reminds us, also need to be remembered and recuperated alongside those of the Civil War. Morgan argues: 'The properties of terror, houses or other sites, are ones that, should we imagine horrible things unfolding, we would imagine them unfolding *there*' (Morgan 2002, 184; italics in original); the difficulty is that *there* no longer has any stable meaning. It is worth reminding ourselves here of Giddens's conceptualisation of place in a globalised circulation: 'place – permeated by distant influences – becomes like a dream or phantom' (quoted in Buonanno 2008, 20). The Gothic house become a free-floating phantom in its own right, and the notion that it has a fixed location becomes itself no more than a haunting idea that suggests its own loss. This loss is, of course, a key reason why Spanish critics lament genre and prefer history: a sense of place is lost in the circulation of contemporary Gothic. We should remember that a feeling of loss may not be shared by all viewers of horror film; they may not have the same investment in perceiving a film in terms of its geography and concomitant history.

The slipperiness of location of the house is a microcosm of Gothic and horror in relation to the recuperation of Spanish memory. In an article which dismisses the efforts of many Spanish films to marry genre and memory, Àngel Quintana argues that 'The internationalization of film industry models represents a break from the cultural movements and traditions that have sustained Spanish cinema for years.' And:

> Today, when the topic of memory is at the heart of current political debates, we are faced with a situation where the blindness of the industry could halt the process of recovery and revision of that memory in contemporary cinema. (Quintana 2014, 13)

Quintana's argument here presumes a moral obligation on the Spanish film industry that is highly debatable. State funding might, of course, imply a degree of responsibility on the part of those directors and producers who get funding, though this sort of funding has, in any case, suffered severely in the wake of the economic crisis of the last few years. I would also argue that Quintana's suggestion that these moves are a genuine break from older models of film-making is also questionable. Genre cinema at the very least – comedy, in particular, but also horror – has had a sustained history well before the so-called 'commercial turn' of the 1990s. In any case, Núria Triana-Toribio notes the turn to genre cinema as a compromise between establishment desires for quality cinema and the lowbrow productions that were nonetheless more profitable. Part of the original emphasis on quality cinema, she points out, was a desire to sell Spanish cinema abroad (Triana-Toribio 2014, 68): what has changed is the fact that quality cinema is now, as often as not, genre cinema such as *The Others*. The suggestion that the international model of film-making has ruptured the link to the past is therefore not as clear-cut as Quintana claims. Quintana's comments, however, chime with those of reviewers, such as Pérez Morán and Rubín de Celis, in their distaste for genre, an attitude that continues to prevail in much Spanish film reviewing, and an emphasis on a specifically Spanish history as the only thing that can redeem films such as *NO-DO*. Quintana implicitly harks back to a presumed Golden Age of oppositional, auteurist cinema in which commercial values did not feature strongly. He explicitly laments the desire of contemporary Spanish directors to follow an 'international' model of cinema even though the oppositional cinema of the 1960s and 1970s also drew on cinematographic models from outside Spain. Age may also be a factor in the perception of the current trend to genre cinema. Paul Julian Smith observes that 'While filmgoers in Spain, as elsewhere, tend to be teenagers, directors, mainly middle-aged men, turn their back on the public to pitch quality projects (such as Civil War dramas) aimed at pleasing government-funding bodies more than audiences' (quoted in Triana-Toribio 2014, 69). Triana-Toribio warns against a simple generational split, as many younger critics and film professionals are in favour of the older forms of cinema promoted by older auteurs (75). While we should rightly heed such a warning, Smith's comments nonetheless draw our attention to a rift between older and younger forms if not film-goers; and, as we have seen, there is little patience on the part of the critics with the younger forms today. In a similar manner, interpretations in terms of national history within Spanish studies have sometimes imposed an analytical straitjacket that separates films from the industrial context from which they came.

Quintana's references to the film industry and their desire to make commercial products raise another question evoked by Mighall's comments quoted above: that of people actively seeking out Gothic film, not to recuperate historical memory, but for the fear and terror it produces. Quite why audiences should want to watch such films for pleasure has exercised quite a few scholars, as mentioned above. As Hills suggests (2005, 3–4), academics tend largely to understand pleasure in horror as a problem or puzzle that needs to be solved and thus, implicitly or explicitly, perceives pleasure in horror as a negative thing. Such a position echoes the negative attitudes to popular horror and the insistence on historical readings that have been considered here. There are, perhaps, possibilities to marry history and pleasure in the study of the Gothic house. Andrew Tudor (2002) calls for a historical approach to the pleasures of horror that would chime well with interpretations that call upon historical trauma:

> If we really are to understand horror's appeal, and hence its social and cultural significance, we need to set aside the traditionally loaded ways in which 'why horror?' has been asked. For the question should not be 'why horror?' at all. It should be, rather, why do *these* people like *this* horror in *this* place at *this* time? And what exactly are the consequences of their constructing their everyday sense of fearfulness and anxiety [. . .] out of such distinctive cultural materials? (Tudor 2002, 54)

Tudor poses questions rather than answers (and acknowledges that answering his questions would involve a gargantuan amount of work for the researcher; 53). But his questions can be applied just as much to the matter of Gothic as a product of a particular film industry as to hauntology as part of the theoretical discussion about Spanish twentieth-century history. Tudor, in fact, goes some way towards answering Quintana's gripe that film-makers want to make commercial films rather than those that engage with the Spanish past, as least as far as the Gothic and horror are concerned. This is a different way in which directors, scriptwriters and viewers have the opportunity, if they wish to take it, to confront the traumas of the past. It is their way of performing memory in *this* place at *this* time. But we have already seen that the idea of *this* place is not as straightforward as we might like to think. And, as scholars, we also have to recognise that this is just one use than can be made of such films.

In her valuable book on the challenges and opportunities of the Spanish historical memory debate, Alison Ribeiro de Menezes discusses the position of the 'consciousness-raising, recuperative politics that seeks to uncover and give voice to silenced and forgotten histories', a position to which the interpretations of ghost films in terms of history arguably belong to a greater or lesser degree. Ribeiro says of this position:

> I fully support such a position at the same time as I regard it as insufficient – insufficient, because it is too limited, unself-critical, and unreflexive a response to memory's debates and dilemmas. The time has come to move beyond this. (Ribeiro de Menezes 2014, 8)

I fully concur. The haunted houses discussed in this chapter point to some ways to do this. As Andrew Smith suggested, we need to give due acknowledgement to other discourses, such as genre and the history, culture and industry that surround it. In addition, we need to recognise that the link of a specific story to a specific time is attenuated by the slipperiness of motifs, such as the haunted house, which eludes efforts to tie it to a fixed place. Instead, the haunted house is part of a mobile discourse, a travelling narrative that can be appropriated for local purposes but which can never be contained by them.

Notes

1. The pact of forgetting, or the agreement among the political parties of a newly democratic Spain that the injustices of the Franco era would not be pursued. This was in order to ensure a peaceful transfer of power from the regime.
2. The main actors are: Anna Paquin (Canadian), Iain Glen (Irish), Lena Olin (Swedish), Stephan Enquist (Swedish/Spanish), Giancarlo Giannini (Italian) and Fele Martínez (Spanish). None of them, ironically, are American – a further disconnect between the house and nationality.

CHAPTER 5

The Gothic Camera:
Javier Aguirresarobe at Home and in
Hollywood

This chapter looks at the Gothic work of renowned Spanish cameraman Javier Aguirresarobe. Aguirresarobe is one of the leading directors of photography in Spanish cinema's contemporary era, having had a long career in Spain arising from the vanguard of Basque film-making in the 1980s. This included working with Imanol Uribe, the leading Basque director throughout the 1980s. In the 1990s he worked regularly with Pilar Miró, Spain's leading female director of the era, while, over the years, he has also worked with prominent Spanish directors such as Julio Medem, Pedro Almodóvar, Alejandro Amenábar, Víctor Erice and Fernando Trueba. From the turn of the century, he has also established an international reputation through working with Woody Allen, Miloš Forman, and James Ivory. Much of his current output emanates from Hollywood, and this includes involvement in Hollywood's highly successful and perhaps most notorious recent franchise, the *Twilight* series, based on the books by Stephenie Meyer. The cameraman's resumé demonstrates work across a wide variety of genres and is not by any means confined to horror and Gothic film-making; some of the most successful films he has worked on, however, come from this genre.

In the discussion here, I shall first focus on two examples of Aguirresarobe's explicitly Gothic landscapes that he created on Spanish soil: *La madre muerta* (The Dead Mother, Juanma Bajo Ulloa 1993) and *The Others* (Alejandro Amenábar 2001). I shall then discuss his more recent work in the United States and, specifically, his work on *The Twilight Saga: New Moon* (Chris Weitz 2009), the second instalment in the *Twilight* film saga, to look at the ways in which Aguirresarobe's work contributes to an idea of Gothic cultural exchange. The notion of a specifically Spanish contribution is from the outset undermined by Aguirresarobe's roots in the Basque Country and his contribution to the establishment of a specifically Basque cinema. This has occurred primarily through his work with Uribe, particularly on key films, such as *El proceso de Burgos*

(The Burgos Trial, 1979), *La fuga de Segovia* (The Flight from Segovia, 1981) and *La muerte de Mikel* (The Death of Mikel, 1984), which remain landmarks in the development of a specifically Basque cinema after the end of the Franco dictatorship. Nonetheless, the work developed by the cameraman in his career in both Basque and Spanish cinema is what has allowed him to establish his particular style, a style that now circulates beyond Spain.

There is a notable trend in much of Aguirresarobe's work for colder landscapes with watery light which dovetail with traditions of Gothic landscape. Gothic exteriors are often craggy and misty, dotted with ruins and castles; interiors are shadowy and labyrinthine. Above all, such landscape appeals to sight, though lived experience of such landscapes might draw on the other senses as well. In cinema, however, sight and, to a lesser extent, sound are the only means of experiencing such landscapes. And sight requires light so that the work of lighting and camera becomes crucial to the cinematic Gothic experience. While all directors of photography are necessarily concerned with light, including the play of light and shade, nevertheless bleaching and attenuation of light are clear markers of Aguirresarobe's individual style. It applies to much of the cameraman's work regardless of genre, as in, for instance, Graham Fuller's reference to lemony amber light in *Vicky Cristina Barcelona* (Woody Allen 2008) (Fuller 2009, 25), the lemon contaminating the amber with its coolness and acidity. According to Alberto Mira, the noir film *Beltenebros* (Pilar Miró 1991) is the start of Aguirresarobe's mature period, and Mira argues that 'he moved away from realistic atmospheres into more creative, expressionistic approaches to light and atmosphere' (Mira 2010, 5–6). The word 'expressionistic' is key to the particular style of light and atmosphere, suggesting the twilight world of the Gothic. 'Increasingly [. . .] one can appreciate Aguirresarobe's taste for working with muted light and experimenting with *chiaro oscuro* [*sic*], together with a feeling for cold moods and unreal spaces' (6).

The book on Aguirresarobe's work by Jesús Ángulo, Carlos F. Heredero and José Luis Rebordinos (1995) carries the title *En el umbral de la oscuridad*, on the threshold of darkness, which readily suggests the match between his camera style and that of the Gothic. They remark: 'La luz, el sol, el color. Siempre da la sensación de que Javier Aguirresarobe tiende, de manera refleja, a defenderse de ellos' (Light, colour, sun. You always get the feeling that Javier Aguirresarobe tends quite consciously to resist them'; 34). Aguirresarobe himself concurs: 'Es muy importante que haya poca luz. Los momentos verdaderamente interesantes empiezan, precisamente, cuando la luz pierde intensidad y gana en posibilidades' (It's very important that there isn't much light. The truly interesting moments start exactly when the light becomes less intense and gains in possibilities; 57). The authors go on to say: 'Parece [. . .] que su mirada se hace más incisiva y más aguda cuando atraviesa el territorio fronterizo en el que la luz y la oscuridad se contaminan mutuamente' (It seems that his gaze becomes sharper and more incisive when it crosses the border territory in which light and darkness bleed into each other; 57–8). The suggestion of border territory and mutual contamination readily implies Gothic principles, the encounter of light and dark and the tendency to chiaroscuro style and theme.

Aguirresarobe's propensity for dim lighting, however, stems not simply from a preference but from what seems almost a schizophrenic antagonism towards the light and thus, by implication, his own role as cinematographer which depends on light (however attenuated) to function. Light is a negative entity that must be combated:

> Si se pretende crear una iluminación creíble, lo primero que ha de fijarse es cuál ha de ser la fuente de luz que proporcione esa credibilidad. Aguirresarobe busca esa fuente de luz, no para serle fiel, sino para destruirla y, posteriormente, recrearla de la forma más conveniente. (Ángulo, Heredero and Rebordinos 1995, 36)
> (If you want to create credible lighting, the first thing to note is what the source of light must be that gives it credibility. Aguirresarobe seeks out that source of light, not in order to be true to it, but to destroy it, and afterwards recreate it in the most suitable form.)

This suggests that Aguirresarobe seeks to dominate light through destruction and recreation: light will ultimately be faithful to his own vision. In this chapter I am not necessarily seeking to establish his approach as something equivalent to auteurism in which one individual (usually the director) might have a unifying vision across all films. As we shall see, different directors with whom Aguirresarobe worked differed in their input to the lighting process but Aguirresarobe did not necessarily have total control. I do, however, wish to claim that Aguirresarobe has a deliberately Gothic approach to light and camera that has as its nexus the Basque Country, a place that itself has had a semi-detached and problematic relationship with the Spanish nation. This approach adapts itself to the Gothic in many settings and contexts: it is an approach that travels.

In Aguirresarobe's Gothic films, light becomes synonymous with death: either it kills directly or exposes to view death as the secret hidden in the Gothic shadows. Yet the light is bound up with photography which is impossible without it, a schizophrenic attitude to capturing the image. Warner, writing on the invention of magic lanterns and cinematic projection, argues:

The association between diabolical phantoms and spectral phenomena influenced the content and material of optical illusions, and shaped the characteristic uses and development of those varied and wonderful technological devices that have been used to represent the supernatural, to make present what eludes the senses and to make visible the invisible. Magic lantern shows sharpened the question that haunts the double: are such visitations phantoms conjured by external, diabolical forces, or are they ghosts within? (Warner 2002, 177)

From the very inception of cinema, then, technology has given rise to Gothic questions about the veracity of the image, prone as it is to illusion. But, if technology can make the invisible visible, the opposite is also true. Misha Kavka argues that: 'Rather than the horror film's challenge to the audience to open their eyes and see, the feared object of Gothic cinema is both held out and withheld through its codes of visual representation' (Kavka 2002, 227), of which light and shadow form one such code. The notion of both offering and withholding the Gothic as visual coincides with the position of a Gothic camera operator attempting to film what is ultimately unrepresentable and can only be hinted at or approached obliquely through Gothic conventions. By controlling the light, the cinematographer is able to dictate how much we see but, nonetheless, depends on the light for his or her very existence *as* a cinematographer.

Kavka goes on to state: 'in Gothic film the dialectic between seeing and not seeing is visualized as a manipulation of space and frames that materializes the impossibility of representations actually grasping the thing "beyond"' (227). Monleón offers a similar principle: 'The destruction of representation through representation – such will be the new paradox that will haunt the twentieth century' (Monleón 1992, 140). Indeed, the paradox haunts the twenty-first century as well. Nonetheless, despite Kavka's argument that Gothic film both raises and forecloses visual representation, there is an irony in that film versions of the Gothic proliferate, yet the very proliferation exacerbates the difficulties of the visual Gothic. Botting suggests: 'Since Walpole, Gothic has emerged as an effect of and an engagement with a crisis in the legitimacy and authority of the structured circulation of social exchanges and meanings over which the father figure presides' (Botting 2002, 282). This crisis in legitimacy today includes the circulation of images within cinema and specifically within Hollywood: Aguirresarobe certainly implies a reverse transatlantic crossing which undercuts the centrality of the Anglo-American to the Gothic mode. The link between the Gothic and father figures expresses itself in ideas of possession, of who can lay claim to anything, of the determination of meaning. If Aguirresarobe controls meaning through the manipulation of light, offering and foreclosing meaning, this suggests that the father figure of authority has not disappeared.

But, if Aguirresarobe is part of a globalised circulation, there is also insistence on his roots, not so much in Spain as more specifically in the Basque Country, which has its own schizophrenic position as part of Spanish territory but with a culture of resistance to Spain. Rob Stone, interviewing Aguirresarobe concerning his work on the film *Tierra* (Julio Medem 1996), quotes the cinematographer's emphasis on being born in October (like Medem) and comments: 'Being born in autumn, when everything else is dying, is perhaps a requisite for sensitivity to notions of duality, especially when that autumn is Basque' (Stone 2007, 114). Ángulo, Heredero and Bordinos link the landscapes of attenuated light to Aguirresarobe's roots in the north and the Basque Country (1995, 30), and further insist:

'Me defiendo continuamente del color; no lo puedo remediar, reconoce este operador que viene del norte y que ha educado sus ojos allí donde la luz es avara y debe luchar, casi continuamente, para abrirse paso entre los filtros de las nubes. (60)
('I constantly resist colour: I can't help it' acknowledges this cameraman, who is from the north and who has trained his eyes there, where the light is sparse and constantly fights to make its way through the clouds that act like filters.)

Aguirresarobe implicitly points to the possibility of an uncanny Basque Country when he refers to a sad and grey San Sebastián in the film *27 horas* (27 Hours, Montxo Armendáriz 1986) which would thus appear 'diferente, extraña, cargada de cierto pesimismo' (different, strange, laden with a certain pessimism, 132). This strangeness can be found in his Gothic films that increasingly move from an uncanny rendering of a specific location (the Basque capital, Vitoria, in *La madre muerta*, the first of the films to be discussed in detail below) to a Spanish landscape masquerading as something else (northern Spain as ostensibly the Channel Islands in *The Others*) and a departure from Spain altogether (the American town of Forks in *New Moon* and *Eclipse*, though much of New Moon was made on Vancouver Island in Canada). Aguirresarobe's landscapes thus retain a trace of his Basque roots but this Gothic light becomes increasingly detached from any notion of national space.

A touch of otherness can nonetheless be detected behind the dominant, indeed patriarchal, association of the Gothic with Anglo–American culture (which itself often displaces the Gothic on to foreign locations, including Spain as in Lewis's *The Monk* and Maturin's *Melmoth the Wanderer*). In the work of Aguirresarobe, this translates into a transatlantic continuum which moves from Spain to the United States in what appears to be a seamless pattern of generic Gothic landscapes. The landscapes considered here move from a specifically Spanish/Basque location to one that is Spanish while masquerading as the Channel Islands, and then to an ostensibly American location. The interplay of light and landscape, however, gives rise to Judith Halberstam's excess of productivity and meaning in terms of space and place (Halberstam 1995, 4; I shall discuss her arguments in more detail in Chapter 6) which, in turn, leads to, if not a crisis, then a great problematisation of the legitimacy of Gothic images over which the Anglo-American presides.

Botting argues that:

> In the context of a movement from a modernity associated with rational production to a *post*modernity linked to accelerated technological consumption, Gothic images and horrors seem less able to restore boundaries by allowing the projection of a missing unifying (and paternal) figure. No single framework stabilizes social meanings and identities. (Botting 2002, 281)

We could perhaps argue that there is a single Gothic framework, possibly a globalised one, possibly transnational but, in any case, a travelling one facilitated by the very technology Botting refers to. Such a framework has, of course, been largely shaped by the anglophone Gothic tradition. Botting understands this new situation, arising from a global economy, as tainting the Gothic: 'as global economic practices change in the twentieth century and industrial production cedes to postindustrial consumption in western societies, excess, waste, and useless activities come to the fore and transform the significance of the Gothic genre' (285). Yet one effect of 'excess' is the rise of new materials from outside the tradition: hence the rise of global Gothic. Excess seems to be the breaching of the anglophone boundaries to allow in all sorts of traditions and frameworks with new meanings which may then be adapted and indigenised elsewhere.

Aguirresarobe is an example of this process of deterritorialisation, providing another example of Spain as nexus, with his roots in the Basque Country and his work first in the Spanish film industry and now in Hollywood. And, in terms of a unifying paternal figure, it could be worth remembering those ghosts behind the film texts, the director, scriptwriter and crew. In terms of Gothic light, Aguirresarobe is one such figure, his actions manifest while he himself is hidden (behind the camera, though the technological advance of DVD extras makes him visible again. He is easily to be seen, for instance, in the DVD extras in *New Moon*). Efforts at control of light suggest him as a father figure who nonetheless dissolves boundaries rather than maintains them. Aguirresarobe travels 'excessively' in the sense that he breaches his own national boundaries (to the extent that, as Núria Triana-Toribio says (2003, 162), it is hard to know where to place a film like *The Others*). Yet his actions are far from excessive as they close down vision. There is an irony in the simultaneous flow of Aguirresarobe's cinematographic style within and beyond Spain, and its denial of the Gothic secret that is crucial to many Gothic plots. Now that secret is denied to many more of us while more of us know that such a secret exists. David Punter observes the rise of what he calls 'schizophrenic Gothic' which is 'the presentation of worlds of cognitive and hallucinated disjunction in which there is no access below the surface, in which everything has been "closed down"' (Punter 1996, 213). I am arguing that Aguirresarobe's Gothic work exemplifies what Punter is talking about. The three films I discuss here also demonstrate how that approach is increasingly deracinated as Aguirresarobe's lighting and camera move further away from Spain, yet the trace of a Basque penumbra still remains even as the cinematographer reaches Hollywood.

La madre muerta

If Aguirresarobe was noted for grey and shadowy landscapes, director Juanma Bajo Ulloa picked him to work on *La madre muerta* for that very reason, for his 'concepción eminentemente tenebrista' (eminently gloomy approach: Ángulo, Heredero and Rebordinos 1995, 66). Bajo Ulloa has said that he feels the Gothic as something very close to him, possibly because of the climate he grew up in (the clouds of the Basque Country) as well as the house he lived in which had little light. He was not fond of the sun (Heredero 1997, 126). Given Bajo Ulloa's predilection for Gothic light, Aguirresarobe's style fitted neatly. Ángel Camiña (1994, 292) complemented Aguirresarobe on his beautiful, superb photography, arguing that the collaboration with the director results in very painterly interiors, with an emphasis on chiaroscuro like that of Ribera, Valdés Leal or Caravaggio (reminding us of his painterly style as observed by reviewers of *Goya's Ghosts* in Chapter 2). Camiña's remarks readily suggest the shadows of the Gothic but they also explicitly signal Aguirresarobe's contribution to the Gothic process and, in the notion of painterly interiors, a certain amount of excess in image, distinct from the real, a process similar to the one we saw in relation to the heritage Gothic of Goya in which spectacle and a museum aesthetic prevailed over narrative. Spectacle veils the secret that is crucial to the plot of *La madre muerta*.

The plot concerns Leire (Ana Álvarez), a young woman suffering from mental illness and loss of speech, the result of severe childhood injury during a burglary in which her mother was killed. The killer, Ismael

(Karra Elejalde) glimpses the adult Leire and, fearful she will recognise him and betray his guilt, kidnaps her. Leire is looked after by Ismael and his girlfriend Maite (Lio). Increasingly, however, Ismael begins to feel some sort of love for Leire – it is unclear whether this affection is sexual or paternal or both although we do not know if his love is returned. Maite's increasing jealousy leads her to shoot Leire and then commit suicide. Ismael takes the wounded Leire to hospital and then goes on the run. At some later point (the film leaves it vague as to exactly when),[1] Ismael passes the nursing home when he originally saw Leire and finds she has returned there. He gives her some chocolate and she embraces him in turn, while he weeps. A wound he sustained earlier begins to bleed, however, and Leire starts to cry at the sight of the blood. She and Ismael struggle, attracting the attention of the home's staff who beat up Ismael while the director (Elena Irureta) leads Leire away. Then Leire breaks away from the director and returns to where Ismael is lying on the ground but simply to pick up the chocolate which she dropped in the struggle.

The setting of *La madre muerta* is not explicitly established but is identifiably Vitoria (or Gasteiz, the town's Basque name), home to the Basque government (in fact, the nameplate for the station is briefly visible in one shot of the railway sequences in the film). Vitoria is an ambiguous location in that, though symbolising Basqueness by being the seat of Basque government, it is also the capital of a region, Álava, which has been more ambivalent about adherence to the Basque nationalist project than its neighbouring regions, Vizcaya and Guipúzcoa. Yet its connections to the Basque Country counter any simplistic identification with Spain. One could arguably posit Vitoria as a schizophrenic city that coincides with the schizophrenic principles to light applied by Aguirresarobe. In the director's commentary on the DVD, Bajo Ulloa frequently describes Vitoria and its buildings as Gothic, and this is confirmed by the old house in which Ismael and Maite keep Leire a prisoner upstairs, in Gothic tradition. The house appears old and decaying both inside and out, and its interior is shabby, gloomy and labyrinthine. The characters' subsequent hideout is an abandoned and ruined cathedral, another traditional Gothic space of shadows and cobwebs. The shots of Vitoria's old quarter, as well as the railway tracks and the paths leading to them, also have a Gothic sensibility to them; and this is where Aguirresarobe's taste for bleaching his landscapes of light begins to be marked.

By day, exterior spaces are seen in a grey wash, a light typical of the winter season in which the sequences were filmed, yet Bajo Ulloa insists more than once in his director's commentary that Aguirresarobe provided an atmospheric, rather than a realistic, lighting. Thus, the grey tones suggest the borders of the Gothic in which light and dark are blurred, rather than a simple seasonal setting. Night-time exterior sequences carry a blue depth in which what light there is looks sickly and weak, as in the first visit to the railway tracks where Ismael plans to kill Leire. As they approach, beams of cold light penetrate the darkness but only to light up a grey, crumbling wall. As they stand waiting for a train, the occasional tree is picked out with a wan lemon light that, far from piercing the darkness, seems only to emphasise the latter's power: the light, though offering a rare yellow tone, is still bleached and cold. Interior sequences also possess a blue light that seems to turn Ismael's very skin bluish so that he merges seamlessly into his background. The cathedral interiors also use a light that Bajo Ulloa calls violet which he perceives as pointing towards death (DVD commentary). At this point in the film, Maite has murdered Leire's carer Blanca (Silvia Marsó) and threatened Leire herself with a gun; and she will later shoot Leire in the back and subsequently kill herself. Jo Labanyi sees the use of light in terms of beauty but also power:

> Both locations – the railway tracks and the cathedral – are given an apocalyptic feel by the intensity of the blue light, which turns scenes of devastation and impending doom into scenes of stunning visual beauty. This is a beauty that does not allow detached aesthetic contemplation but that overwhelms us physically. (Labanyi 2008, 157)

Thus, narrative gives way to spectacle; we are distracted from the terrible secret at the heart of the film. The power and beauty are magnified by the insistence of the film on Gothic landscapes; Vitoria becomes a labyrinthine city without sun, perpetually immersed in a penumbra from which there is no escape. For even the care institution to which Leire ultimately returns is bathed in the same Gothic light that Aguirresarobe bestows on other spaces and places.

Bajo Ulloa emphasises, in the DVD director's commentary, the monochrome tones in which we find one focal point of colour (such as the red balls in the early hospital scenes). The general tone seems to be drained of colour to form a blue-grey that seems to tint even the skin tones, particularly of Ismael. The only exception to the oppression of the cold greys, blues and violets is the room in which Leire is held prisoner, dominated as it is by red walls which give a warmer tone that seems in key with Ismael's growing affection towards his prisoner, and, above all, in the scene that takes place in this room when he daubs himself with red lipstick and acts as a clown in a desperate attempt to make Leire laugh. The saturation of red in this scene is itself oppressive, however. Aguirresarobe still attenuates the light so that the red tone becomes heavy and crushing, underscoring

Figure 5.1 The Gothic hideaway of *La madre muerta*.

the ponderous significance of the violent blood ties between Ismael and Leire. In addition, many commentators on the film (including Bajo Ulloa himself) note the tendency for each sequence to contain a splash of colour (usually red) which contrasts with the general lack of bright colour that pervades the settings (DVD director's commentary; Ángulo, Heredero and Rebordinos 1995, 162; Labanyi 2008, 147, 151). Thus, Bajo Ulloa comments on, for instance, the use of red balls in some of the scenes at the care home while Labanyi remarks on the opening sequence:

> filmed in blue-tinged monochrome, with one important exception: the blood that we see trickle over Leire's mother's point-of-view shot as, dying on the ground, she sees the feet of little Leire approach, cutting to an all-red screen as her vision is blotted out. (Labanyi 147)

Though red is not always the colour used by Bajo Ulloa and his artistic director, it is by far the most common and is a constant reminder of the secret at the heart of the film that Ismael killed Leire's mother and irreparably damaged Leire herself – a fact of which Leire appears to be unaware precisely because of that damage. Labanyi associates Aguirrsarobe explicitly with the violent meaning of red: 'director of photography and cameraman, Javier Aguirresarobe, has noted that most of the frames contain a red object, which stands out against the pale or gloomy background like a gash or wound' (Labanyi 2008, 156).

Hogle argues that a Gothic tale uses 'antiquated or seemingly antiquated space' and, within such spaces, some past secret is contained that haunts the characters (2002, 2). Within these decaying spaces of Vitoria, the spots of colour pierce the grey decay with its reminder of the secret that haunts Ismael. Given that Aguirresarobe shuns colour, as has been observed above, his light reveals and yet denies the secret: it underscores it and yet forecloses it. The light reveals only the darkness embodied by the violent red splashes of colour and is therefore schizophrenic and excessive in its contradictory meaning. It is like the dead mother, the thing never seen (since our only glimpse of Leire's mother is while she is still alive and confronting the burglar who has intruded into her home). The secret of her death remains hidden. Leire's mother is an art restorer, rather like Aguirresarobe in being hidden and yet applying light and colour. These notes of colour do not occur regularly in Aguirresarobe's later work: with one minor exception, we shall not find them in *The Others*. We shall, however, find vivid splashes of colour again in the scenes of *New Moon* set in Italy; the bright yellow car in which Alice drives Bella through the Italian countryside; the red robes as people gather for the ceremony in which Edward intends to immolate himself.

Labanyi stresses the visual beauty of the film over coherent meaning, as the beauty encourages us to 'give ourselves up to its visual and acoustic pleasures' that ensure *La madre muerta* can be analysed only at the performative, rather than the representational, level (2008, 160). She also observes:

> It is not clear whether *La madre muerta* can be read as a redemptive narrative. Any redemptive message it may offer comes not from language, but from the beauty of its images and musical soundtrack – that is, from those aspects of cinema that impress themselves on the body. This is a kind of redemption that comes not from transcending the abject but from plunging into it. (156)

Redemption is, of course, the opposite of loss; therefore, if Labanyi is correct, the visual display is a surrender to loss. As Kavka would have it, it materialises, impresses on the body, representations grasping the thing beyond. The secret is hinted at through the lighting and the splashes of colour that penetrate it: we simultaneously revel in the spectacle of portrayal while losing sight of what the spectacle distracts us from. Kavka notes that: 'Gothic mutability derives from the limits of representation, because it deals in those liminal regions of being, whether social or existential, which can be only fleetingly represented in words or images' (Kavka 2002, 212). *La madre muerta* is a film steeped in liminality, a world outside society in which the criminality of Ismael, the hysteria of Maite and the muteness of the damaged Leire point to its Gothic nature. Within this world, Aguirresarobe offers fleeting images that suggest the mutability which Kavka mentions, the schizophrenia wherein representation is both offered and withheld, leading to loss and a lack of redemption.

The Others

Alejandro Amenábar's *The Others* functions by coincidence (as far as Aguirresarobe is concerned) as a halfway house between *La madre muerta*, set in the Basque Country and with a fair proportion of Basque actors and crew, and the full-blown Hollywood of the *Twilight* films. This duality arises from the film's production backing by Tom Cruise and use of anglophone actors, including Nicole Kidman in the central role of Grace, while using Spanish crew (including, of course, Aguirresarobe) and Spanish sets, including exterior locations in northern Spain, the landscape marked out by Ángulo, Heredero and Rebordinos as typically Aguirresarobian. In the introductory chronology to *The Cambridge Companion to Gothic Fiction*, the year 2001 is marked thus: 'Full-blown Gothic reappears on film in *The Others*, with Nicole Kidman' (Hogle 2002, xxv). The film is thus recognised as some sort of Gothic landmark although the film's Spanish roots manage to go unacknowledged and covered over by the reference to Kidman. Scholars of Spanish film have been swift to interpret *The Others* in terms of Spanish culture (such as Acevedo-Muñoz 2008; Smith 2001). It is possible to detect an underlying trace of Spanish identity beneath the Jersey fog of *The Others*. Ernesto Acevedo-Muñoz argues that the film refers allegorically to Spain's traumatic past and the present need to deal with it, such concerns being adapted to 'a more universal language' (Acevedo-Muñoz 2008, 202), and further suggests that, despite the co-production arrangements, Spanish historical referents, such as Roman Catholicism and repression, are still discernible (211).

On the other hand, Amenábar himself pointed out that *The Others* was thought by his producers to be a genuinely Anglo-Saxon production (Andrade 2001, 221, 222). He comments, in relation to casting British actor Christopher Ecclestone, that 'daba ese aire alienado y fantasmagórico que buscábamos' (he provided the alienated and phantasmagoric impression we were looking for), while Spanish actors would not have fitted in this role (221). Triana-Toribio, however, observes that, while the Spanish film industry and surrounding discourse acclaimed *The Others* as a successful Spanish export, Spanish viewers watch a version dubbed over the original English. The bulk of funding came from America (Miramax), the producers were American, and the film competed with English-language films in the Golden Globes (Triana-Toribio 2003, 162). Triana-Toribio concludes her discussion of the film – and, indeed, of the state of Spanish cinema generally:

> perhaps *The Others* is a wake-up call to the future, to indicate that national cinemas should be prepared to be challenged about the national mindset in which they have been immersed and accept that, in order to make films that are relevant to a large number of people it is necessary to pool resources and think globally. (163)

Amenábar himself compares the haunted house of *The Others* to other Gothic houses from the anglophone tradition: (Henry James's *Turn of the Screw* (1898), Peter Medak's *The Changeling* (1980), Charles Laughton's *The Night of the Hunter* (1955); Úbeda-Portugués 2005, 147). Originally he planned to set the film in Latin America but was finally persuaded by his producers to film in English. One of them, José Luis Cuerda, told the director that the film had no Latin elements (Cuerda himself knows no English; 151). Amenábar argued:

> No creo demasiado en los nacionalismos ni en las nacionalidades; yo hago mis histo-rias y procuro que conecten conmigo y con un colectivo. Yo creo en la película, no en el cine de tal sitio o de tal otro, y la película funciona o no funciona. Cada proyecto te exige lo idóneo para la historia que planteas. Y si la historia reclama el inglés, si transcurre en algún paisaje desolado y sin identificar o en un lugar del mundo donde se habla inglés, pues habría que hacerla en inglés, pero siempre sin forzar. (148)
> (I don't believe too much in nationalism or national identities: I create my stories and try to make them connect with me and with a collective. I believe in the film, not in the cinema of this place or that, and either the film works or it doesn't. Each project demands of you whatever is appropriate for the story you're creating. And if the story needs English, if it takes place in some desolate, anonymous landscape or in a part of the world where English is spoken, then you should tell the story in English but without making it seem forced.)

He saw the film in retrospect in terms of a transatlantic crossing:

> I never thought that [the original story] would end up being my next movie, or that that little boat, that is a project when it is born, would cross nothing less that the Atlantic, and would put us in contact with 'the others', the Americans [. . .] (quoted in Kercher 2015, 212)

As Kercher herself observes immediately afterwards, these are 'metaphors usually applied to Columbus's encounter with indigenous peoples', a comment that raises its own spectre of colonial crossings. Kercher later suggests that the slightly American accents of Victor and his family come to symbolise America being chased off screen; she feels that Amenábar may be looking to a Spanish cinema with a British or European accent (222). In the case of *The Others*, Kercher suggests a comparison with

Hitchcock's *Rebecca* (1940), with the house in Amenábar's resembling Manderley (215). We should not, however, overlook the fact that Kercher is, on the whole, writing about the influence on Spanish cinema of Alfred Hitchcock who himself absorbed many influences from Europe but for whom America loomed very large in his thinking.

Certainly the plot stresses the halfway-house nature of *The Others*. The setting is the Channel Islands, belonging to the United Kingdom, but dual natured in the use of English and French (though no French is heard in this film) and rendered ambiguous through its occupation by German forces during World War II. Amenábar obliquely reminds us of this by the plot detail that Grace is waiting for her husband Charles (Christopher Ecclestone) to return home from the war. The fog that surrounds the house of Grace and her children, Anne (Alakina Mann) and Nicholas (James Bentley), serves to cut off the setting still further. Grace is obsessed with keeping the sunlight out of the house, keeping curtains drawn and using a complex system of keeping doors shut to protect Anne and Nicholas who suffer from extreme sensitivity to light and who can therefore be harmed by exposure to sunlight. As the film opens, new servants, led by Mrs Mills (Fionnula Flanagan) arrive. Anne and Nicholas are convinced the house is haunted while Grace investigates strange noises and occurrences. Eventually, however, she realises that she, the children and the servants are the ghosts haunting the house while the strange noises come from the living people who occupy it – until, finally, the living family can stand no more and flee. Grace had murdered her children and then killed herself out of madness and grief since Charles has not returned home.

Kercher argues that, in *The Others*, 'The essential tool of cinematography, the manipulation of light, becomes a narrative *leitmotif*' (2015, 215). Mira talks of light in *The Others* as 'a narrative theme and something of a protagonist' (Mira 2010, 6). Ángel García Romero sees light and shadow as almost a central character of the film:

> La cámara en *Los otros* se mueve con elegancia y funcionalidad, encuadra con delicadeza a todos y cada uno de los personajes, y retrata los interiores de la casa como si luces y sombras fueran protagonistas de la historia. (Garcia Romero 2005, 126)
> (In *The Others* the camera moves elegantly and purposefully, framing each and every one of the characters with sensitivity, and portraying the interiors of the house as if light and shadow were main characters in the story.)

Unlike *La madre muerta*, however, where Bajo Ulloa had clear ideas of what he expected in terms of lighting (Ángulo, Heredero and Rebordinos 1995, 108), Amenábar admitted that light was the element he had the least grip on in his film-making (Andrade 2002, 234). Thus, implicitly, he was quite dependent on his director of photography. Aguirresarobe himself talked at some length about his work on *The Others*, arguing that:

> Mi intención, la intención de la luz, ha pretendido sumergirnos en espacios de cuento, en tinieblas reales, en ambientes que, alguna vez, nos han envuelto y nos recuerdan el deleite por el cosquillo del miedo. (Aguirresarobe 2001: 215)
>
> (My intention with the light was to try to immerse us in story spaces, in real shadows, in environments that have at some point in time enfolded us and which remind us of the delight of a frisson of fear.)

This is an approach that clearly suggests the film's subsequent Gothic aesthetic. Oti Rodríguez Marchante, writing about Amenábar's work, argues that a feeling of cold is important to Aguirresarobe's films. Aguirresarobe looks to film in autumn, with cloudy landscapes, believing that any heat in the film should come from the characters (Rodríguez Marchante 2002, 137). Aguirresarobe confirms this, observing that: '*Los otros* nos desliza hacia [. . .] cuentos con fondos de luz crepuscular, sonidos de ventanas que aletean por la fuerza de un viento frío en aquellos inviernos lluviosos del norte.' (*The Others* draws us towards [. . .] stories with a twilight background, sounds of windows swinging back and forth from the force of a cold wind in those rainy northern winters.)

He goes on to add: 'Estas sensaciones son la que tocaron mi piel y las que provocaron una idea estética y formal para esta historia de casa solitaria entre nieblas [. . .]' (These sensations are the ones that made me shiver and which produced a formal and aesthetic idea for this story of a lonely house in the mist; Aguirresarobe 2001, 213). To this extent, we have a similar approach to the cold landscapes of *La madre muerta*. Unlike *La madre muerta*, however, where the light and the landscape emphasised atmosphere and power above realism, here the repeated note is on restrained realism. So Aguirresarobe himself also talks of looking for settings that *naturally* created Gothic spaces and shadows (2001, 214). Amenábar tells of how Aguirresarobe lit the fog to look natural (Andrade 2001, 239) while Barry Jordan speaks of a rejection of excess Gothic style in favour of a 'heavily restrained naturalism' in decor (2012, 161). Yet Aguirresarobe also noted that creating this natural and restrained look took a good deal of work (2001, 214). Kercher suggests that the muted tones were 'accommodations to Kidman's star status and to expectations of classical Hollywood cinema' (2015, 213) which echoes Aguirresarobe's comments in that the natural look is not, in fact, natural but driven by a deliberate aesthetic. The restrained naturalism that Jordan speaks of is a code of visualisation that aims to hide the demands of film-making (though, of course, these critics have spotted the effort).

Figure 5.2 The murky landscape of *The Others*.

The result is, nonetheless, a similarly minimalist sense of interiors and exteriors in which details become subordinate to the foreclosure of light. Colin Davis observes of the film:

> we cannot be sure what this world contains because the absence of light makes it impossible to see properly; doors open and objects move without apparent cause; voices are heard where no person is visible. (Davis 2010, 69)

The first shot after the credits is an exterior one of the house in mist, cool colours, greens; and the exterior shots from then on maintain these cool colours. Different interior scenes are bookmarked with brief shots of the house from the outside, and these scenes are grey, cold and shadowy. The trees in close-up cast menacing black shapes. It is intriguing that, when there is more light in theory, as in the final exterior shot which I discuss briefly below, in practice the house still seems gloomy and grey, cold; the light is bleached and seems to lose the very potency that Grace fears when she shields her children from exposure to sunlight. We also see lighting and colour motifs previously used in *La madre muerta*. As Grace walks through the wood in search of the priest, the only time she escapes from the confines of the house and its grounds, the greenery also becomes bleached and the forest turns grey, so she is the only note of colour in her coat, but muted in plums and purples. This is a modified form of the colour splash in *La madre muerta*, tentatively marking out Grace as the source of the secret at the heart of the film, the murderer of her children, though this is a secret we do not as yet know at this point in the film. Similarly, in the scene where the children walk through the grounds at night, in search of their father, cold blues replace the misty greys, with a sickly yellow light reminiscent of *La madre muerta*.

Terrie Waddell observes of the exteriors that the landscape is bleak and sterile: 'The large expanses of lawn fringing the house are reduced to paths of grass amidst grainy barren soil. The exterior shots are muted in a grayish-blue haze that gives the impression of an enveloping mist.' The fog suggests entrapment but also, because it shifts, the possibility of uncovering secrets (Waddell 2006, 82). Just as in *La madre muerta*, light and visibility both cloak and reveal the secret at the heart of the film, in this case the house and the ghosts it contains, who flicker in and out of visibility like the mist, seen by Victor and the medium but not by Victor's parents. Pamela Ellayah argues that the fog underscores the confusion between the ghosts and the living (2011, 119) but, in fact, all those who live in the fog are ghosts, as it turns out. As Grace and the children end the film claiming 'this house is ours', some shots occur where the house is now full of light, yet grey light. But, as the living family leave and Victor turns to look up at the windows, there is a shaft of sunlight as birds sing (the first time we hear them) yet the sun is not in shot and the light appears weak compared to the surprisingly dominant grey. The final shot is of the house behind its gates and, though as Victor's family drives away the sun clearly persists, yet the house still appears to be framed in blue and grey. The weak sunlight distinguishes the living from the dead but its very weakness suggests the only tentative hold that life has in this Gothic setting.

Light is very muted throughout but there is a strong connection between the grey fog of the outdoors and light as rendering things and people ghostly and bleached. Much of the house in which Grace and the children live is deprived of outdoor light because of the children's photosensitivity but what light there is in these darkened rooms tends to be warm, the yellow of firelight or lamps, enhanced by the brown tones of the wood-panelled walls. Where exterior light filters into interior rooms it turns everything grey. In particular, when Grace is in the attic, trying to detect the source of noises, the light is in striking and ironic contrast to the shadowy light elsewhere in the house but it washes out Grace's skin tones and ironically renders her white as a ghost. When Grace first talks to Mrs Mills and her companions looking for work as servants, the room appears cold and bleak, framed with grey stone arches. Grace insists to Mrs Mills that the light can kill but, in fact, the grey light illuminates the ghostly chill of characters who will turn out to be already dead.

Nevertheless, the idea that light kills is not without its force, given the children's sensitivity to light. Susan Bruce notes that the problem of light-sensitivity 'isn't absence of light *per se*, but fear of what the light might do, or, put even more simply, fear of the light'. And herein lies a pun: Grace's photophobia is not only fear of the light but also fear of the photograph (Bruce 2005, 28). She is appalled by the photos of dead people that she finds (29). Technology has enabled the ghost to coexist daily alongside the living so that the photograph is a gateway to the dead. As Warner says:

> The ubiquitous electronic voice has become domestic now, the everyday magic of hearing the voice of someone dead or faraway; likewise photography has established former selves and the presence of people as they were when they were alive in every corner of everyday experience. (Warner 2002, 163)

So what, then, of the status of the director of photography in such a film? Amenábar told Aguirresarobe as a working premise that light kills (Andrade 2002, 239), an idea that the cinematographer much appreciated, an appreciation that, in turn, struck the director (Rodríguez Marchante 2002, 128). This is reflected not only in the plot point concerning the children's light-sensitivity but also the fact that all that the light serves to record is the fact of death, the secret to be uncovered. Yet the Gothic light and landscape immediately absorb the secret again, hence the contrast between the sunshine of the living and the fog of the dead. Light and photography appear to hold out the secret as representational, yet simultaneously suggest the light as destroying or casting out what it represents. It shows up the ghostliness of Grace and her household, yet the household and the house that contains it remain ultimately in the shadows.

As in *La madre muerta*, we see from *inside* the Gothic light, we finally see the secret and then realise that we have seen it all along. In a similar way, we peer like Grace with horrified fascination at the post-mortem photographs, then belatedly realise that, right from the very beginning, we have seen nothing but ghosts: the living appear only briefly at the very end. But, as Labanyi suggested of *La madre muerta*, there is no redemption. Grace, Anne, Nicholas and Mrs Mills remain in the shadows and recognise it as where they belong, their home. Yet, for all this visibility, the traumatic event that gives rise to the Gothic adventure is never seen: the death of the mother and damage to the daughter in one film; the deaths of mother and children in the other. Both films occur largely (*La madre muerta*) or totally

(*The Others*) after the fact. It is not that they cannot show these traumas but that they refuse to do so. We come back to Kavka's concept of the simultaneous revelation and withholding of the object of horror through light, and this coincides with Davis's comment on *The Others*: 'reality is *screened*: both presented to us on a screen and screened from us, made inaccessible even as it is offered to us' (Davis 2010, 66). He continues: '*The Others* records a collapse of faith in the very terms with which we might talk about the world. The erosion of conceptual certainties is matched by the confusion of perceptual data.'

Davis goes on to talk about various perceptual tricks and illusions in the film where people are seen who are not, in fact, there (such as a portrait on a wall) or who ought to be visible but are not (such as Charles's missing reflection in a mirror) (72). Sometimes, Davis argues, there are moments when we expect logically to see the camera reflected in a mirror (and, by implication, ourselves as spectators) but cuts and effects frustrate this expectation. He adds 'The danger here, for our comfort as spectators, is extreme. If the mirror points straight at us, and we cannot see ourselves, where are we? Do we exist? (ibid.). Davis's remarks bring us back to the role of the camera that manages to keep itself hidden while nonetheless having a material role in challenging our expectations of what we see. Aguirresarobe is actively involved in the confusion of perceptual data to which Davis refers and which Kavka conceptualises for Gothic film as a whole. The camerawork forms part of a strategy of representation in which lighting also plays a part, as we have seen. *The Others* erodes the conceptual certainties that Davis talks of to the extent that its location, too, is uncertain. As Davis also says, where are we? Where are the characters we see? As in the previous chapter, the haunted house has only a tenuous link to any fixed geographical location. Aguirresarobe's style contributes to this sense of deterritorialisation.

New Moon

By the time of *The Twilight Saga: New Moon*, Aguirresarobe's transatlantic career seemed assured. Until *The Others* he did not work in America or with American personnel. After that film, however, he soon had work on an Eric Clapton documentary, and the first feature-length American film in his portfolio, *The Bridge of San Luis Rey*, came out in 2004, the same year in which the cinematographer contributed to Amenábar's Oscar success with *Mar adentro* (The Sea Inside). For a few years, Aguirresarobe juggled films for the Spanish and American film industries: this included the film *Goya's Ghosts* discussed in Chapter 2. But, with *Vicky Cristina*

Barcelona, a new phase of his career opened up and Aguirresarobe began to work primarily in the American industry with occasional excursions to make Mexican films. Of the American films, he has mostly worked on horror films, such as the remake of *Fright Night* (Craig Gillespie 2012), or comedies, such as *Identity Thief* (Seth Gordon 2013). The commission to work on *New Moon*, as well as its follow-up *Eclipse* (David Slade 2010), is thus of a piece with the emphasis on popular genre film in his American work. If Aguirresarobe's style of cinematography was rooted in the light and colour of the Basque Country, by this point it now seems almost wholly deracinated. Director Weitz, in conversation with editor Peter Lambert on the DVD commentary, refers to language difficulties, communicating with his director of photography in French as that was the language the two had in common, a factor that underscores the sense of dislocation.

As with *The Others*, such deracination causes problems of critique in terms of a national cinema. This time, however, no one rushed to claim any part of the film for Spain, far from it. It is in some ways difficult to introduce, into a discussion of Spanish texts, Aguirresarobe's work on the *Twilight* series, box-office hits that were film adaptations of the highly successful series of vampire novels by Stephenie Meyer. This is not simply because the novels and films are firmly set in the United States (in the town of Forks, Oregon) but because the series has given rise to a great deal of negative critique for being pulp fantasy stories for teenage girls, stories that offer as desirable a subordinate and, indeed, masochistic position for young women in romantic relationships. Tim Robey's review is fairly typical and fairly cruel:

> Teenage girls everywhere who have woken up clutching their tickets for the Twilight sequel will love it whatever I say. Not much of their schoolwork is going to stick, I'm guessing. [. . .] It barely needs to be competent storytelling, and isn't, really. (Robey 2009)

The series is centred on the love of the protagonist Bella, a teenager, for Edward, a vampire. Bella's all-consuming desire for Edward leads her to neglect all other ties to family (particularly her father) and friends, and dictates all her decisions and plans. Her desire is masochistic in that she surrenders any sense of self and submits herself entirely to Edward, an uncomfortable fit for older commentators who see Bella and the Twilight narratives as a retrograde step in terms of women's position in society, a poor example for young women. The debate as a whole is more complex than this commonplace dismissal suggests (see Crawford 2014, Ch. 5, for an excellent detailed discussion). Its scope is beyond that of my study here though it is worth briefly declaring my own position. I do think the stories offer a worryingly masochistic version of sexual desire for young women, and one that can be moreover unpleasantly self-absorbed, but I also feel concern that a glib dismissal of these texts can encompass a dismissal of the desires of teenage girls as irritating, inconvenient, valueless and taste-less, as is demonstrated by the horror of regular cult convention-goers at having their space invaded by apparently hysterical fans, as has frequently happened at the major convention Comic-con (Crawford 2014, 224–5). Nor should we assume that all teenage girls identify with the heroine Bella or, indeed, that all fans of the series are teenage girls. My focus here, however, is the work of Aguirresarobe on one of the two films in the series, *New Moon*, in terms of his Gothic photography.[2]

Nonetheless, a sense remains that these texts of all texts do not belong in a study deriving from the discipline of Hispanic Studies, and not simply because they are texts steeped in American culture. Those of us who work in contemporary Spanish (and Latin American) film studies have by now become familiar with the possibility of discussing films that are not simply far removed from Hispanic cultures but are not even in Spanish. *The Others* is one such film. Triana-Toribio rightly defined it as problematic for the Spanish canon of films, as we saw earlier, but Hispanists are 'allowed' to consider it nonetheless. Aguirresarobe has worked on other Hollywood films, notably Allen's *Vicky Cristina Barcelona* mentioned earlier, but the aura of glossy airbrushing of the *Twilight* films is hard to stomach alongside the earlier intense spareness of *La madre muerta* or minimalist gestures to realism of *The Others*. Yet the emphasis on earth tones and cool greys and blues is not so far removed from the autumnal Basque feel attributed to Aguirresarobe by Ángulo, Heredero and Rebordinos.

Perhaps part of the problem with any academic consideration of the film lies not simply with worrying gender politics but also with the blockbuster success of the franchise. Such concerns are demonstrated by an intriguing aside made by Robey in his review quoted above: 'The phenomenon is more than critic-proof: it basically consigns us to the dust-heap' (Robey 2009), implying an underlying fear that analysis and value judgements on the part of critics – and academics – are ultimately irrelevant. Such a fear is, of course, reminiscent of Botting's concerns that we saw in the intro-duction. Milly Williamson suggests the Twilight films

> remind us of the link between venerated Romanticism and the vilified Gothic. However, it is another step to simply applaud any offering from what is an increasingly consumerist, merchandise-bound, branded and profit-driven cultural field, simply because it is consumed by non-dominant social groups. (Williamson 2014, 85)

Williamson goes on to qualify such a stance, arguing that 'those critics who ridicule the fans of *Twilight* and other more mainstream vampire stories, as being dupes of consumer capitalism, ignore how cult or quality home films address their own audience' (86). She goes on to demonstrate such an address by giving as an example *Låt den rätte komma in* (Let the Right One In, Tomas Alfredson 2008) which, Williamson notes, was equally the subject of careful marketing to cult audiences (87). A first response to Williamson might lie with the subtlety of the latter's plot, the starkness of the *mise en scène*, the complex relationship between the two central characters, one vampire child, one human (though the projected future for the human child is not ultimately promising nor the vampire ultimately benign). Yet critical distaste for a film such as *New Moon* (for example, Bradshaw 2009, Ebert 2009, Robey 2009) is not simply based on preference for quality or even on snobbishness. There seems to be an implicit (and sometimes explicit) fear that viewers of *New Moon* have no critical faculties themselves. Its very success is against it: Williamson goes on to say that *New Moon* 'grossed $309 million at the box office, $160,000 million in video/DVD sales' (85). A perception of the film as consumerist indulgence is closely akin to Botting's dismissal of Gothic viewers as passive, 'becoming woman in the process' (Botting 2007, 173). Therefore, comparing Aguirresarobe's work on *New Moon* with the other two, more 'tasteful' films I have discussed in this chapter aims to challenge the ambivalence about a Gothicised circulation in that some Gothic texts and style are more worthy of consideration than others. This goes against the perennial association of the Gothic with the perceived dangers of popular culture that any scholar of the Gothic has to live with.

The plot of *New Moon* leads on from the end of the previous film *Twilight* (Catherine Hardwicke 2008) where Bella (Kristen Stewart) and Edward (Robert Pattinson) have become a couple. That happy ending is undercut when Edward and his vampire family, the Cullens, decide to leave their home in Forks because people are gradually becoming aware that the Cullens are somehow different. In addition, Edward insists that Bella cannot be a part of his world and breaks their relationship. After a period of despair, Bella turns to her friend Jacob (Taylor Lautner) who is in love with her. Jacob turns out to be a werewolf: he and the other werewolves protect Bella from the murderous threat of Victoria (Rachelle Lefevre), a hostile vampire. Edward's sister Alice (Ashley Greene) returns to Forks to say that Edward now thinks Bella is dead and he is going to the Volturi (a form of vampire royalty) in Italy to end his own life. Alice and Bella go to Italy and Bella offers her own life to the Volturi in place of his. Edward and Bella are reconciled and, once back in Forks, he asks her to marry him.

New Moon is undeniably a Gothic film. Carole Veldman-Genz (2011, 48) has identified Bella as the traditional Gothic female victim, always helpless. In addition, *New Moon* functions as an example of ecoGothic, the marrying of the Gothic with ecocriticism and environmental concerns (see Smith and Hughes 2013). In terms of setting, Tara K. Parmiter argues that Gothic monsters are associated with 'dark corners' and 'ancient castles'. 'The landscapes they inhabit are landscapes of terror, where our most irrational and unnatural fears come horribly true.' But in the Pacific northwest of America, where the *Twilight* novels and films are set (though, in fact, *New Moon* was filmed in Canada), the greenery means that 'although death and decay are essential to this landscape, they are part of the natural cycle, sustaining the life of the forest' (Parmiter 2011, 221). But, while lush green landscapes of the forests near Forks stress nature, they also stress a fear of it from a human populace largely alienated from the natural world. The vampires and, above all, the werewolves are the chief inhabitants of the woods, indicating that the humans are right to be wary. Nonetheless, Parmiter points out that Edward and his family not only live in the woods and undertake outdoor activities whenever they can but show a concern for their environment. Edward's discussion about their hunting practices suggests a concern for a balanced ecosystem. By getting closer to Edward, Bella learns to love the environment of which he is a part. But she also gets closer to the dangers it represents (226). Parmiter points out 'it is telling that the most dangerous activities she can imagine take place in wild spaces' (227).

Parmiter is writing of the novels but her points hold true for the films as well, and the lighting and photography reinforce the notion of the natural made uncanny. Wickham Clayton argues that, in contrast to the cold colours of *Twilight* and *Eclipse*, *New Moon* uses 'earth tones, highlighting browns and deep greens' though he immediately appears to contradict himself by mentioning the reds and yellows of the opening sequence (Clayton 2014, 89). What strikes Clayton here is the emphasis of the colours of nature and the outdoors, rendering them strange and thus a Gothic space. The wider setting of Forks (actually Vancouver Island, the shooting location) repeats the green scenery and grey skies of *The Others*: it is a space noted for rain (which is one reason why vampires are drawn to it, because of the lack of sunlight). If the lack of light attracts the vampires to this environment, because it allows them to exist, it also hides them from sight as well. The woodland, however, seems oppressive because of the dim lighting. As the werewolves hunt the vampire Victoria, her red hair becomes the mark of the secret that stands out from the earth tones of the green forest and the grey and brown wolves. Shafts of sunlight (a similar sickly yellow to that

Figure 5.3 Nature made uncanny: Edward in the woods of *New Moon*.

occasionally found in *La madre muerta*) illuminate the battle but, as Bella wanders through the forest (wrapped in her own Gothic melodrama and oblivious of the battle around her), the light is grey and the forest apparently impenetrable. Eventually, she throws herself off the cliff to be surrounded by grey waters in which Victoria's red hair is again the only contrast. Interiors can demonstrate a similar pattern: the confrontation with the Volturi takes place in a large, domed chamber with windows high up that shed a sickly light in which only the red eyes and lips of the vampires stand out. The green tiles and green marble walls fade into grey, aided by the dry ice that Aguirresarobe applied to the set that gives it a Gothic appearance once again. These spaces are all supernatural ones where humans rarely venture and are in danger if they do. These are places where werewolves can truly be werewolves, and vampires can truly be vampires, rather than imitations of elegant American living as in the Cullens' upmarket house. This is the secret that Aguirresarobe simultaneously pinpoints and veils. We are human ourselves, and the film takes us into these spaces where humans normally fear to tread. Only love for the vampire seems to override this fear: for Bella, for the vampire groupies dotted around the Volturi's palace, and for us, keen to see a story about vampires, for whatever reason. (The only exception is Bella's father, who knows nothing of the struggle between vampires and werewolves or his daughter's part in it but who goes to the forest in search of his daughter, drawn by a love of his own.)[3]

Yet these spaces are also marked as places where we do not belong. Kavka argues that 'Monsters, by definition, exceed spaces of enclosure – such as the screen itself – whereas humans are diminished and oppressed by Gothic space' (Kavka 2002, 216). The prevailing ethos of these places goes beyond anything that humans can conceive of, one reason why Bella is dwarfed both physically and metaphorically by the supernatural spaces.

These supernatural spaces are also impossible spaces both thematically and technically. Bella's fantasies about Edward always include a space that is impossible for him, the woodland where he is comfortable but with shafts of sunlight that highlight his beauty but which would in reality destroy that beauty. The beams of sunlight have been added through computer-generated imagery, CGI, including what director Weitz calls diamond shots when Edward's skin appears to sparkle in the sunlight. The sky behind Jacob, as he and Bella talk on the beach, appears a slate grey but, in fact, the sun was shining in that shot, and the grey sky was added digitally afterwards. These digitally enhanced spaces are like the CGI-enhanced vampires and werewolves: the apparently natural ecosystem is, in fact, nothing but (rather like the treaty that keeps the vampires and werewolves in a pact of coexistence). The technical aspects of these spaces remind us of the restrained naturalism of *The Others* that was actually care-fully crafted: these are fake landscapes created by special effects to which the cinematographer contributes and, in so contributing, he marks these places impossible through rendering the light bleached or deliberately artificial. The light forms part of a code that appears to render these spaces invisible while also gesturing at erasure through bleaching, or drawing attention to their counterfeit nature through saccharine colouring.

As with *La madre muerta*, the splashes of red point up the secret that this is a supernatural place but the dim lighting and *mise en scène* suggest that this secret is veiled from humanity, as are the ghosts of *The Others*, only perceptible in the fog. The dream sequences, in which Bella is lying in a field, employ an odd saturation of colour which is deliberately artificial and creates unease with the same sickly ambience that was also to be found in *La madre muerta*. In the scene in which Bella tries (or not) to come to terms with the break-up, the camera revolves around the view from her room as she stares unseeingly out of the window like an imprisoned princess in her tower. The months change but the light remains oppressive and, indeed, there is little difference between exterior and interior light. All is dim. Clayton argues that the closer Bella gets to Edward, the brighter and more vivid is the colour palette (2014, 90). Yet, even the sunlit sequences in Italy, initially so bright in contrast to the greens and greys of the landscapes at home, prove at a second glance to be slightly bleached with a similar lemon wash to that which Aguirresarobe used in *Vicky Cristina*. This is exemplified, in particular, by the pale-blue sky behind the clock striking the fateful hour of midday as Edward emerges to allow himself to be burnt up in the sunlight. The strong contrast to the more traditionally Gothic sequences underscores once again the notion that light kills. As Edward emerges into sunlight, the light again threatens to kill, and it bleaches him, surrounds him in a hazy mist. The destructive power of the light is here at its most overt, revealing Edward for what he is and, at the same time, threatening to destroy him as sunlight traditionally does for vampires. In these washed-out sequences, Alice's bright-yellow car and then, more ominously, the massed red cloaks as Bella runs through the town square to save Edward, stand out more prominently. The red cloaks are, of course, strongly reminiscent of *La madre muerta*. Clayton also notes the red splashes of colour in the sequence of Bella and Jacob fixing Bella's motorbike but observes that it, too, is muted and that, throughout the film, 'Despite occasional expressionistic uses of this bright red [. . .] the washed-out colouring dominates the bulk of the compositions' (Clayton 2014, 90). If we reverse this, however, the splashes of red imply violence. The red cloaks assemble to watch Edward's immolation, red marks out Victoria, the Volturi's red eyes are emphasised, and Bella's bike comes to symbolise her self-destructive tendencies once Edward has left her. As with *The Others*, then, the vampires of *New Moon* suffer from their own form of light-sensitivity that Aguirresarobe reflects through sickly sunshine, washed out and lacking vibrancy compared to the colour of the vampires' eyes and occasional props, such as Alice's car, and the recurring notes of red. The only exception is the Cullens' home which is in direct contrast to the traditional Gothic castle, with warm but subdued lighting, but this becomes another impossible space because the Cullens decide to vacate it.

The style of lighting in *New Moon* reveals a consistency of approach that has spanned the entirety of Aguirresarobe's career and that repeats itself across Gothic films in a variety of locations both real (Vitoria) and fake (northern Spain for Jersey, British Columbia for Washington State). Dim lighting and plenty of fog are, of course, staples of Gothic film, as is the schizophrenic form of the Gothic film proposed by Kavka. Aguirresarobe's lighting and camera, however, are Gothic ones that permeate all his cinematography. The cinematography is also one that exceeds borders and detaches itself from nationality while, nonetheless, retaining an ambiguous trace of Basque culture. Aguirresarobe functions as a unifying authority figure but one that remains hidden, his authority manifesting itself in his aesthetic that both reveals and screens while he himself is screened from view by the camera and light monitors that he directs. His Gothic cinematography hints at multiple layers of seeing and not seeing, both in terms of the narrative (the secret that is highlighted and obscured) and of the film form that contains it (the visibility of the camera's actions while the camera itself is invisible). When the mirror in *The Others* reveals precisely nothing, it is an indication of the invisibility of Aguirresarobe and his crew: the camera is never reflected.

Botting argues that 'Gothic styles, while concerning themselves with disturbing, duplicitous powers of representation and simulation, inevitably remain effects of the representational techniques' (Botting 2002, 280). The lighting and camerawork of Aguirresarobe comprise one such technique, showing a duplicitous mastery that grants him a certain measure of authority, providing a single framework of meaning that Botting thought to be missing from contemporary Gothic. It is a framework that stretches beyond the Basque Country and beyond Spain, the secret that, on one level, is visible to us but which nevertheless works hard to frustrate our reliance on what we see. We know what we are looking at but, simultaneously, our trust in what we see is undermined. That is the case not only for our knowledge of what we see but also for our knowledge of where we are. Even in a film as sentimental as *New Moon*, and certainly in *The Others* and *La madre muerta*, the light never offers us the redemption or the comfort of clarity.

Notes

1. The compressed time frame of the plot, and Ismael's injuries and wounds, suggest that this scene takes place roughly within twenty-four hours of Leire being shot and taken to hospital. If only one day has passed, then Leire has recovered remarkably quickly if she is able to return to the home after being shot and seriously wounded. If more time has passed, however, why is Ismael still wounded and bandaged up? How did he get those wounds if not from the struggle with Maite?
2. I have concentrated on *New Moon* and omitted *Eclipse* because the former emphasises external landscapes while the latter does not. The emphasis on interiors in *Eclipse* comes with a loss of emphasis on the Gothic woodlands and cliffs that I believe illustrate more clearly Aguirresarobe's schizophrenic approach.
3. In other films in the series, the father, Charlie (Billy Burke), ventures into the forest in pursuit of law and order: he is the local sheriff.

CHAPTER 6

Gothic Medicine:
Written on the Body

The final chapter takes up another aspect of the debate about the contemporary Gothic, to consider examples of the Gothic body in Spanish culture. Spooner observes that

> Contemporary Gothic discourses are [. . .] dual-natured: in their emphasis on surfaces, they may offer a lack of resistance to simulation; but in their foregrounding of the body they offer scope for their use in an entirely opposite way, for the reinstatement of depth into a superficial culture. (Spooner 2006, 58)

In saying this, Spooner suggests the body as resistant to the fears of ephemerality and empty circulation that were discussed in the Introduction. She observes the emphasis on the body in contemporary Gothic and the possibility of the body's reduction to simulacra (63) but also suggests that the grotesque and monstrous body which characterises many recent Gothic outputs can also be understood as 'an attempt to reinstate the physicality of the body in an increasingly decorporealized information society' (65). The particular focus of this chapter is both the emphasis on the body in contemporary Spanish Gothic but also the response to it, the efforts to control the body's materiality. One way in which this occurs is through the efforts of medicine to contain it or reshape it.

This medicine is itself Gothic, however, in its simultaneous recognition and repression of the problematic, diseased, disruptive or dead body. Andrew Tudor observes the central position of science as dangerous in the horror film and notes that 'all mad scientists share one characteristic. They are volitional. Disorder in these movies is a direct consequence of individual scientists' actions' (Tudor 1989, 133). The mad scientist causes, and then exacerbates, the supposed challenge he (and it is nearly always he) tries to contain. He is the one who chooses to see the body as a problem which can be countered only by his control, yet the body will ultimately elude the scientist, though at considerable cost to itself. The chapter begins with a study of the body as Gothic excess in

Pedro Almodóvar's *La piel que habito* (The Skin I Live In, 2011), and then considers the displaced body of the actress Belén Rueda who has become strongly associated with Gothic texts. The focus here is on two recent roles: the wandering eyes and sight of *Los ojos de Julia* (Julia's Eyes, Guillem Morales 2010) and the wandering body of *El cuerpo* (The Body, Oriol Paulo 2012).

To explore these ideas further I shall draw on the conceptual positions put forward by Judith[1] Halberstam (1995). Halberstam sees Gothic in terms of excess but her approach seems less pessimistic than some of the other Gothic commentators we have considered. Nonetheless, she is at least ambivalent about the Gothic audience. She suggests that 'The Gothic, in fact, like the vampire itself, creates a public who consumes monstrosity, who revels in it, and who then surveys its individual members for signs of deviance or monstrosity, excess or violence' (Halberstam 1995, 12). The vampire is itself an embodiment of Gothic monstrosity as well as symbolic of a public simultaneously eager for, and censorious of, the monstrous body: unlike Botting's feminised consumers, however, this public is not a passive one. The Gothic, on Halberstam's reading, creates a predatory public. Gothic medicine enacts a similar dichotomy and with a similar result, as we shall see below, particularly as regards *La piel que habito* where the surgeon desires the body he has recreated while simultaneously punishing the original body which was the basis for his design. Christopher Frayling, in his survey of the mad scientist in film, observes that film itself produces a similar dichotomy that is ironic:

> A medium that owed its existence to a spin-off from science has spent much of its history playing to public anxieties about the activity that gave it birth. And yet, 'doing science' involves a significant amount of making visible, or dramatizing images or inventing scenarios or imagining situations. (Frayling 2005, 43)

I am not arguing that the Gothic scientist (or, more specifically here, the medic) or, indeed, the film form, stand in for the predatory audience so that, somehow, the audience must inevitably take on the viewpoint of the mad scientist. I do, however, believe that these parallels ensure a saturation of the filmed body with Gothic meaning in that questions of control of the body, and images of such control, are fundamental to the renewed emphasis on corporeality in the contemporary Gothic. What I believe we see in Halberstam's and Frayling's comments is the constant oscillation between horror of, and fascination with, the body and a similar horror of, and desire for, control: an oscillation that the film form makes visible. Film itself becomes another manifestation of this ambivalence towards both the body and science, demonstrating the malign power of the scientist over the body but also the power of science over a body that eludes control.

For there is further ambivalence about the body owing to the fact that, while it implies materiality and the concrete as opposed to the ephemera and simulacra that many Gothic theorists posit, it also implies instability as the body is moving, changing and decaying. The role of the body in Halberstam's Gothic reading is crucial from the outset, as her title (*Skin Shows*) demonstrates, with references to the monster and to skin. The subtitle (*Gothic Horror and the Technology of Monsters*) captures the importance of technology (which, in this chapter, will be considered in the light of medicine as a technology of the body), the body as manufactured and human intervention in the shape and disposition of the body, the idea of 'disposition' including the concept of disposal of the body as well. The materiality of the body offers a different emphasis from Botting's concerns about the Gothic as ever-circulating ephemera but we also need to bear in mind that the body itself is not necessarily fixed. Halberstam observes: 'The danger of monsters lies in their tendency to stabilize bias into bodily form and pass monstrosity off as the obverse of the natural and the human. But monsters are always in motion and they resist the interpretive strategies that attempt to put them in place' (85). The body thus paradoxically suggests stability and instability. Such a position is supported by Dani Cavallaro:

> The monstrous body is not fixed, despite its persecutors' attempts to frame it as conclusively evil, demonic or simply repugnant. In fact, it has a proclivity to undergo baffling metamorphoses that are frequently literal [. . .] Yet, such metamorphoses are also occasioned by rhetorical interpretations of the anomalous: monsters are shapeshifters to the extent that we read their anatomies differently, depending on whether we wish them to conform to a regulatory discourse of order or to a carnivalesque narrative of excess. (Cavallaro 2002, 173)

And by Jack Morgan: 'Our bodies are not hardwired structures unto themselves; rather they situate a nexus of life, an intimate experience of the natural order' (Morgan 2002, 3). And, indeed, Botting himself implicitly challenges Spooner's supposition, with which we began, that the body resists the reduction of the Gothic to sheer simulacra. The body, too, collapses into superficiality:

> To see the body cut up, transformed, as nothing but a mask, an illusion of integrity, reality and coherence, is to expose a hollow, a formlessness that may be formed and re-formed by programmes or corporations. The horror, here, arises in identifying something that is both unbearable and all-too familiar. The return to the body does not, however traumatic or painful, sublimely evoke a sense of self in its delivery of an

essence or reality underlying existence: on the contrary, it hollows out and carves up an existence assumed to be solid and immutable. (Botting 2008, 148)

I do not, however, think that Spooner is necessarily wrong in consequence. Spooner herself gestures in Botting's direction when she argues that the body in contemporary Gothic is 'simply one more feature in the procession of simulacra: endlessly repeated, endlessly manipulable'. But she goes on to reassert the physicality of the body and, in doing so, she mentions that the body feels pain (Spooner 2006, 86). Botting himself refers to pain and trauma as well. The sense of self that Botting finds missing is, indeed, problematic: *La piel que habito* will readily demonstrate that. Nonetheless, the body as a locus for pain returns us to the importance of that physicality that Spooner emphasises. In fact, the body becomes a nexus or crossing point for all the Gothic processes done to it and the slippages to which it is subject but pain suggests that it remains a physical body for all that.

Morgan further suggests that 'in the gothic, the nexus of the supernatural and the natural is corporeality' (Morgan 2002, 3). Not all of Gothic, however, necessarily deals with the supernatural. Gothic science, and more particularly Gothic medicine, suggest that the crossing point is the natural with the unnatural. Gothic medicine, far from attempting to stabilise the body and return it to normality (however defined), deliberately induces or exacerbates monstrous instability. In this sense I am concerned with what Halberstam describes as 'excessive productivity':

The Gothic novel of the nineteenth century and the Gothic horror film of the late twentieth century are both obsessed with multiple modes of consumption and production, with dangerous consumptions and excessive productivity, and with economies of meaning. (4)

Halberstam's excessive productivity differs from the fears of the simulacrum of other Gothic critics in that production and consumption are not seen as a simple tired recycling of Gothic motifs. What I shall argue here is that it is Gothic medicine, the efforts on the part of others to control the body through rendering it monstrous, that results in excessive productivity and meaning. Indeed, Halberstam later notes that 'The suppleness of monstrosity allows for numerous interventions in the business of interpretations' (144); and I would argue that Gothic medicine is literally in the business of interpretations. Gothic medicine tries to intervene in the body in order to interpret how it should be but that interpretation is often at odds with the prevailing interpretations of society. The quintessential bodily intervention is, of course, Frankenstein's use of body

parts to create a new being that will turn out to be a monster beyond
Frankenstein's control, yet the monster, an outcast from society, exists
only because of Frankenstein's scientific intervention. The fascination
with Gothic medicine and its hubris is demonstrated in the popularity
of Mary Shelley's original story and the numerous cinematic remakes.
Halberstam's remark about economies of meaning, cited above, also ties
in with the notion of profit – not always monetary profit but the idea of
personal gain. What economy of meaning does this have for us, here and
now, in our own specific materiality? Or, to pick up on a motif I touched
on briefly above, what pain can this cause me – physically, emotionally,
materially? With this I return to the concept of nexus. The possibility of
deterritorialisation is still there, chiming with the theoretical concerns
noted earlier, but still the body inherently suggests a moment in space or
time that is Gothic, a moment of pain. I place the nexus at the point of
this contradiction.

The potential instability of the Gothic body has implications for that
body as a nexus of cultural flow. Halberstam remarks: 'It is the propensity
for the monster to deconstruct at any time, to always be in the process
of decomposition, that makes it/him/her a fugitive from identity' (37).
The ever-present possibility of deconstruction and decomposition –
phenomena to which all bodies will necessarily succumb – suggests flux
that coincides with the ability of the body to flow across national borders.
Halberstam further argues, however, that 'Monstrosity as the bodily
manifestation of evil makes evil into a local effect, not generalizable across
a society or culture' (162) but then goes on to suggest that modernity and
Nazi Germany have removed such a comforting thought because evil now
becomes a system. These comments stress once again the contradictory
notion of the body as both stable and thus localisable, and as unstable and
the embodiment of a principle applying indiscriminately to all areas. Such
a contradiction overlaps with that of evil as a system because the system
is now all-encompassing and inescapable but simultaneously suggests
circulation and flow precisely because the system reaches to all areas. As
Halberstam goes on to observe: 'Monsters within postmodernism are
already inside – the house, the body, the head, the skin, the nation – and
they work their way out' (ibid.). If the body is therefore a contradictory
site of cultural flow, I shall argue here that this should help shape our
thinking with regard to Gothic medicine. As I have suggested above,
Gothic medicine implies a deliberate attempt to render the body unstable,
to deconstruct it and decompose it. As an example of such an intervention,
we need go no further than Spain's most prominent director worldwide in
the democratic era, Pedro Almodóvar.

Almodóvar *La piel que habito*

La piel que habito fits well with a Gothic mode, given the isolated country house that acts as a hideaway in which a mad scientist performs experiments on the body of another, and the dangers of dominance by a corrupt patriarchal figure. The scientist concerned, Robert Ledgard (Antonio Banderas), carries out surgery on Vicente (Jan Cornet), a young man who Ledgard thinks has raped his daughter Norma (Blanca Suárez). It is not, in fact, clear if the encounter between Vicente and Norma was rape but Norma (already mentally fragile, having previously witnessed the suicide of her mother, Gal) is traumatised as a result. Ledgard kidnaps Vicente and turns him into a woman, Vera (Elena Anaya): he also refashions Vicente/Vera's body to resemble Gal. Eventually, Vera shoots Ledgard dead and escapes, returning home to an uncertain reception from his mother (Susi Sánchez).

The very title of Halberstam's book, *Skin Shows*, seems an apt description of Almodóvar's film, *La piel que habito* or The Skin I Live In. Though the Gothic surgery carried out in the film goes deeper than the skin, *La piel* is, indeed, a skin show. Firstly, though the central surgical act of the film is the carrying out of vaginoplasty on a young man without his consent, the film spends a good deal of time focusing on the surface of the resulting young woman, Vera, first in terms of her carefully made-up face and the body stockings she wears (often hinting at the naked skin beneath), and later in the designer dress she wears. Early in the film, Ledgard sits and watches his experiment through a one-way screen, and zooms in on her face so that the face and its skin dominate both his screen and ours. Secondly, Ledgard also conducts experiments in synthetic skin to facilitate plastic surgery. Some early sequences portray the experiments and the application of the new skin to Vera's body. Alessandra Lemma suggests that the skin show we have in *La piel* is the true source of the film's horror: 'the real horror of the film lies in its seductive aesthetics'. She further observes that, while Vera looks flawlessly beautiful, her smooth skin covers over the violence done to her. 'Vera's flawless skin, which conjures up unreality in its perfection, covers up a profound traumatic injury which, unlike the new skin grafted on her by Ledgard, never heals' (Lemma 2012, 1299). The trauma is ironically exacerbated by the fact that Vera can no longer feel pain as a result of Ledgard's experiments with skin. This body is a locus of trauma, and part of that trauma is precisely the inability to feel pain.

The strong focus on surface and on aesthetics has given rise to some troubling possibilities. Darren Waldron and Ros Murray observe that 'By framing its representations in such ways [here Waldron and Murray refer to the use of cold colours and clinical angles devoid of tension], the film could be criticized for reducing the themes of transgender/gender subjectivity to grounds for an exercise in style' (Waldron and Murray 2014, 63). Waldron and Murray frame this potential criticism – style at the expense of theme – in terms of scientific rationality. Paul Julian Smith (White and Smith 2011) addresses a parallel dichotomy when he argues that the film is 'deeply unhealthy' and takes '(un-)pleasure in disappointment and distress': he finds that the aesthetics of the film, however, its skin, are the only potentially redeeming element of this negative narrative, mentioning as examples the shreds of dresses ripped up over the floor of the woman's cell. There is an uncomfortable parallel here with Halberstam's comment:

> Gothic reveals the ideological stakes of a bourgeois realism – namely, there is no one generic form that resembles 'life' and another debased form that deviates from the natural order of things. There are only less or more fantastic costumes, less or more Gothic interpretations of reality. (Halberstam 1995, 62)

Halberstam's suggestion here coincides to some extent with the postmodernist nihilism that Botting sees in the Gothic, in that reality becomes simply a matter of Gothic interpretation. In that sense, Smith is right to highlight concerns within Spain that specific realities, such as the country's economic crisis, become buried under a play of fantastic costumes. And *La piel* is in itself just such a play of costumes, the fascination of Vicente's makeover into the smooth surface of Vera. We can, however, also observe that *La piel* exposes the violence that goes into these different Gothic costumes, and that underlying violence behind the pleasures of the surface, the skin, is also important to recognise. The idea of such performance as a show chimes with Halberstam's notion of predatory and yet judgemental viewers, revelling in the beautiful finished product of the woman while simultaneously being aware of the violence that made this possible.

Delight in violence and trauma is, of course, an uncomfortable element in the Gothic and horror, as both genres or modes entail witness to the fear or suffering of another, and the problem that pleasure poses has already been touched on in my earlier discussion of Gothic ghosts and historical traumas (see Chapter 4). In such a scenario, aesthetics, in this case the skins that cover Vera, both distract and detract from the horror that Vicente/Vera suffers. Yet it is hard not to admire the beauty that Ledgard has created even while being aware of the trauma that has gone into its making (and the trauma is not only Vicente's): I believe this mismatch between the beauty and the trauma undermines the complacency of *La piel* posited by Waldron and Murray and by Smith. The beauty and the horror reinforce each other.

It is the deliberate intervention of another person in the case of Gothic medicine that interests me here, as I shall argue that it is that intervention, in particular, that destabilises the body. Nonetheless, I should like to dwell a little more on the idea of skin before considering the matter of who pierces it. Xavier Aldana Reyes argues that 'The skin as hybrid opens up a door for the perception of identity as both transmorphic and unyielding' (Aldana Reyes 2013, 828). He thus echoes the idea posited above that the body is both fixity and flow. Skin, posing as a natural barrier that hinders flow and implies fixity, is, of course, breached by bodily openings, including the pores of the skin itself. But it is also breached by the surgeon's knife and needle. In *La piel*, skin comes to involve excess of meaning, as skin here means both Vicente *and* Vera, particularly at the end as Vera, beautiful surface on display in her dress, reclaims her identity as Vicente. It is, however, Ledgard that causes such excess through his surgical intervention (and Ledgard throws in a further identity to the mix, that of his dead wife Gal whom Vera resembles).

It is not incidental that Aldana Reyes foregrounds the female body. The female body appears to be an unchanging entity identifiable by certain body parts which, in theory, fix the sex of the body but the malleability and, indeed, potential loss of the body contradict this and add to the flow. The female body, perhaps more than the male, captures this bodily double bind. On the one hand, traditionally women have been less able to 'rise above' their bodies through the use of the mind and rational thinking: they are more bound to the earth, less cerebral. On the other hand, and also traditionally, the female body had its own sexual mobility, a constant sexual temptation if no control was exercised, because women were thought to be more naturally promiscuous. This supposed promiscuity arose, of course, from the female emphasis on the body over the soul, on this traditional reading, but it simultaneously suggests a fixity and a fluidity from which has arisen over the centuries many paradoxical perceptions of women. Gothic surgery is not confined to the female, as the example of the Frankenstein story readily shows: in Mary Shelley's original story of 1818, the original Gothic surgery was carried out in order to create a male (while women were kept well away from the scene). If we are talking about the manipulation and control of these bodies through medicine, however, it is hardly surprising that women become victims.

The surgical processes and the surgeon who carries them out are nonetheless also of vital importance in considering medicine as Gothic. It is quite telling, I think, that most academic criticism of the film focuses on

Vera/Vicente and the difficulty of gender definition. In a sense, this is right, particularly with regard to the ways in which female bodies might be perceived. If, as I said earlier, the body is the nexus of physicality, pain and of a shifting deterritorialisation and simulation of what the body represents, then it is an obvious place to focus our attention. Yet this also occurs precisely because Vera becomes a skin show: we are drawn to the surface even if, as many of the commentators do, we try to distinguish between surface and soul or argue for the close imbrication of the two. Perpetration receives far less attention. I am intrigued by the fact that, at the time of writing, the most in-depth studies of Ledgard's character come from the field of psychoanalysis rather than from Hispanic studies and film studies (see Di Ceglie 2012, Lemma 2012). For Gothic scholarship, however, the perpetrator is as crucial as the victim. Francisco A. Zurián comments that 'The effect on the spectator watching the film is one of an increasing sense of terror, an experience that is rare in the Almodóvar filmography.' He compares this to another new element: 'the terror that results from the exercise of absolute power, unchecked by any type of moral or ethical counterweight (Zurián 2013, 263) The source of this terror is the doctor's power as

> judge, jury and executioner, lacking in any capacity for empathy or remorse [. . .] The force of the scalpel and the madness of absolute power converge in the millimetrically precise actions of a brilliant mind with a will of steel. (ibid.)

Ledgard is thus familiar to us as a mad scientist.

Almodóvar underlines the importance of Ledgard by using the very recognisable face of Antonio Banderas, one of Spain's most international

Figure 6.1 The mad scientist: Ledgard at work.

stars. In a sense, Almodóvar is remoulding Banderas who is recognisable but, with his face given a new cast, made to look sinister: a far cry from his familiar persona (cf. Perriam 2004) of a Latin lover or voicing Puss in Boots in the *Shrek* films. A 'making of' featurette on the DVD reminds us of the parallel between the director and his character as a controller of bodies (and with the ability to cut them up or edit them): it shows all the bodies of the actors in turn being observed by Almodóvar and his crew, just as Ledgard observes Vera. Our first sight of Ledgard is a close-up of Banderas's face: his first line, as he addresses a group of doctors, is 'El rostro nos identifica' (the face identifies us, or alternatively, the face gives us identity). As he gives his paper, graphics reveal faces coming apart and being remoulded. From his very first appearance, then, Ledgard underscores the importance of skin to our identities but also his ability to reshape that identity. Though Ledgard's persona sounds initially benign (as yet we do not know his past history), his face contradicts this. He looks menacing. The actor's heavy eyebrows are shot from a slightly high angle, particularly when we encounter Ledgard at his podium, so that the brows cast a shadow over his eyes that makes him appear more sinister. Ironically, given his comment that our face identifies us, this face clearly identifies him as a Gothic scientist.

While Banderas has played dangerous and violent characters before, and particularly in earlier Almodóvar films [such as *La ley del deseo* (The Law of Desire, 1987), to take just one example], in *La piel* Almodóvar gives Banderas a clinical air. Almodóvar himself commented:

> No mueve ningún músculo porque así se lo impuse. Antonio es muy expresivo y aquí le pedí lo contrario. Desde el principio había decidido que como la historia de La piel . . . es tan bestia, el tono debía ser muy austero. Aséptico. Y Antonio se ajustó perfectamente a lo que le pedía. Se sorprendió al principio, pero se sometió de inmediato. (Harguindey 2012, ellipsis in original)
> (He doesn't move a muscle because I insisted he didn't. Antonio is very expressive and this time I was asking him to do the opposite. From the beginning I had decided that because *La piel* . . . is so crude, the tone had to be very austere. Aseptic. And Antonio adjusted perfectly to what I required of him. He was surprised at first, but he immediately agreed to it.)

There is, then, an irony in Manohla Dargis's review when she says: 'it's a pleasure to experience a performance from Mr. Banderas that peels away his persona and burrows under the skin' (Dargis, 2011). Dargis here hints at the surgery that Almodóvar himself carries out on Banderas's star image, and the reference to skin is hardly incidental. While the dominance of Ledgard, impervious to the warnings and criticisms of other characters, stands in strong contrast to the Latin lover that has been a particular feature of Banderas's Hollywood career, Perriam observes that the actor's earlier films and, in particular, those with Almodóvar, such as *La Ley del deseo*, *Matador* (1986) and *¡Átame!* (Tie Me Up! Tie Me Down, 1989), involve sexual ambiguity, transgression, and occasionally mental disturbance (as in his character in *Matador*, for example). Perriam notes that: 'Off-screen considerable effort went into disavowing the particular emphasis on disturbance, psychic splitting, sexual ambiguity and mother fixation to point up less challenging Antonios for certain important sectors of the public' (Perriam 2004, 48). He goes on to observe that 'The comedy and action roles of later, Hollywood years went some way towards erasing or at least flattening out the perverse and excessive notes in Banderas's first career' (though Perriam also observes that Banderas's performances in *Interview with the Vampire* (Neil Jordan, 1994) harks back to notes of perversion and excess: 65). The role of Ledgard appears to be casting against type on one level, one reason why Banderas's performance initially seems quite startling. Nevertheless, the earlier perverse traces remain within his performance in this film.

Ledgard is the film's dominant male; his own traumas at the loss of his wife and subsequently his daughter are masked by his lack of emotion and rationality even as he exercises power over both Vicente and Vera. Ledgard's house suggests his personality: Julián Daniel Gutiérrez Albilla observes that the architecture of El Cigarral resembles the oppressive authority within and covers over the disorder and irrationality beneath while the iron bars at the entrance suggest a prison (Gutiérrez Albilla 74, 75). Here we have another example of a haunted house, haunted by the ghosts of Gal, or Norma, and even of Vicente. Similarly, Gutiérrez Albilla points to the initial setting of Toledo as implying the weight of the past, arguing that Almodóvar offers us a 'fused time' with the past and present coexisting in the same space (73). Ledgard is haunted by his past and, in consequence, Vera will be haunted by it, too. Lemma observes of them both, 'As he gradually remodels her body to uncannily resemble that of his deceased wife, we are exposed in a most disturbing manner to repeated and violent projective processes/surgeries through which Dr Ledgard manages the unbearable losses he cannot mourn' (Lemma 2012, 1293). This lack of mourning is indicative of Ledgard's inability to come to terms with the failure to manage his wife's body, through her infidelity and her subsequent suicide following disfigurement after a car crash. His refusal to accept what happened is the source of his Gothic surgery, remaking the world to the way he wishes it to be.

As we have seen above, it is the instability of the female body and its relation to identity that are principal thematic threads in *La piel*. Yet the creation and manipulation of the female body are arguably either not confined to gender or something inherent to the male. Philip French, being careful not to give away the plot twist, argues that

> at different times and in different places, a pair of related characters appear – in a seemingly natural way and with great tenderness – to be creating new beings. In one case a man makes scarecrow-like women with twigs and straw to take their place in the window of a chic boutique as mannequins wearing vintage dresses; in the other a woman makes copies of doll-like creatures from wool and cotton, modelled on Louise Bourgeois sculptures. (French 2011)

The parallel French draws here between Vicente, working in his mother's boutique, and Vera, trying to express herself, is perhaps more sinister than he makes out. There is another parallel to be made, with Ledgard. For, after all, who is the first person we see manipulating bodies and creating a form of skin? Immediately after the title credits, the film's first main sequence reveals an as yet unidentified Vera in her room, with shots (as yet unexplained) of detached heads. The first person we see working with a form of skin (in fact, cloth) is Vera, cutting and applying cloth to her model figures. Her first words of dialogue involve her asking the housekeeper Marilia (Marisa Paredes) for more cloth, and then for scissors and a needle, which she is refused. Vera then puts on one of her own dresses, looks at herself in a mirror, and starts to hack away at the dress with an emery board, in this way acquiring more material for herself. At this point in the film, we do not know anything about Vera, not even her name, nor why she might be making models or why she is denied scissors and a needle. These scenes introduce a strong equation between cloth and skin. I understand the joint action of Vera putting on the dress and then tearing at it as a clear ambivalence about her status as woman and her role as manipulator of skin on heads and bodies, a role that is ultimately marked as masculine in *La piel* because both Ledgard and, as we shall see, Vicente handle skin/cloth in similar ways. I feel, nonetheless, that the salient element of this scene for my purposes is the latter: Vera refashions bodies and deals in skin. Elsewhere in the film she makes surgical gestures that demonstrate her resistance to her imprisonment and the violence done to her body. Shortly after surgery, Vera, recently transformed from Vicente, tries to escape: when she fails to get away she slits her throat, piercing her own skin. This gesture echoes Vera's suicide attempt at the beginning of the film (though chronologically later in time than her first attempt, seen halfway through the film): on this occasion the camera dwells on her body as Ledgard lovingly patches up her skin. Increasingly, then, Almodóvar breaks down the divide between perpetrator and victim.

Vera is nonetheless only continuing the interest in shaping women's bodies that Vicente had. In flashback we see Vicente dressing the mannequins in his mother's second-hand clothes store: like Vera, he is applying a layer of skin on them and, indeed, turning them into women. As such he is carrying out surgery on them, applying pins to hold the 'skin' in place. As we see him dressing a mannequin in a shop window, he lightly massages a breast, as he will do to Norma at the end of their botched encounter. This parallel suggests an inability to distinguish between mannequins and women, an idea reinforced by the fact that, in this same scene in the shop, Vicente wants to dress his mother's assistant Cristina (Bárbara Lennie) in a particular dress, the very designer dress later worn by Vera, a point to which I shall return. Dresses appear to be a form of control over women, as is skin, the idea reinforcing cloth and clothes as simply another form of skin. As a lesbian, Cristina eludes Vicente's control and is immune to his flirtation, so his desire to dress her is an effort to impose some sort of control. (Nonetheless, in her brief appearances, Cristina always wears jeans, suggesting her ability to elude being dressed.) As part of that same scene, a man (the regular cameo of producer Agustín Almodóvar) enters to sell the clothes of the wife who keeps leaving him in his attempt to reassert control (because the next time she returns she would have to leave naked). Some commentators have also picked up on Almodóvar's suggestion that the dresses hanging in the shop are like the ghosts of the women who wore them. White quotes Almodóvar's comment and adds: 'there's also this haunting dimension of becoming-inhuman (vampire, alien, ghost, doll) that makes *Skin* so interesting to me'. In this way, White argues, the film opens us up to the possibility of the uncanny (White and Smith, 2011). Gutiérrez Albilla similarly observes that the second-hand dresses in the window carry with them the traces of the female bodies that wore them (Gutiérrez Albilla 2013, 81–2). Vicente's work with clothes is therefore not so far removed from Ledgard's work with skin, and it can also be seen in negative terms for women, as Aldana Reyes observes: 'if Vicente's attempt to have sex with Ledgard's reluctant daughter is never consummated, the overwhelming epistemic attack on the female body is still manifest in his behaviour' (Aldana Reyes 2013, 829).

If Cristina resists Vicente's effort at remaking her, other women resist Ledgard's efforts at transformation. Norma, after her encounter with Vicente, is hospitalised: despite Ledgard's insistence she refuses to wear dresses or fitted clothing, and hides in a cupboard, crying, when her father comes to see her. This is her form of resisting male control over her body. The doctor advises Ledgard that Norma associates him with the possible rape. Ledgard, of course, denies this but it is an intriguing conflation with Vicente. Lemma observes that Legard wants to refashion reality by asking the psychiatrist to get Norma to put on a dress: he wants to change 'the surface of the body' (Lemma 2012, 1294). In his efforts to clothe Norma, he is, of course, acting just as Vicente does in trying to clothe Cristina and thus both change the surface of her body and exercise some sort of control. Norma's mother, Gal, also tried to flee Ledgard and, after her disfigurement in a car crash, she commits suicide (an escape route that Norma will follow in her turn). One particular object of Ledgard's refashioning of Vicente is not simply to turn him into a woman but to turn him into a replica of Gal, as is recognised by those who knew her. It is clearly his attempt to regain control of the wife he lost. The most sustained resistance, however, is that of Vera. While Vicente makes no attempt to resist, Vera tries to escape the first moment she gets, and cuts her own throat when finally caught. Subsequently, Vera's ripping of the dresses, in revolt at imprisonment and in having been refashioned as a women, demonstrates her resistance by refusing to be dressed as a man dictates: those dresses will later become the materials for her own creations, the skin she will control. She uses eyeliner pencils as materials to draw on the walls of her room which again suggests a resistance to Ledgard's dictation of how she must look. Like the dresses, Vera assigns a new purpose to the pencils, suggesting the assertion of her control. As Aldana Reyes observes, 'the type of desiring being portrayed in the character of Vera/Vicente is testimony to the transformative quality available in the act of resistance itself' (Aldana Reyes 2013, 830).

So what does it mean that Vera eventually wears the dress with which Vicente tried to clothe or cover Cristina? The improbability of such a dress still being available after six years have passed can perhaps be overlooked in the interests of melodramatic coincidence. Yet the dress is also ironically a ghost of a *man* because it is that dress, and the story attached to it, that enable Cristina to identify Vera as Vicente at the end of the film. Aldana Reyes argues that:

> liminal identities do not rely on a rhetoric of materiality, but instead [. . .] all gendered 'being' is necessarily disembodied and out of joint, permeable and able to stretch beyond the pure material significance of sex. [. . .] As the yoga teacher in Vera/Vicente's television reminds us, we should never confuse 'la forma' (the shape) with 'el fondo' (its inner depth). (Aldana Reyes 2013, 830)

Perhaps rather than rendering woman uncanny, then, both Ledgard and Vicente between them render a sense of gendered subjectivity, perhaps any subjectivity, uncanny. The intervention of the surgeon, whether supplied with a scalpel or a sewing needle, is reminiscent of Richard Davenport-Hines's observations on the Gothic body:

> The late twentieth-century gothic preoccupation with fetishistic body mutilation or transgressive decoration of body surfaces is not just a counter-cultural version of cosmetic surgery (though it is certainly that). It also registers dissent from God's arrangements for humankind; it expresses our self-disgust and death-wish; it recognises that demoralisation is one of the most effective modes of seduction [. . .]

Thus far, Davenport-Hines's comment reminds us of both Ledgard's and Vicente's desire for the body to be otherwise, a desire that is more than skin deep (or cloth deep). But Davenport-Hines goes on to say:

> it declares that adult acts of self-reinvention are ultimate acts of freedom, certainly as enriching and liberating as searching for an inner true self through anxious introspection, or seeking a heavily mediated identity based on childish experience and childish perception. (Davenport-Hines 1998, 5)

We cannot be sure how far Vicente has reinvented himself as Vera: the film ends with his reclamation of his old identity, and yet he is transformed. Vicente can never, in fact, escape the effect of Ledgard's efforts to control his body and the bodies of women. He is, however, both the cause and the result of his own efforts to control women's bodies: he embraces both identities. By putting on the dress, but acknowledging her original name, Vera accepts the excess of meaning that she now embodies, and is therefore free of bodily control. Nonetheless, the intervention of Gothic medicine has radically altered her. Vera has the effects of Gothic medicine written on her body but she ultimately eludes its control.

Vera/Ledgard as Cultural Nexus

The place of Pedro Almodóvar in a Gothic cultural flow is an unusual one. Almodóvar has come to represent Spain and Spanish film in a number of very reductive and problematic ways. Abroad, his films have, to a great extent, come to stand for what is perceived as a specifically Spanish style of humour that challenges heteronormativity in a zany style, drawing on popular culture and kitsch in order to do so. As Almodóvar is by far the best-known Spanish director abroad, his style has often been understood as quintessentially Spanish (an approach that neglects the wide range of Spanish cultural styles and modes on offer). Yet he is also known for his intertextual references, pointing to international influences on his film-making. A good example here is *Mujeres al borde de un ataque de nervios* (Women on the Verge of a Nervous Breakdown, 1988) which cited films such as *How to Marry a*

Millionaire (Jean Negulesco 1953), *Rear Window* (Alfred Hitchcock 1954) and *Johnny Guitar* (Nicholas Ray 1954): *Mujeres* has strong associations with the American screwball comedy tradition, involving unlikely coincidences and strong reliance on dialogue. There are touches of humour, drawing on Spanish and international references, throughout his films but it is also clear that Almodóvar's films grew more serious and even more dark as the director's career developed, although humorous elements remained. *La piel que habito* is easily the darkest of all, in which humour is intermittent at best and much of that is based on the rape scene involving Zeco (Roberto Álamo) who is dressed in carnival costume as a tiger. Its darkness may be one reason why Almodóvar reverted to a high dosage of camp comedy with his following film, *Los amantes pasajeros* (I'm So Excited, 2013).

There are Spanish precedents for mad-doctor films though, to my knowledge, no indication that Almodóvar was influenced by any of them. In their portmanteau review of Spanish horror, López and Pizarro (2014) mention, for instance, the examples of *La cara del terror* (The Face of Terror, Isidoro M. Ferry and Willian J. Hole Jr 1962) (89), and *Santo contra el doctor muerte*[2] (Santo against Doctor Death, Rafael Romero-Marchent 1973) (237–8). There is also the connection with Jess Franco's Dr Orloff films in terms of Gothic surgery (Lázaro-Reboll 2012, 271). Nonetheless, international referents prevail. *La piel* is itself an adaptation of the French novel *Mygale* (Tarantula 1984) by Thierry Jonquet, though French respondents surveyed by Waldron and Murray by and large felt the film to be ultimately Almodóvar's work: 'Although his success at rendering the tale his own is by no means unquestioned, a large section of the postings depict *La piel que habito* as unmistakeably an Almodóvar film' (Waldron and Murray 2014, 64). Almodóvar himself, in the film's pressbook, suggests *La piel* as part of a transnational Gothic flow:

Una historia de estas características me hacía pensar en Luis Buñuel, Alfred Hitchcock, todos los Fritz Lang (desde lo gótico al noir). Pensé también en la esté-tica pop del terror de la Hammer; o en el más psicodélico y kitsch del giallo italiano (Dario Argento, Mario Bava, Umberto Lenzi, Lucio Fulci . . .) y por supuesto en el lirismo de Georges Franju en 'Los ojos sin rostro' [. . .] Es imposible no pensar en 'Frankenstein' de James Whale, o en 'Vértigo' y 'Rebecca' de Alfred Hitchcock [. . .] (quoted in Zurián 2013, 267)
(A story with these characteristics made me think of Luis Buñuel, Alfred Hitchcock, all the Fritz Lang films (from Gothic to noir). I also thought of Hammer horror's pop aesthetic or the Italian *giallo* at its most psychedelic and kitsch (Dario Argento, Mario Bava, Umberto Lenzi, Lucio Fulci . . .) and, of course, in the lyricism of Georges Franju's *Eyes Without a Face* [. . .] You can't help thinking of James Whales's *Frankenstein* or Alfred Hitchcock's *Vertigo* and *Rebecca* [. . .])

Almodóvar's comments coincide with the sense of a lack of place observed by Paul Julian Smith:

> [. . .] the claustrophobia of *Skin*'s enclosed settings and the hermeticism of its self-reference go hand in hand with an indifference to time and place. Where once Almodóvar offered a heightened vision of Madrid that somehow intersected with the real city, now he seems, literally, all over the place. So we start with a showy shot of landlocked Toledo, although the film was mainly made in damp coastal Galicia. And one minor character inexplicably carries a copy of *La Vanguardia*, the Barcelona newspaper. Even the names (Ledgard, Marilia, Gal) seem to come from nowhere. (White and Smith, 2011)

Almodóvar also used Jean-Pierre Melville's *Le Cercle rouge* (1970) as a model for Banderas's clinical portrayal of Ledgard (Harguindey, 2012). The French connection did not go unnoticed by *El País*'s acerbic critic Carlos Boyero, no fan of Almodóvar:

> Impone a Banderas el hieratismo, no hacer el mínimo gesto ni manifestar emociones, una mezcla de lo que pretendían lograr con sus actores y actrices Jean-Pierre Melville y Robert Bresson. En el caso de los maestros franceses, esa impuesta sobriedad expresiva servía para algo frecuentemente fascinante. (Boyero 2011)
> (He imposes solemnity on Banderas, who mustn't move a muscle or express any emotion, a mixture of what Jean-Pierre Melville and Robert Bresson aimed to do with their actors. In the case of the French maestros, this expressive sobriety imposed on the actors offered something frequently fascinating.)

Thus, Boyero implies that, in the case of *La piel*, the expressive sobriety offered no fascination at all.

French (2011) specifically links Almodóvar to Buñuel's *Tristana* (1970) as both films are set in Toledo, though French does not make the further link to the prosthetic female body of both films: the eponymous character of *Tristana* suffers the amputation of her leg after illness and subsequently wears a prosthetic limb. Dargis spots a reference to *Citizen Kane* (Orson Welles 1941) in the entrance through the gates to El Cigarral, reminiscent of Kane's mansion. Ian Olney sees *La piel* as an inheritor of what he calls Euro horror, the trashier end of European horror production from the 1950s to the 1980s (Olney 2013, 232). Domenico Di Ceglie notes the similarities to Shelley's Frankenstein but also to Danny Boyle's theatre version which told everything from the point of view of the monster. In that version, Di Ceglie argues, it is clear that Frankenstein 'could not relate at all to the emotional world of the creature he had given life to', like Ledgard (Di Ceglie 2012, 1309).

Aldana Reyes speaks of the interest in surgery in other texts: he refers to American television series that explore plastic surgery and sees *La piel* as deriving from this newer trend. 'In the horror genre, this has translated into a shift in tone and thematic concerns, meaning that horror no longer takes its cues from Gothic narratives but exceeds them representationally' (Aldana Reyes 2013, 822). Aldana Reyes goes on to consider the surgery occurring in Frankenstein films and observes that the scientists of these films 'are obsessed with the creation or alteration of life as we know it [. . .] these figures are always ineluctably male'. He further observes: 'In *The Bride of Frankenstein* (1935) [. . .] woman is artificially manufactured' (825). The interest in horror surgery is not confined to America: 'Another example of beauty terror where the construction of woman remains flawed, indeed impossible, is Georges Franju's *Eyes Without a Face*' (825), an obvious reference for *La piel*. French also says:

> Inevitably reducing his stature in our minds, the audience recognises him [Ledgard] as that celebrated movie figure, the mad scientist, whose most famous antecedent is Dr Frankenstein, and most infamous current avatar the loony doctor in the Dutch horror flick *The Human Centipede*.
>
> Robert is a hubristic scientist, a man questioning the nature of what we have traditionally been taught to regard as natural. He is also that part of all of us that in one way or another attempts to reshape the world according to our own devices and desires rather than accepting things as they are. In this way he resembles Scottie Ferguson, the detective played by James Stewart in Hitchcock's *Vertigo*, one of Almodóvar's favourite films, who transforms a woman he meets by apparent accident into the ideal image of one he has lost and feels guilty over. (2011)

Dargis pinpoints the exoticism of Vera as Legard watches her reclining on her couch:

> she's stretched out in the classic recumbent pose of the odalisque: that exotic Turkish harem dweller and Orientalist fantasy painted by the likes of Goya, Ingres and Manet, and given opulent new life and reverberant meaning by Mr. Almodóvar, a master of his art. (Dargis 2011)

Gothic surgery has thus provided a seam of international film-making that suggests cultural flow but also transnational cinema once Almodóvar gets his hands on this plot. Almodóvar incorporates this plot into his own style of film-making, as suggested above with regard to the reshaping of the body in order to change sex, as in *La ley del deseo* and *La mala educación* (Bad Education 2004). This is a tricky case of 'indigenisation' given the complexities of Almodóvar's relationship with Spanish culture but, given his status abroad as *the* Spanish director, it could also be argued as indigenisation from outside.

The idea of *La piel* as part of a transnational Gothic continuum comes up against specifically Spanish demands of its cultural texts.

Paul Julian Smith has remarked that 'some Spaniards do say that, secluded by celebrity, Almodóvar is out of touch. And the claustrophobia of *Skin*'s enclosed settings and the hermeticism of its self-reference go hand in hand with an indifference to time and place.' He goes on to slate the film for a lack of engagement with Spain's current situation and argues: 'There's a transparent disconnect between the supposed present of *Skin*'s perverse but cosseted cast and the reality of contemporary Spain, reeling from the financial crisis and wracked by popular protests' (White and Smith 2011). Smith's comments raise considerable questions about the function of Almodóvar's recent work in Spanish culture: it is hard to overestimate the severity of the economic crisis in Spain and I certainly would not want to dismiss the real pain and suffering involved. I wonder, however, how far an Almodóvar film would work as an appropriate vehicle for connecting up with (that is, reversing the disconnect of which Smith speaks) the impact of Spain's economic problems. After all, his follow-up, *Los amantes pasajeros* (which, of course, was released well after Smith was commenting), took a sideswipe at the habit of regional governments in Spain to build white elephants such as the barely used Castellón airport. This waste of money clearly angered Almodóvar (Vallín 2013) but, ultimately, the film's final scene at the empty airport becomes little more than an in-joke.

The ability to spot intertextual references has obviously entertained a few critics but the use of them might be considered to have a negative accent. Waldron and Murray (2014, 63) note that: 'For some viewers the film's intertextual borrowings may undermine its potentially controversial implications, reassuring them that *La piel que habito* is a harmless homage to a cult cinematographic legacy.' It also implies detachment from one's roots, as Smith suggests: 'Perhaps the final moral of this unsettling film is quite simple, and one that applies to character and director alike: that, after such knowledge (such experience), "You can't go home again"' (White and Smith 2011). As far as the specificities of the Spanish crisis are concerned, I am reminded of the comments of Fernando Savater, discussed in Chapter 4, that we can and should remember more than one trauma. All the intertextual references do not disguise the very real physical and mental trauma undergone by all the 'ghosts' of the house, Gal, Norma and Vicente. The burden of this trauma is left for Vera to carry by the film's end. The sensuality of skin and of clothes hugging the body does not hide this pain. Almodóvar is both taking from and contributing to an international tradition of Gothic surgery and, in doing so, gives his own twist to it. Given his position within Spanish cinema, his film indigenises the theme of Gothic medicine to demonstrate that, ironically, the body is subject to change and to the pain of change, regardless of where in the world it is.

Belén Rueda

In this section I shall consider the actor Belén Rueda as an example of another nexus, between the textual and actual body. Rueda may at first seem an odd choice with regard to cultural flow because she is far from being a transnational actor. Though some of the films she has appeared in have had international distribution and success, especially *Mar adentro* (The Sea Inside, Alejandro Amenábar 2004) and *El orfanato*, her career has been firmly based in Spain. Her only major foreign credit is *Séptimo* (7th Floor, Patxi Amezcua 2013), made and set in Argentina with well-known Argentinian actor Ricardo Darín as the male lead. (Even here, director Amezcua is himself Spanish.) Rueda also has a role as a minor character in the British film *Savage Grace* (Tom Kalin 2007) alongside other Spanish actors playing bit parts, such as Elena Anaya, Simón Andreu and Unax Ugalde. Otherwise, Rueda's portfolio to date is therefore largely confined to Spain.

Rueda is not known simply or necessarily as a Gothic actor because she has appeared in other genres. She first came to public attention as a television actor: firstly in the highly successful *Médico de familia* (Family Doctor 1995–99; Rueda appeared in five episodes in 1997) and then in the also successful *Periodistas* (Journalists, 1998–2002). In *Periodistas* Rueda was a regular character, reprising her character Clara Nadal from *Médico de familia*: she then moved to play Lucía in the successful series *Los Serrano* (The Serranos, 2003–08). Her big break into films came with her role in the Oscar-winning biopic *Mar adentro*. It was her next film, however, that rapidly established Rueda's association with the Gothic. *El orfanato* had its own transatlantic touch with Mexican director Guillermo del Toro as producer: his name was used as a brand in publicity. Rueda played the central character, Laura, the focus and pivot of the action: there were hardly any sequences that did not feature her to some degree. *El orfanato* features a haunted house (as mentioned in Chapter 4) and Laura is the Gothic heroine seeking not only to find her missing son but to solve the mystery of the disappearances of other children (see Davies, 2011). The success of this role led to other Gothic roles in the films *Los ojos de Julia* (Julia's Eyes, Guillem Morales 2010) and *El cuerpo* (The Body, Oriol Paulo 2012), and the television series *Luna: el misterio de Calenda* (Luna: the Mystery of Calenda 2012–13) where Rueda's character investigates a mystery involving werewolves. In many of her roles Rueda is playing a mother but whether she is a good or bad mother varies considerably. As a main character in *Periodistas*, she is both a single mother and a press photographer trying to juggle her responsibilities while, in *El orfanato*, her function as mother is paramount, both as regards her own son and the mothering role she carries out towards all the dead children at the end of the film. She is also a concerned mother in *Luna: el misterio de Calenda*. On the other hand, as Delia in *Séptimo*, her love for her children leads her to pretend to kidnap them in order to take them to Spain and deprive them of the care of their father Sebastián (the character played by Darín). When Sebastián finds out, he ensures that Delia boards her plane alone, in effect banishing her from her family. In another film, *No tengas miedo* (Don't Be Afraid, Montxo Armendáriz 2011), she plays a mother who is either unaware of, or prefers not to acknowledge, the fact that her husband is sexually abusing their daughter.

Another particular aspect of the roles that Rueda plays – a factor particularly important to the current discussion – is the fragility of her body in key roles. This is clearest in the part that propelled her into the front rank of Spanish actors, *Mar adentro*, in which she plays Julia, a lawyer suffering from a degenerative disease deemed to be incurable. She considers suicide but, in the end, cannot go through with it, and the last sequence of the film shows how the disease has her firmly in its grasp. As a final sequence, this is striking because her role is as support to central character Ramón Sampedro (Javier Bardem), a paraplegic campaigning for the right to die. Sampedro's death (by assisted suicide) is the climax of the film, yet the coda reinforces Rueda's star persona. Rueda also played the one-eyed Princess of Éboli in the television miniseries of the same name (2010). Small details can reinforce this association of Rueda with the fragile body: in *El orfanato* the mysterious little boy Tomás (Óscar Casas) traps the hand of her character Laura in a door, injuring her quite badly. In some cases, the fragility of the body is displaced on to her children. In *No tengas miedo* the moral blindness of Rueda's character (known simply as the Mother) contributes directly to the bodily suffering of her daughter Silvia (Michelle Jenner) as a result of the sexual abuse of Silvia's father (Lluís Homar). This motif of displacement also holds true for *El orfanato* even though Laura is not the biological mother of her son Simón (Roger Princep). Simón has inherited AIDS through the biological mother. The motif is further underscored by the fact that Laura and her husband (Fernando Cayo) are converting their house into a home for handicapped children. Similarly, in *Luna: el misterio de Calenda*, Rueda plays a character with power, the judge Sara Cruz. Playing a principal role in the investigation of the mysterious crimes in Calenda, Sara is required to act quickly, run fast, and endure physical suffering, particularly in the final episodes where she is trapped in a cave after a cave-in. Sara's body needs to be strong. Therefore the series displaces fragility and instability on to the characters who surround her: her daughter, and the son of her assistant (who share a home with Sara), both suffer debilitating illnesses. These fragile and unstable bodies seriously compromise Sara's power.

The fragile and unstable body of Rueda's roles applies also to Rueda herself (as it does to many stars); there is a need for bodily control which itself implies the unstable body. Botting observes:

> Image, it seems, is everything. It wages war on the ever-expanding meat that it leaves slumped before its screens, screens across which assorted monsters and horrors flicker and fade. Hollywood, of course, lies in the forefront of the image imperative: all excess corporeality, given that the camera's gaze is reputed to add pounds, must be cut away. [. . .]
>
> When value is calibrated to dress size, huge expenditures on losing weight are demanded: diets and fitness regimes, nutritionists and personal trainers, abused medication and banned pharmaceuticals, become a major growth area. Continued employment depends on turning the body into an image, reducing it to the thinness of celluloid two-dimensionality. (Botting 2008, 149–50)

Botting here reiterates his scorn for the vapid spectators 'slumped before the screen' that demand perfect bodies even as their own bodies balloon. He also, however, neatly demonstrates the need to control the body to the point of invisibility but also the foregrounding or visibility of that body. The star bears the weight (ironically) of this impossible excess of meaning. Part of Rueda's star persona is the portrayal of unstable bodies while publicity emphasises how well she maintains her own. The body may be turned into an image (rather as Vicente's body is turned into Vera) but the body retains its materiality nonetheless. Far from the body being reduced to simulacra, in fact stories about the female body demonstrate that some of the older Gothic narratives of violent patriarchy continue to pertain. If Vicente's punishment is to become one of the female bodies he used to dress and control, Rueda's roles reveal that Gothic medicine is not only the production of 'unnatural' female bodies but also a fearful response to women presumed to be unnatural. To explore these ideas I should first like to give brief consideration to the film *Los ojos de Julia* before analysing *El cuerpo* in more detail to consider the effect of Gothic medicine not only on the character but also on the star.

Los ojos de Julia

Julia and Sara are twin sisters (both played by Rueda) who suffer from a disease that makes them go blind: the only solution is replacement eye surgery with no guarantee of success. At the beginning of the film, Sara is now blind even after surgery, and apparently commits suicide, but Julia

Figure 6.2 Julia struggles to adapt after her operation.

suspects murder. She investigates with the reluctant help of her husband Isaac (Lluís Homar) and discovers that Isaac and Sara had a brief affair but also that a mysterious man seems to have accompanied or shadowed Sara everywhere. Isaac commits suicide and Julia collapses, waking up to find she has been operated on and now has new eyes (we discover at the end of the film that the eyes are Isaac's, donated by him). But Julia must keep her eyes covered for some days in order to ensure that the operation is a success and, to help her through this period of time, she has a carer. She will subsequently discover that her original carer has been murdered and substituted by Ángel (Pablo Derqui) who also murdered Sara. Eventually the two of them will fight a battle to the death from which Julia emerges the winner while Ángel, cornered rather belatedly by the police, commits suicide in his turn. But to fight Ángel Julia has had to remove her bandages and, as a result, her operation fails and she goes blind.

The focus of Gothic medicine in the film is clearly the eye, the immediate object of the surgeon's knife and, more grimly, Ángel's needle as he pierces the eye of his mother Soledad (Julia Gutiérrez Caba), shown in extreme close-up. There are also, unsurprisingly, many close-up shots of Rueda's eyes. Yet the eye comes to stand for the unstable body which, in its totality, is foregrounded right from the very beginning when Julia collapses at work, apparently in telepathic response to the death of her twin sister Sara. Of course, the mere idea of twins suggests the instability of the body, that can divide and multiply itself, and frustrate a simple equation of the body with a fixed identity. The central section of the film, after the operation, focuses on Julia's attempt to manage day-to-day living while her eyes are still bandaged and she cannot see. There are protracted sequences wherein Julia learns to manage basic tasks, such as picking up the phone, all without sight. Rueda herself noted in an interview the ways in which the body becomes foregrounded, becomes difficult, for both character and actor. Julia and Rueda's experience is all about the body:

> Tenía que interpretar con el cuerpo, sin caer en la exageración, todo lo que no podía transmitir con los ojos. La angustia de mi personaje es interna y externa. Sin visión, los peligros se multiplican por mil y lo más cotidiano se transforma en un obstáculo mortal. (Ponga 2010)
> (I had to interpret with my body, without succumbing to exaggeration, everything I couldn't convey with my eyes. My character's distress is both internal and external. Without sight, the dangers are multiplied a thousand times and the most ordinary thing becomes an insurmountable obstacle.)

Director Guillem Morales had his own mission to ensure that Rueda looked good ("'Los ojos de Julia'", 2010), despite her character's blindness. Thus, there is pressure not only on the character's body but also on the actor's. A demand for excess meaning is placed on the latter which must respond to the requirement to look both beautiful and flawed.

Gothic medicine is here clearly represented by Ángel. The first time Julia and we see him is a brief glimpse in a hospital ward, apparently as a nurse. In a sinister prefiguration of what is to come, there is a woman sobbing in the background, the patient he is administering to. (How? We do not know but, in retrospect, it is easy to believe his intentions were malign.) Once Julia leaves hospital after her operation, Ángel poses as her carer, advising her how to cope with her temporary loss of sight; in fact, in his assumed medical capacity, he is controlling her. That control becomes more violent as he begins to suspect that she does not trust him, and rightly, for, by now, Julia has risked removing the bandages from her eyes and knows she is in danger. He holds the point of a knife very close to her eyes to test her (false) claim that the operation failed; he dopes her tea (she switches the mugs of tea around); and finally he confronts her with the body of her original carer whom he murdered. His efforts at control thus become increasingly violent, right up to the end of the fight to the death and the arrival of the police. But even though he does not live to see it, Ángel's control is ultimately successful because Julia goes blind as a result of removing her bandages too soon. In a similar way, he blinds his mother after realising belatedly that she lied to him previously about being blind; her lies are an indication that women need control. With his trademark little leather case of scalpels and syringes, Ángel marks himself out as a worrying form of the Gothic surgeon.

But beyond Ángel, who is emphasised as monstrous by his violence, there is a more ingrained association between surgery, patriarchy, and control of women that passes for normal. This occurs through medical intervention on Julia's eyes. The continued threat to her sight clearly derives from the actions of a patriarchally motivated madman; she is finally confirmed in her suspicions when she gazes upon Ángel's photo-montage of violent images, so sight becomes the sense that finally confirms the truth. Yet the threat to her subjectivity also comes from her husband Isaac. Isaac posthumously donates his eyes to her after his suicide, sur-renders his eyes and thus his gaze. But then his gaze replaces hers; she no longer sees with her own eyes. This is underscored by the final scene, as Julia is informed that the operation has failed and she will go blind. As she stares into the mirror, the film cuts from her reflection to an image of the universe (a reference to an earlier, romantic conversation confirming their love for each other). Her vision collapses into the panorama of the universe that is the final shot of the film. This ending may seem romantic (as cued by the accompanying strings and the apparently loving voice-over of Isaac from beyond the grave). Ironically, however, the film contrasts the anonymity of the universe, the loss of subjectivity, with Julia's last desper-ate sight of herself as she struggles to observe and capture her own reflec-tion in the mirror. This scene is the culmination of a general tendency among the principal male characters to prevent a woman seeing for herself. Thus, Isaac tries to prevent Julia from finding out and 'seeing' the truth, particularly as to his affair with Sara, in particular stealing CCTV footage that proves his infidelity. Moreover, after her operation, Julia dreams that Isaac attempts to remove her bandages, despite her protests; at this point, the removal of the bandages would blind her. Her neighbour Blasco (Boris Ruiz) also relies on her lack of sight to grope her. Ángel's mania is simply an extreme or excessive version of this more general tendency.

By taking the viewpoint of Julia throughout the film, *Los ojos de Julia* ensures that Gothic medicine is the secret that Julia uncovers; while she solves the mystery of her sister's death she also discovers the malignant desire to control the female body through surgical modification that leads to pain and death. None of the women in the film survives unscathed. Sara dies, as does Blasco's daughter Lia (Andrea Hermosa), gruesomely stabbed by Ángel as she attempts to help Julia to escape. Soledad is hor-rifically blinded by her own son while Julia's blindness is the risk she took in her efforts to save her own life. The common suffering shared by the women emphasises the extent to which Gothic medicine is a patriarchal matter. Like Vera, Julia will always carry the mark of Gothic medicine with her, her body indelibly marked by male efforts at control, forced to adopt a male gaze, and that only until another male ensures that she will never have any gaze of her own again. Nevertheless, the female body is also shown to be flawed from the start; the sight and body of both Julia and Sara are inherently diseased from the beginning. The female body may be subject to malign male control but, in itself, it lacks material integrity, both through its disease and through the doubling potential symbolised by twin sisters. Such instability furnishes another example of the fragile body that is integral to Rueda's star persona, a persona that proves fundamental to the understanding of our final film, *El cuerpo*.

El cuerpo

El cuerpo is a blend of the Gothic and noir thriller. Its plot begins with the discovery that Álex (Hugo Silva), head of a successful pharmaceutical company, has just murdered his rich wife Mayka (Rueda) whose body subsequently goes missing from the mortuary. Álex is called to the mortuary by Inspector Peña (José Coronado) and his investigative team to inform him of the disappearance and ask him some questions. Increasingly, Álex comes under pressure as a result of questioning that seems to point to his guilt; the pressure is increased by the frantic phone calls of his mistress Carla (Aura Garrido) who is herself trying to find out what is going on. Flashbacks to the time leading up to Mayka's death reveal how Álex committed the crime but we also have flashbacks from the viewpoint of Peña who remembers the death of his wife Ruth (Silvia Aranda) in a car crash. Eventually, Álex confesses. Mayka's body is found in some woods. Peña then tells Álex that he and Carla, who is actually Peña's daughter, have framed Álex in revenge for Ruth's death. A final flashback reveals that Álex crashed into Peña's car, causing Ruth's severe injuries; she might have been saved if Álex had summoned help but Mayka, a passenger in Álex's car, exhorts him simply to drive away. In a final return to the present, Peña tells Álex that he has poisoned him, using the same pharmaceutical product that Álex used to kill Mayka. The film ends as Álex writhes in pain, abandoned in the woods.

The film's title stresses the link between medicine and the body, the tight intertwining of the two. While the film is about Álex and the link between his private life and his profession as a pharmaceutical chemist, the body mentioned in the title refers to that of Mayka, murdered by Álex so that he can continue his affair with Carla while keeping Mayka's money. In the 'making of' DVD extra, director Oriol Paulo suggests that Álex is a man of science looking for a rational answer to something that is not rational. Álex felt, like Ledgard, that, by using his scientific skills, he could control Mayka's body yet, in the mortuary, itself a setting within which medicine takes place, he seems to see the body move about, come

Figure 6.3 *El cuerpo*: Mayka's body is found in the woods.

to life again, rearrange itself in different positions and spaces within the building, and finally escape the confines of the mortuary as it apparently transfers itself to the woods. He had thought he had controlled the body but now he cannot believe his own science. (By the time he discovers the rational explanation, he is no longer in control of his own body, and his medicine is used against him.)

Álex's actions are, at bottom, rather like Ledgard's in *La piel*, in that he is trying to gain mastery over a woman's body, a mastery that ultimately eludes him; and his efforts at mastery, the skills he draws on, are medicinal. He uses his medicine, like Ledgard, to gain the woman he desires. The story is told from Álex's viewpoint so that, in fact, we learn more about him than about Mayka. Like Ledgard, his actions are terrible although the motivation for them lies in his position as a powerless husband at the whim of his powerful wife. Mayka is not a sympathetic character, as is clear from the moment we see her alive in flashback on her wedding day when she embarrasses him in public by initially refusing to marry him as a joke. A later flashback (at the moment of poisoning) reveals Mayka phoning her office to say he is fired: it also turns out to be a joke. Yet his knowledge of pharmaceuticals gives Álex power, too, and, like Ledgard, it is this access to medicine that initially gives him power over the female body though, like Ledgard, he will ultimately lose control of it, forced to delve deep into the abject. Failing to flush away in the toilet a piece of paper with a giveaway message, he is forced to remove the paper from the toilet bowl and swallow it as a policeman approaches. Later he must delve into a body bag and thrust his hand past a dead body in order to extract a mobile phone (which is ringing inside the bag). The person who ultimately has real control is Peña, the corrupt member of patriarchal authority who is stage-managing the whole show in revenge for the death of his wife. Aldana Reyes suggests that 'the body gradually becomes the object under attack by tyrannical individuals or, in some cases, corporations or institutionalised systems of punishment' (Aldana Reyes 2014, 145). The irony here is that Mayka's dead body is the immediate victim of her own corporate control. Álex resents the fact that Mayka dictates what he does and that being her husband is the price of his success in her pharmaceutical company. Yet Álex's own actions are visited on himself as he, too, dies through ingesting the same poison that he gave to Mayka, and one created by himself in his laboratory. This poison is administered through an authority figure, Peña. In his own personal vendetta against Álex he is hardly representative of the police force for which he works but it is precisely through his role as detective that he manipulates both Álex and Mayka's body. He uses the latter as simply a prop in his own scheme but he also bears ultimate responsibility for Mayka's death since he, through his daughter, instigated Álex's own plot to kill his wife.

Mayka's body exemplifies the instability posited by both Halberstam and Cavallaro discussed at the beginning of this chapter. Halberstam notes that rendering the body as monstrous is a gesture towards the fixity of bias, yet the monstrous body's instability constantly undermines this. Mayka's body is portrayed in the film as monstrous in that she tries to ward off the ageing process by taking a younger husband, adopting a consciously flirtatious pose, dressing in short and revealing dresses which are aimed at a younger demographic, and acting in a childish manner (such as her behaviour at her own wedding). The fear of the ageing body is an essential element of the presentation of Mayka's character as unsympathetic; the revelation at the end of the film indicates that she is the ultimate villain, allowing Ruth to die, and so deserves no sympathy. The audience might feel some compassion when Mayka finally confesses her fears, backing them up with her insistence on playing the song 'November'. The song reveals her own vulnerability in the face of ageing, living in the autumn of her life, and therefore her own fear of bodily instability. Álex does not share that compassion. He is, among other things, punishing the ageing female body and trying to control what is appropriate behaviour for middle-aged women.

There are both contrasts and parallels with Rueda's position as star. In the 'making of featurette' on the DVD, the make-up artist Caitlin Acheson talks of the problems of making up Rueda who at times appears as dead, at other times as a ghost haunting Álex; yet also of recognising that this is, nonetheless, Rueda who has a certain look and is beautiful. Publicity surrounding the film emphasised Rueda's body as lovely, implying a contrast to her role. Rueda was praised for an ideal body after scientific tests carried out for the magazine *Quo* (García, 2013). This event seems to be no more than an elaborate publicity stunt that fitted neatly with her work in *El cuerpo* which is cited as a reference. The emphasis on the ideal body goes some way both to promoting Rueda as an actor but also to counter the negative ways in which her body was shown in the film. Rueda's efforts to distance herself from her body image in the film (or alternatively, the efforts of her publicity team) lead to some intriguing contradictions as, for instance, when she is interviewed during a fashion shoot for *El País:*

> «Soy consciente de que ya no soy tan joven», una reflexión que comparten Belén Rueda y Mayka Villaverde, su personaje en *El cuerpo*, el *thriller* psicológico de Oriol Paulo [. . .] en el que trabaja junto a José Coronado y Hugo Silva. «Nunca me he considerado *sexy*. Pero comprendo esa sensación de haber sido en otro momento el centro de todas las miradas y ahora sentir que pasan los años y que llegan otras generaciones en las que se posan los ojos. Afortunadamente, no me afecta». Todo lo contrario que a su personaje. «A ella este temor le da un toque decadente», dice mientras se recoge el pelo. (Torrecillas, 2012)
>
> ('I'm aware that I'm not so young now', a reflection shared by Belén Rueda and Mayka Villaverde, her character in *El cuerpo*, the psychological thriller directed by Oriol Paulo [. . .] in which she appears alongside José Coronado and Hugo Silva. 'I've never considered myself to be sexy. But I understand that feeling of having previously been the centre of attention and now being aware that the years are passing and all eyes are on the upcoming generations. Fortunately, it doesn't affect me.' In total contrast to her character. 'This fear gives her a decadent air' she says as she pulls back her hair.)

The photo shoot also features Silva and Coronado, the other lead actors of *El cuerpo*, but the central focus is on Rueda, talking about her views on life and on the position of women in society. Though she does not claim to be a feminist, she welcomes the changes that have seen women reach positions of power (German Chancellor Angela Merkel is mentioned) and allowed them to take control of their own lives. The piece is titled 'Belén Rueda se pone los pantalones' (Belén Rueda wears the trousers) and, indeed, Rueda wears trousers in all the fashion shots. Such a title suggests female power in a man's world that is reminiscent of Mayka but there is irony in that the focus on both the star and her character is through the body. While Rueda argues that she is unaffected by being the object of the gaze, she is still subject to promotional needs for the film. She is arranging her hair even as she comments on Mayka's fears about her own ageing body.

Rueda's body, as opposed to Mayka's, may itself be a form of revenge of a younger generation of directors. An Agencia EFE press release observes the following:

> La actriz redondea con este filme su calidad de musa del nuevo terror español, aupada por una generación de directores que crecieron viéndola como dulce azafata

de ingenuos programas de televisión como *El juego de la oca* que, años más tarde, decidieron hacerle sufrir en la gran pantalla. ('Hugo Silva y José Coronado buscan 'El cuerpo' de Belén Rueda', 2012)

(With this film the actress rounds off her standing as the muse of contemporary Spanish horror, helped by a generation of directors who grew up with her as the sweet hostess[3] of simple television programmes such as *El [gran] juego de la oca* [The Great Goose Game] who, years later, decided to make her suffer on the big screen.)

Rueda's function as Gothic muse is noted here, a common term in the Spanish press for a favourite actress but also suggesting passivity and a lack of power in the face of the director. The comment seems to be almost a form of revenge on the mother, the woman who oversaw the innocent childhood years of her director, and thus it refers back to her star persona with the maternal element I described above. Mayka's body and the indignities done to it – displaced, dumped in passages and lifts, flung into some woods – are also experienced by Rueda, suggesting revenge on the actor as well as the character.

Rueda's Films and International Gothic

Los ojos de Julia, like *La piel que habito*, comes with a fair number of international referents. The scriptwriters recommended to Rueda that she watch films such as *Alien* (Ridley Scott 1979), *Wait Until Dark* (Terence Young 1967), and also films that did not refer to blindness, such as *The Shining* (Stanley Kubrick 1980) and *The Birds* (Alfred Hitchcock 1963). According to Rueda, the script was originally written in English, with the intention of filming in Scotland (Ponga 2010). Phelim O'Neill, in (briefly) reviewing the film for *The Guardian*, made much of the involvement of high-profile Mexican director Guillermo del Toro, and cited a couple of international references (Dario Argento and Brian de Palma; also Alfred Hitchcock, if only to say how far removed is *Los ojos de Julia* from the work of the master). These references take up half the review; for the rest, O'Neill describes the film as good, if overlong, and with unlikely plot twists (O'Neill 2011). Director Morales himself saw Rueda in terms of 1950s Hitchcock ('"Los ojos de Julia"', 2010). In addition to these references, of course, *Los ojos* draws from a wider tradition of films about mad scientists and doctors.

El cuerpo offers a similar opportunity to spot intertextual references and influences. Jordi Costa (2012) compares the film to Aldo Lado's *La corta notte delle bambolle di vetro* (Short Night of Glass Dolls 1971), a film told from the point of view of the corpse; though this does not occur in *El cuerpo*, the corpse is central to uncovering the crime. Costa also cites Andrea Bianchi's *Nude per l'assassino* (Strip Nude for Your Killer 1975) and observes that the film is influenced by the *giallo* but also by a taste in Spanish horror film for Gothic paradoxes. In a review that is as much about referencing outside influences as discussing the film itself, Costa closes with a comparison to George-Henri Cluzot's *Les Diaboliques* (1955). Rueda herself sees *El cuerpo* as an example of travelling styles if not narratives: 'Lo bueno de los nuevos directores es que tienen una formación de cine muy americana a nivel visual, pero siguen contando las historias de una manera muy europea, muy desgarradora.' ('Hugo Silva y José Coronado buscan "El cuerpo" de Belén Rueda' 2012). ('The great thing about the new directors is that they have a very American cinema background when it comes to the visual, but they still tell stories in a very European manner, very heartrending.)

Both of Rueda's films, then, have indigenised a recognisable international Gothic and horror tradition, especially through Rueda's position as a Spanish actor, the inspiration of this particular national cinema which takes revenge again and again on her body, one that represents the duality of the mother figure. The directors mentioned by the Agencia EFE press release have become very much like the predatory audience we met at the beginning of this chapter. They look with fascination at the unstable maternal body. In doing this, they, too, resort to a Gothic form of technology to allow the repeated efforts at bodily control, as Botting indicated. If film is one technology that captures the body in an oppressive and repressive double bind, then so does Gothic medicine. The syringes, chemicals and scalpels demonstrate that the body is both material and unstable. These technologies aim to restore the bodily bias of which Halberstam talked and, in doing so, they render the body more monstrous than before. These bodies demonstrate an excess of meaning and production in that Vera is and is not Vicente; Julia's eyes are and are not her own; and Mayka is both dead and alive.

If these technologies give rise to an excess of meaning and production, so then do the intertextual references grafted on to the films discussed here. Almodóvar and Rueda's work becomes a nexus of cultural flow that ensures these particular films exceed their local context. The constant game of guess the reference, that critics indulge in, goes beyond the usual intertextual knowledge of horror reviewers to become a mainstream critical activity within Spain and beyond. Nevertheless, it is also true that Almodóvar and Rueda are bringing it all back home to say that the pain and trauma, the materiality and instability, of the body are also matters for local audiences. For local audiences, too, there is never just one meaning.

Notes

1. Also known as Jack Halberstam: I have kept to the gender convention of referring to Halberstam as 'she' in acknowledgement of the gender claimed by the author for this particular work.
2. Even here, however, this film uses the Mexican figure of Santo who travels to Spain in search of a mad scientist.
3. According to the Internet Movie Database (IMDb), Rueda was not a host on *El gran juego de la oca* but a guest, appearing on the long-running show exactly twice.

CHAPTER 7

Conclusion

In a recent talk, the Gothic scholar Lucie Armitt spoke of the Gothic as inherently about crossing points (Armitt 2016). The occasion was a symposium at my home institution of the University of Stirling to celebrate the opening of an archive relating to the author Patrick McGrath. I attended the symposium primarily to listen and to support colleagues, and found myself fascinated by the insights of speakers on McGrath and the Gothic more widely. Some speakers were fully immersed in Gothic scholarship but others came from different disciplines and sometimes apologised for the fact, as if they were trespassers. Armitt's own paper came at the end of the day, and I believe her remarks might help us understand that the Gothic is not so much all-pervasive but a nexus in which subjects, themes and disciplines might intersect; for, in a world where universities promote interdisciplinary research, the Gothic is more interdisciplinary than most. It positively invites trespass. As Armitt says, the Gothic crosses lines, including those of academic disciplines. McGrath himself suggests: 'The idea of the "real man" – or the "true self" or the "essential identity" – has no validity in the Gothic. The Gothic recognizes the fluidity, the multiplicity, the contingency of identity' (McGrath 1997, 156).

Armitt and McGrath's ideas suggest a different approach to the Gothic, one that counters the fears of other Gothicists that the Gothic is reduced to ever-circulating simulacra. It also suggests a different approach to the fear of trespassing arising from other disciplines. There is no essential identity but that is not to say identity does not exist at all. The idea of circulation, which I have addressed in this book, is fluid but it is also contingent, originating and/or travelling through a particular place and time, the crossing of lines to which Armitt referred, the nexus which I have been talking about throughout this study. Or it travels through a particular discipline, so that each informs the other. These metaphors, I hope, demonstrate the value of the Gothic for Spanish studies, and the value of Spanish studies for the Gothic.

Or we could apply another metaphor, that of the circulation and movement of seeds and spores. Warner, talking of the fairy tale, suggests the value of the fairy tale's spread and repetition that applies equally well to the Gothic:

> The audience is not necessarily assembled in one place at one moment – the circle loops out across the centuries, forming a community across barriers of language and nation as well as time. Think of it as a plant genus, like roses or fungi or grasses, which seed and root and flower here and there, changing species and colour and size and shape where they spring. [. . .] The stories' interest isn't exhausted by repetition, reformulation, or retelling, but their pleasure gains from the endless permutations performed on the nucleus of the tale, its DNA as it were. (Warner 2014, 44–5)

This way of considering the Gothic would again be a positive one, seeing it as one genus sharing DNA but changing according to its environment. As in plants, so the Spanish Gothic has also lain dormant or hidden away on occasion, only to flower and flourish sporadically. This again raises doubts about how far we can claim the Gothic to be ubiquitous. The Gothic may be everywhere but it is not everywhere at once, while its specificities can vary from location to location without totally losing touch with its origins or with other Gothic flowerings elsewhere. There is a sense of cross-pollination occurring frequently but not necessarily continuously. The nexus, then, is a more optimistic way of perceiving and studying the Gothic; and it enables us to see how the Gothic works in a particular culture without having to be too prescriptive as to where the boundaries of that culture lie. The concepts of circulation and cultural flow do not assume a Gothic that is ever on the move but one that comes to rest here and there, rather like the copies of *Las nueve puertas* that move around Europe in *El club Dumas*. At these resting paces and crossing points the Gothic can be seen in operation. The seeds and spores of the Gothic can also come to rest in any discipline, offering new permutations on the original Gothic DNA. What I hope to have done in this book is to outline some of these permutations in a particular area subject to its own disciplines: contemporary Spanish culture.

Much of this book has addressed film specifically which has a strong link to the Gothic in its very form. Moreover, however, the circulation of film is linked to the uncanny animation of the celluloid (or computer-generated) image, allowing places and people to 'come alive' in places far away from their origin. As Elisabeth Bronfen argues:

> Images imprinted on celluloid (or now digital cyberspace) that seem to come alive and whose movements render palpable an immaterial world hover between the actual

and imaginary, the present and the past. Neither the actors nor the locations where they perform are really present; they are perceptible only as remnants of a location that once existed. Although what we see and hear took place when the film was being shot, the world the actors move in is purely immaterial. We, in the audience, are really partaking in a shared experience of ghost-seeing. (Bronfen 2014, 107)

But Gothic cinema itself is haunted, as Bronfen argues, by the older forms of Gothic from which it derived, including photography and theatre as well as literature (112): she could also have cited the magic lantern shows that Warner studies (2002, 2006).

Spain can be seen in a similar way, an entity that haunts the Gothic, all the more so for commonly being unrecognised yet adding its own DNA to the Gothic mix. Though he is not writing about the Gothic per se, Brad Epps's comments on the modern period in Spain (for him, 1893–1939) suggest Spain itself as some sort of Gothic ghost flickering at the corner of our vision:

So vexed is the state of the Spanish nation in the modern period that the very notion of 'seeing Spain' is dubitable; at the very least, it is fraught with blind spots, omissions, and partialities that cast the designated object – Spain – into an impossibly ideal position and that makes it as elusive a sight, *toutes proportions gardées*, as death itself. And yet, for all the difficulties, some mortally flecked part of Spain does appear to come into view amid a welter of works in which death, disease and suffering figure prominently. (Epps 2005, 118)

Epps goes on to point out that many of the artists and writers who produced such works had 'transnational contacts and cosmopolitan cravings' so that we should not simply obsess about the local dimension (ibid.). As this book has shown, that is very much true for the contemporary era as well, in which the transnational dimension of Spanish culture is more than apparent and yet sidelined in much of the writing on Spanish culture in favour of the local. Spanish culture as Gothic nexus shows that both the local and the transnational are inextricably entwined. Spanish Gothic film, then, suggests multiple layers of haunting; it offers up palpable instances of the immaterial world of which Bronfen speaks and, within this, the Spain of which Epps speaks is a flickering presence even to people far away. Epps's comment indicates that Spanish Gothic has existed for far longer than scholars previously might have supposed and, furthermore, that Spanish Gothic is both local and transnational. Knowing this may help us to see the contemporary Spanish Gothic in new and more positive ways, as a fluid process in which deterritorialisation and indigenisation constantly recur, and sometimes together in the same text. This process creates the interstitial space of which Bronfen speaks and yet in which Spain is still visible, if only out of the corner of our eye. Yet, equally, Spanish culture becomes immaterial though not ephemeral; it is something we can equally lose sight of.

I hope to have traced out in this book some of the ways in which this process occurs. It is not always a comfortable process as we see with biopics of Goya where the power of Goya's art is overlain with a museum aesthetic that distances us, and where the rebellious figure of the artist is still at times co-opted into a museum gaze. Goya's work was steeped in his own time and place but heritage Gothic detaches it from its context. Surely, here, if anywhere, is an example of the danger of indifferently floating Gothic simulacra. Yet, if pastiche and costume drama infiltrate the Gothic (something that is hardly new), the reverse is also true. Goya's images are no longer confined to the museum or to Spain but the heritage biopic nonetheless insists on his original perspective. And if Goya can be deterritorialised, that deterritorialisation is itself indigenised in *Goya en Burdeos* by a renowned Spanish art-house director who has rarely strayed too far from Spain in his subject matter. On the other hand, the Spanish context is perhaps all too prominent in previous analyses of haunted-house texts in Spanish cinema, for this runs the risk of erasing other traumas and other pleasures which need to be recognised and incorporated if we are to have a more nuanced perception of memory texts and the work they do. The cinematic haunted house is part of a wider tradition and uncomfortably detached from any national location; and films that appear to offer a clear link to Spanish history, such as *NO-DO*, demonstrate equally clear links with films such as *Darkness* that avoid any contextualisation altogether. This transnationalism of a national trauma may be deeply uncomfortable but it is also an opportunity for a more profound consideration of narratives of national trauma as a part of an intricate web of narratives that provoke a plethora of responses which do not map neatly on to a simple framework of recuperation. Any catharsis involved in *NO-DO* and *Darkness* may have nothing to do with the recognition of past history. In both the case of Goya and of the haunted house, the films concerned are operating in interstitial spaces.

The case of Javier Aguirresarobe provides evidence of a gradual deterritorialisation but also a sense of interstitial space, and not only in terms of the confusion of the geographical locations in which the films concerned were made. The ambivalence with which the cinematographer approaches the question of Gothic light gives rise to an oscillation between revelation of Gothic secrets and blurring them to ensure they remain concealed. Light, far from being a positive element in the films, is actually dangerous: in *The Others* and *New Moon* it can kill while, in *La madre muerta*, light signifies discovery. If the Basque Country is the source of Aguirresarobe's style, as critics suggest, then already the whole concept of Spain is interrogated because of the difficult and often violent history between the two. This is pushed still further by Aguirresarobe's movement in time and space from a Basque film (but made in Spanish), a film by one of Spain's most successful directors (but made in English) and an American film in which French becomes the lingua franca between cinematographer and director. The Gothic work of Aguirresarobe is another of Bronfen's interstitial spaces, and an occasion in which, as Epps says, a mortally flecked Spain comes into view in works where death, disease and suffering are to the fore. Nonetheless, this Spain is not always recognised; it is visible and yet invisible within Aguirresarobe's work.

While Aguirresarobe has moved seamlessly between different countries and locations with his cinematographic style, Almodóvar and Rueda are generally home-based members of the Spanish film industry. *La piel que habito*, *El cuerpo* and *Los ojos de Julia* are peppered with international textual references but the style of Almodóvar and the star persona of Rueda refigure these references for a home audience and for their own cultural cachet. This is a form of indigenisation but the subject matter of the films under discussion, Gothic medicine and its effect on the body, raises questions, which are endemic, over the extent to which the body can be fixed. The discourse around Rueda's star persona suggests the pressures on the body remain fixed but also the pressures to be perfect (and thus in need of fixing) to conform to a different model imposed by someone else, someone with the power to ensure that model will be followed. Yet, as we have seen, that body ultimately eludes control. Just as the body's materiality goes against the notion of simulacra, so it suggests the materiality of place, the fact that the body is being controlled in this place at this time. Nevertheless, if the body is unstable and shifting, it points back once again to the suggestion of interstitiality.

Film, then, is itself an interstitial space that opens itself up to other interstitial spaces, the crossing points of the Gothic. This is also true for literature albeit in a different way. Here, too, there is an emphasis on the form of the book, its physical copies, the process of writing it. Nevertheless, its material form is open to question: is it authentic? And, with that question, we find ourselves in a similar position to the one we must adopt when it comes to the Gothic body. The book is an unstable entity, open to forgery and destruction, and the focus of unhealthy obsessions. Like film but in a different way, the book enables us to travel vicariously while creating and preserving characters long beyond their natural lifespan. The book itself shifts and travels, however, moving around Europe as in *El club Dumas* or back and forth between Spain and France as in *La sombra del viento*. I have included these two novels in a study otherwise dedicated to film because the novels by Pérez-Reverte and Ruiz Zafón are the most pervasive of Spanish texts worldwide today. Of the films I have discussed, only *The Others* and *The Twilight Saga: New Moon* can compete but, in these two films, any sense of Spanishness is well hidden. On the other hand, while the two authors are marked and acknowledged as Spanish, their narratives render Spain interstitial. Lucas Corso travels around Europe in search of a book; the dark motivation for his journey lies behind him in Spain, and to Spain he must return for the denouement but *El club Dumas* emphasises the ways in which both a book and its guardian must travel, and also that travel, or circulation, is essential if the book is to remain a healthy entity. *La sombra del viento*, on the other hand, insists on its Barcelona setting yet that Barcelona becomes hard to pin down in the confusion of local and international readings and the fear of, or appeal to, tourism. Ruiz Zafón's Barcelona is itself in any case a ruin, a mortally flecked part of Spain, in Epps's words, but also interstitial in its identification with Catalonia, potentially at least semi-detached from Spain, rather like Aguirresarobe's Basque Country.

Contemporary Spanish culture, then, functions as a Gothic nexus and, in this book, I have explored just some of the crossing points that exist within it. The examples I have selected are the ones that fascinate me most but there are plenty of other examples waiting to be explored. In making one last comment on the condition of contemporary Spanish Gothic, I would like to extend Armitt's metaphor a little further. The contemporary Spanish Gothic is not *just* about crossing lines but about lines that criss-cross, that loop round and round themselves, crossing over themselves and each other in elaborate curlicues and dizzying spirals and zigzags that reveal complex layers of nuance. The designs they produce are fascinating. Far from taking fright at what the contemporary Gothic has become, we should relish the complex patterns it creates and the myriad opportunities to step outside rigid disciplinary boundaries and explore the lines that cut across our own.

Filmography

27 horas (27 Hours, Montxo Armendáriz 1986)
9.99 (Agustín Villaronga 1997)
Acción Mutante (Mutant Action, Álex de la Iglesia 1993)
Algo amargo en la boca (Something Bitter in the Mouth, Eloy de la Iglesia 1969)
Alien (Ridley Scott 1979)
Los amantes pasajeros (I'm So Excited, Pedro Almodóvar 2013)
The Amityville Horror (Stuart Rosenberg 1979)
Ana y los lobos (Ana and the Wolves, Carlos Saura 1973)
Angels and Demons (Ron Howard 2009)
¡Átame! (Tie Me Up! Tie Me Down, Pedro Almodóvar 1989)
Beltenebros (Pilar Miró 1991)
The Birds (Alfred Hitchcock 1963)
The Bridge of San Luis Rey (Mary McGuckian 2004)
La cara del terror (The Face of Terror, Isidoro M. Ferry and William J. Hole Jr 1962)
El carnaval de las bestias (Carnival of the Animals, Jacinto Molina 1980)
El clavo (The Nail, Rafael Gil 1944)
La casa sin fronteras (The House Without Borders, Pedro Olea 1972)
Le Cercle rouge (Jean-Pierre Melville 1970)
The Changeling (Peter Medak 1980)
Citizen Kane (Orson Welles 1941)
La corta notte delle bambolle di vetro (Short Night of Glass Dolls, Aldo Lado 1971)
Cría cuervos (Raise Ravens, Carlos Saura 1975)
El crimen de la calle Bordadores (The Crime on Bordadores Street, Edgar Neville 1946)
El cuerpo (The Body, Oriol Paulo 2012)
Darkness (Jaume Balagueró 2002)
Deprisa deprisa (Hurry, Hurry, Carlos Saura 1981)
Les Diaboliques (George-Henri Cluzot 1955)
El día de la bestia (The Day of the Beast, Álex de la Iglesia 1995)
Domingo de carnaval (Carnival Sunday, Edgar Neville 1945)

El espinazo del diablo (The Devil's Backbone, Guillermo del Toro 2001)

El espíritu de la colmena (Spirit of the Beehive, Víctor Erice 1973)

Exorcismo (Exorcism, Juan Bosch 1974)

The Exorcist (Wiliam Friedkin 1973)

El extraño viaje (The Strange Journey, Fernando Fernán-Gómez 1964)

Frágiles (Fragile, Jaume Balagueró 2005)

Frankenstein (James Whale 1931)

Fright Night (Craig Gillespie 2012)

La fuga de Segovia (The Flight from Segovia, Imanol Uribe 1981)

Los golfos (The Delinquents, Carlos Saura 1960)

Goya en Burdeos (Goya in Bordeaux, Carlos Saura 1999)

Goya's Ghosts (Miloš Forman 2006)

Halloween (John Carpenter 1978)

The Haunting (Robert Wise 1963)

How to Marry a Millionaire (Jean Negulesco 1953)

Identity Thief (Seth Gordon 2013)

Interview with the Vampire (Neil Jordan 1994)

Johnny Guitar (Nicholas Ray 1954)

Juana la Loca (Juana the Mad, Vicente Aranda 2001)

Juego de amor prohibido (Game of Forbidden Love, Eloy de la Iglesia 1975)

Låt den rätte komma in (Let the Right One In, Tomas Alfredson 2008)

La ley del deseo (The Law of Desire, Pedro Almodóvar 1987)

Lust for Life (Vincente Minnelli and George Cukor 1956)

La madre muerta (The Dead Mother, Juanma Bajo Ulloa 1992)

La mala educación (Bad Education, Pedro Almodóvar 2004)

Mar adentro (The Sea Inside, Alejandro Amenábar 2004)

Matador (Pedro Almodóvar 1986)

La muerte de Mikel (The Death of Mikel, Imanol Uribe 1984)

Mujeres al borde de un ataque de nervios (Women on the Verge of a Nervous Breakdown, Pedro Almodóvar 1988)

The Night of the Hunter (Charles Laughton 1955)

The Ninth Gate (Roman Polanski 1999)

NO-DO (The Haunting, Elio Quiroga 2009)

No tengas miedo (Don't Be Afraid, Montxo Armendáriz 2011)

Nude per l'assassino (Strip Nude for Your Killer, Andrea Bianchi 1975)

Los ojos de Julia (Julia's Eyes, Guillem Morales 2010)

El orfanato (The Orphanage, J. A. Bayona 2007)

The Others (Alejandro Amenábar 2001)

Para entrar a vivir (To Let, Jaume Balagueró 2006)

Peppermint Frappé (Carlos Saura 1967)

El perro del hortelano (The Dog in the Manger, Pilar Miró 1996)

The Phantom of the Opera (Rupert Julian 1925)
La piel que habito (The Skin I Live In, Pedro Almodóvar 2011)
El proceso de Burgos (The Burgos Trial, Imanol Urobe 1979)
¿Quién puede matar a un niño? (Who Can Kill a Child, Narciso Ibáñez Serrador 1976)
Rear Window (Alfred Hitchcock 1954)
Rebecca (Alfred Hitchcock 1940)
[REC] (Jaume Balagueró and Paco Plaza 2007)
[REC]² (Jaume Balagueró and Paco Plaza 2009)
La residencia (The Boarding School, Narciso Ibáñez Serrador 1969)
Ringu (Hideo Nakata 1998)
Santo contra el doctor muerte (Santo against Doctor Death, Rafael Romero–Marchent 1973)
Savage Grace (Tom Kalin 2007)
Séptimo (7th Floor, Patxi Amezcua 2013)
The Shining (Stanley Kubrick 1980)
Los sin nombre (The Nameless, Jaume Balagueró 1999)
The Sixth Sense (M. Night Shyamalan 1999)
Souperstition andalouse (Andalusian Superstition, Segundo de Chomón 1912)
El techo de cristal (The Glass Ceiling, Eloy de la Iglesia 1971)
Tesis (Thesis, Alejandro Amenábar 1996)
Tierra (Julio Medem 1996)
La torre de los siete jorobados (The Tower of the Seven Hunchbacks, Edgar Neville 1944)
Tristana (Luis Buñuel 1970)
Twilight (Catherine Hardwicke 2008)
The Twilight Saga: Eclipse (David Slade 2010)
The Twilight Saga: New Moon (Chris Weitz 2009)
Vicky Cristina Barcelona (Woody Allen 2008)
Volavérunt (Bigas Luna 1999)
Wait Until Dark (Terence Young 1967)
Wuthering Heights (William Wyler 1939)

Bibliography

Acevedo-Muñoz, Ernesto (2008), 'Horror of Allegory: *The Others* and its Contexts', in Jay Beck and Vicente Rodríguez Ortega (eds), *Contemporary Spanish Cinema and Genre* (Manchester: Manchester University Press), 202–18.

Águeda Villar, Mercedes (2001), 'Goya en el relato cinematográfico', *Cuadernos de Historia Contemporánea* 23, 67–102.

Aguilar, Carlos (1999), 'Fantasía española: negra sangre caliente', in Carlos Aguilar (ed.), *Cine fantástico y de terror español 1900–1983* (San Sebastián: Donostia Kultura), 11–47.

Aguilar, Carlos (2005a), *Cine fantástico y de terror español 1984–2004* (San Sebastián: Donostia Kultura).

Aguilar, Carlos (2005b), 'Fantástico, español, moderno: un cine a caballo entre dos siglos', in Carlos Aguilar (ed.), *Cine fantástico y de terror español 1984–2004* (San Sebastián: Donostia Kultura), 11–42.

Aguirresarobe, Javier (2001), 'Dirección de Fotografía', in *Los otros: una película de Alejandro Amenábar* (Madrid: Ocho y medio/Sociedad General de Autores y Editores), 213–15.

Aldana Reyes, Xavier (2013), 'Skin Deep? Surgical Horror and the Impossibility of Becoming Woman in Almodóvar's *The Skin I Live In*', *Bulletin of Hispanic Studies* 90/7, 819–34.

Aldana Reyes, Xavier (2014), *Body Gothic: Corporeal Transgression in Contemporary Literature and Horror Film* (Cardiff: University of Wales Press).

Amago, Samuel (2013), *Spanish Cinema in the Global Context: Film on Film* (New York: Routledge).

Andrade, Isabel (2001), 'Entrevista con Alejandro Amenábar', in *Los otros: una película de Alejandro Amenábar* (Madrid: Ocho y medio/Sociedad General de Autores y Editores), 217–24.

Ángulo, Jesús, Carlos F. Heredero and José Luis Rebordinos (1995), *En el umbral de la oscuridad: Javier Aguirresarobe* (San Sebastián/Vitoria: Filmoteca Vasca/Fundación Caja Vital Kutxa).

Armitt, Lucie (2016), 'Crossing the Line: McGrath's *Constance* and Railway Phobia', Plenary speech at the symposium 'Asylums, Pathologies and the Themes of Madness: Patrick McGrath and his Gothic Contemporaries', University of Stirling, 16 January.

'Balagueró, pesadilla en inglés' (2014), *Fotogramas* 2054, December, 72.

Baldick, Chris (1993), 'Introduction', in Chris Baldick (ed.), *The Oxford Book of Gothic Tales* (Oxford: Oxford University Press), xi–xxiii.

Baldick, Chris and Robert Mighall (2001), 'Gothic Criticism', in David Punter (ed.), *A Companion to the Gothic* (Malden, MA: Blackwell), 209–28.

Benet, Vicente J. (2012), *El cine español: una historia cultural* (Barcelona: Paidós).

Berthier, Nancy (2011), 'Carlos Saura, cineaste de la temporalidad: el caso de *Goya en Burdeos*', in Robin Lefere (ed.), *Carlos Saura: una trayectoria ejemplar* (Madrid: Visor), 151–64.

Blake, Linnie (2008), *The Wounds of Nations: Horror Cinema, Historical Trauma and National Identity* (Manchester: Manchester University Press).

Botting, Fred (1996), *Gothic* (London: Routledge).

Botting, Fred (2002), 'Aftergothic: Consumption, Machines, and Black Holes', in Hogle, Jerrold E. (ed.), *The Cambridge Companion to Gothic Fiction* (Cambridge: Cambridge University Press), 277–300.

Botting, Fred (2007), 'Flight of the Heroine', in Benjamin A. Brabon and Stéphanie Genz (eds), *Postfeminist Gothic: Critical Interventions in Contemporary Culture* (Basingstoke: Palgrave Macmillan), 170–85.

Botting, Fred (2008), *Limits of Horror: Technology, Bodies, Gothic* (Manchester: Manchester University Press).

Boyero, Carlos (2011), '¿Horror frío? No, horror grotesco', *El País*, 2 September, <http://elpais.com/diario/2011/09/02/cine/1314914404_850215.html> (last accessed 23 May 2015).

Bradshaw, Peter (2009), 'The Twilight Saga: New Moon', *The Guardian*, 19 November, <www.theguardian.com/film/2009/nov/19/twilight-saga-new-moon-review> (last accessed 2 January 2016).

Briefel, Aviva (2009), 'What Some Ghosts Don't Know: Spectral Incognizance and the Horror Film', *Narrative* 17/1, 95–110.

Bronfen, Elizabeth (2014), 'Cinema of the Gothic Extreme', in Jerrold E. Hogle (ed.), *The Cambridge Companion to the Modern Gothic* (Cambridge: Cambridge University Press), 107–22.

Bruce, Susan (2005), 'Sympathy for the Dead: (G)hosts, Hostilities and Mediums in Alejandro Amenábar's *The Others* and Postmortem Photography', *Discourse* 27/2–3, 21–40.

Buonanno, Milly (2008), *The Age of Television: Experiences and Theories*, tr. Jennifer Radice (Bristol: Intellect).

Byron, Glennis (2012), 'Global gothic', in David Punter (ed.), *A New Companion to the Gothic* (Chichester: Wiley-Blackwell), 369–78.

Byron, Glennis (2013a), 'Introduction', in Glennis Byron (ed.), *Globalgothic* (Manchester: Manchester University Press), 1–10.

Byron, Glennis (2013b), 'Gothic, Grabbit and Run: Carlos Ruiz Zafón and the Gothic Marketplace', in Justin Edwards and Agnieszka Soltysik Monnet (eds), *The Gothic in Contemporary Literature and Popular Culture* (New York: Routledge), 71–83.

Byron, Glennis and Gordon Byron (2012), 'Barcelona Gothic: Carlos Ruiz Zafón's *La sombra del viento* and the omnipresent past', *Journal of Romance Studies* 12/1, 72–84.

Camiña, Ángel (1994), '*La madre muerta*', in Equipo Reseña (ed.), *Cine para leer 1994* (Bilbao: Mensajero), 291–4.

Carroll, Noël (1990), *The Philosophy of Horror: Paradoxes of the Heart* (New York: Routledge).

Cavallaro, Dani (2002), *The Gothic Vision: Three Centuries of Horror, Terror and Fear* (London: Continuum).

Clayton, Wickham (2014), '"Where Have All the Monsters Gone? Long Time Passing": the Aesthetics of Absence and Generic Subversion in *New Moon*', in Wickham Clayton and Sarah Harman (eds), *Screening Twilight: Critical Approaches to a Cinematic Phenomenon* (London: I. B. Tauris), 86–94.

Codell, Julie F. (2014), 'Gender, Genius and Abjection in Artist Biopics', in Tom Brown and Belén Vidal (eds), *The Biopic in Contemporary Film Culture* (New York: Routledge), 158–75.

Colmeiro, José (2011), 'A Nation of Ghosts? Haunting, Historical Memory and Forgetting in Post-Franco Spain', *452°: Electronic Journal of Theory of Literature and Comparative Literature* 4, 17–24 <http://www.452f.com/index.php/en/jose-colmeiro.html> (last accessed 14 January 2014).

Cook, Mark (2012), 'The Great British Bake Off Goes Global: from Sweden to Australia the Show is Flourishing', *The Guardian* 12 October, <http://www.theguardian.com/tv-and-radio/2012/oct/12/great-british-bake-off-round-the-world> (last accessed 19 September 2015).

Coomer, Martin (2015), 'Goya: The Portraits', *Time Out* (London), <http://www.timeout.com/london/art/goya-the-portraits> (last accessed 1 December 2015).

Costa, Jordi (2012), 'El caso del cadáver inquieto', *El País* 20 December, <http://cultura.elpais.com/cultura/2012/12/20/actualidad/1356033015_997328.html> (last accessed 22 August 2015).

Crawford, Joseph (2014), *The Twilight of the Gothic? Vampire Fiction and the Rise of Paranormal Romance* (Cardiff: University of Wales Press).

Cumming, Laura (2015), 'Goya: The Portraits Review – The Artist in an Extraordinary Light', *The Guardian* 11 October, <http://www.theguardian.com/artanddesign/2015/oct/11/goya-the-portraits-review-national-gallery-astonishing-show-radical-truthfulness> (last accessed 1 December 2015).

Curbet, Joan (2002), '"Hallelujah to Your Dying Screams of Torture": Representations of Ritual Violence in English and Spanish Romanticism', in Avril Horner (ed.), *European Gothic: A Spirited Exchange 1760–1960* (Manchester: Manchester University Press), 161–82.

Dargis, Manohla (2011), 'A Beautiful Prisoner Lost in Almodóvar's Labyrinth', *New York Times* 13 October, <http://www.nytimes.com/2011/10/14/movies/the-skin-i-live-in-directed-by-pedro-almodovar-review.html?_r=0> (last accessed 9 May 2015).

Davenport-Hines, Richard (1998), *Gothic: 400 Years of Excess, Horror, Evil and Ruin* (London: Fourth Estate).

Davies, Ann (2006), 'The Beautiful and Monstrous Masculine: the Male Body and Horror in *El espinazo del diablo*', *Studies in Hispanic Cinemas* 3/3 (2006), 135–47.

Davies, Ann (2011), 'The Final Girl and Monstrous Mother of *El orfanato*', in Ann Davies (ed.), *Spain on Screen: Developments in Contemporary Spanish Cinema* (London: Palgrave Macmillan), 79–92.

Davies, Ann (2012), *Spanish Spaces: Landscape, Space and Place in Contemporary Spanish Culture* (Liverpool: Liverpool University Press).

Davies, Ann (2014), 'Ghostbusting: Pursuing the Spectres of Spanish Cinema', *Mediático* 17 February 2014, <http://reframe.sussex.ac.uk/mediatico/2014/02/17/ghostbusting-pursuing-the-spectres-of-spanish-cinema/> (last accessed 7 December 2015).

Davies, Ann (2015a), 'The Continuities of Spanish Gothic' in Elena Oliete-Aldea, Beatriz Oria and Juan A. Tarancón (eds), *Global Genres/Local Films: The Transnational Dimension of Spanish Cinema* (London: Bloomsbury), 115–26.

Davies, Ann (2015b), 'Slime and Subtlety: Monsters in del Toro's Spanish-language Films', in John W. Morehead (ed.), *The Supernatural Cinema of Guillermo del Toro: Critical Essays* (Jefferson, NC: McFarland), 41–57.

Davies, Ann (forthcoming) 'Postmodern Gothic Heroines and the Preference for Meaning Over Narrative'.

Davis, Colin (2010), 'The Skeptical Ghost: Alejandro Amenábar's *The Others* and the Return of the Dead', in Esther Peeren and María del Pilar Blanco (eds), *Popular Ghosts: The Haunted Spaces of Everyday Culture* (London: Continuum), 64–75.

Dawson, Nick (2007), 'Milos Forman, *Goya's Ghosts*', *Filmmaker* 20 July, <http://filmmakermagazine.com/1273-milos-forman-goyas-ghosts/#.VksKjk_sLcs> (last accessed 17 November 2015).

Di Ceglie, Domenico (2012), 'Identity and Inability to Mourn in *The Skin I Live In*', *International Journal of Psychoanalysis* 93, 1308–13.

Durham, Carolyn (2001), 'Books Beyond Borders: Intertextuality in Arturo Pérez-Reverte's *El Club Dumas*', *Anales de la literatura española contemporánea* 26/2, 465–81.

Ebert, Roger (2007), 'Goya's Ghosts', <http://www.rogerebert.com/reviews/goyas-ghosts-2007> (last accessed 17 November 2015).

Ebert, Roger (2009), 'The Twilight Saga: New Moon', <http://www.rogerebert.com/reviews/the-twilight-saga-new-moon-2009> (last accessed 2 January 2016).

Edwards, Justin D. and Fred Botting (2013), 'Theorising Globalgothic', in Glennis Byron (ed.), *Globalgothic* (Manchester: Manchester University Press), 11–24.

Edwards, Justin D. and Agnieszka Soltysik Monnet (2013), 'Introduction: from

Goth/ic to Pop Goth', in Justin D. Edwards and Agnieszka Soltysik Monnet (eds), *The Gothic in Contemporary Literature and Popular Culture: Pop Goth* (Hoboken: Taylor and Francis).

Ellayah, Pamela (2011), 'Traces du gothique anglo-saxon dans *Les Autres* (2001) d'Alejandro Amenábar et *Fragile* (2005) de Jaume Balagueró', in Marie-Soledad Rodriguez (ed.), *Le fantastique dans le cinéma espagnol contemporain* (Paris: Presses Sorbonne Nouvelle), 115–22.

Ellis, Robert Richmond (2006a), 'Reading the Spanish Past: Library Fantasies in Carlos Ruiz Zafón's *La sombra del viento*', *Bulletin of Spanish Studies* 83/6, 839–54.

Ellis, Robert Richmond (2006b), 'Detectives, Mad Bookmen and the Devil's Disciple: a Reading of *El club Dumas, La novena puerta* of Arturo Pérez Reverte', *Anales de la literatura española contemporánea* 31/1, 29–45.

Epps, Brad (2005), 'Seeing the Dead: Manual and Mechanical Specters in Modern Spain (1893–1939)', in Susan Larson and Eva Woods (eds), *Visualizing Spanish Modernity* (Oxford: Berg), 112–41.

Fiddian, Robin (2013), '*El espíritu de la colmena/The Spirit of the Beehive* (Víctor Erice, 1973): *To Kill a Mockingbird* as Neglected Intertext', in Maria M. Delgado and Robin Fiddian (eds), *Spanish Cinema 1973–2010: Auteurism, Politics, Landscape and Memory* (Manchester: Manchester University Press), 21–34.

Floyd, Nigel (2011), 'Julia's Eyes', *Time Out* 17 May, <http://www.timeout.com/london/film/julias-eyes> (last accessed 29 August 2015).

Frayling, Christopher (2005), *Mad, Bad and Dangerous? The Scientist and the Cinema* (London: Reaktion).

French, Philip (2007), 'Goya's Ghost', *The Guardian* 6 May, <http://www.theguardian.com/film/2007/may/06/worldcinema.drama1> (last accessed 17 November 2015).

French, Philip (2011), 'The Skin I Live In – Review', *Observer* 28 August, <http://www.theguardian.com/film/2011/aug/28/skin-live-in-almodovar-review> (last accessed 9 May 2015).

Frow, John (2015), *Genre*, 2nd ed. (London: Routledge).

Fuller, Graham (2009), 'No City for Old Men', *Sight and Sound* 19/2 (February), 24–7.

García, Marta (2013), 'El cuerpo de Belén Rueda', *Quo* 27 March, <http://www.quo.es/salud/el-cuerpo-de-belen-rueda> (last accessed 9 August 2015).

García Ochoa, Santiago (2005), 'Goya en el laberinto del autor', in Jean-Pierre Castellani (ed.), *Goya en Burdeos de Carlos Saura* (Nantes: Editions du Temps), 139–64.

García Romero, Ángel, 'Alejandro Amenábar: "Sombra que siempre me asombras"', in Carlos Aguilar (ed.), *Cine fantástico y de terror español 1984–2004* (San Sebastián: Donostia Kultura), 115–31.

Gelder, Ken (2004), *Popular Fiction: the Logics and Practices of a Literary Field* (London: Routledge).

Gómez, Iván and Fernando de Felipe (2013), 'Alegorías de miedo: el cine fantástico español en los tiempos de la Transición', *Studies in Spanish and Latin American Cinemas* 10/2, 197–211.

Gómez García, Iván (2013), 'Alegorías de miedo: el cine fantástico español en los tiempos de la Transición', in David Roas and Ana Casas (eds), *Visiones de lo fantástico en la cultura española (1900–1970)* (Benalmádena: E. D. A Libros), 185–206.

'Goya en el Prado: Volaverunt', <https://www.museodelprado.es/goya-en-el-prado/obras/ficha/goya/volaverunt/> (last accessed 21 February 2014).

Graham, Helen (2012), *The War and Its Shadow: Spain's Civil War in Europe's Long Twentieth Century* (Brighton: Sussex Academic Press).

'The Great British Bake Off: How Its Recipe Translates Worldwide – In Pictures' (2015), *The Guardian* 5 August, <http://www.theguardian.com/media/gallery/2015/aug/05/the-great-british-bake-off-international-versions-in-pictures> (last accessed 19 September 2015).

Gutiérrez Albilla, Julián Daniel (2013), 'La piel del horror, el horror en la piel: poder, violencia y trauma en el cuerpo (post)humano en La piel que habito', *Journal of Spanish Cultural Studies* 14/1, 70–85.

Halberstam, Judith (1995), *Skin Shows: Gothic Horror and the Technology of Monsters* (Durham, NC: Duke University Press).

Hale, Terry (2002), 'Translation in Distress: Cultural Misappropriation and the Construction of the Gothic', in Avril Horner (ed.), *European Gothic: A Spirited Exchange 1760–1960* (Manchester: Manchester University Press), 17–38.

Hanich, Julian (2010), *Cinematic Emotion in Horror Films and Thrillers: the Aesthetic Paradox of Pleasurable Fear* (New York: Routledge).

Harguindey, Ángel S. (2012), 'El abismo Almodóvar', *El País* 13 January, <http://cultura.elpais.com/cultura/2012/01/13/actualidad/1326456677_930721.html> (last accessed 23 May 2015).

Heredero, Carlos F. (1997), *Espejo de miradas: entrevistas con nuevos directores del cine español de los años noventa* (S. L: Festival de Cine de Alcalá de Henares/Caja de Asturias/Filmoteca de la Generalitat Valenciana/Fundación Autor).

Higson, Andrew (2003), *English Heritage, English Cinema: Costume Drama Since 1980* (Oxford: Oxford University Press).

Hills, Matt (2005), *The Pleasures of Horror* (London: Bloomsbury).

Hogle, Jerrold E. (2001), 'The Gothic Ghost of the Counterfeit and the Progress of Abjection', in David Punter (ed.), *A Companion to the Gothic* (Malden, MA: Blackwell), 293–304.

Hogle, Jerrold E. (ed.) (2002), *The Cambridge Companion to Gothic Fiction* (Cambridge: Cambridge University Press).

Hogle, Jerrold E. (2014), 'Introduction', in Jerrold E. Hogle (ed.), *The Cambridge Companion to the Modern Gothic* (Cambridge: Cambridge University Press), 3–19.

'Hugo Silva y José Coronado buscan "El cuerpo" de Belén Rueda' (2012), *La Vanguardia* 3 December, <http://www.lavanguardia.com/cine/20121203/>

54356932073/hugo-silva-jose-coronado-belen-rueda-el-cuerpo.html#ixzz3i
JEDVxsk> (last accessed 9 August 2015).

d'Humières, Catherine (2007), 'La Bibliothèque dans *La sombra del viento* de
Carlos Ruiz Zafón', *SEALS* 53–4, 339–51.

Hutchings, Peter (2004), *The Horror Film* (Harlow: Pearson Education).

Iglesias, Eulàlia (2009),'Grabo, luego existo: [*REC*]², de Jaume Balagueró y Paco
Plaza', *Cahiers du Cinéma España* 27, 41–2.

Jordan, Barry (2012), *Alejandro Amenábar* (Manchester: Manchester University
Press).

Kavka, Misha (2002), 'Gothic on Screen', in Jerrold E. Hogle (ed.), *The
Cambridge Companion to Gothic Fiction* (Cambridge: Cambridge University
Press), 209–28.

Kercher, Dona (2015), *Latin Hitchcock: How Almodóvar, Amenábar, de la Iglesia,
del Toro and Campanella Became Notorious* (London: Wallflower).

Kristeva, Julia (1982), *The Power of Horror: an Essay on Abjection* tr. Leon S.
Roudiez (New York: Columbia University Press).

Labanyi, Jo (2001), 'Coming to Terms with the Ghosts of the Past: History
and Spectrality in Contemporary Spanish Culture', *Arachne@Rutgers*
1/1,<http://www.libraries.rutgers.edu/rul/projects/arachne/vol1_1labanyi.
html> (last accessed 11 June 2013).

Labanyi, Jo (2008), 'Abjection, Trauma and the Material Image: *La madre muerta*
(Juanma Bajo Ulloa, 1993)', in Joan Ramon Resina with the assistance of
Andrés Lema-Hincapié (eds), *Burning Darkness: a Half Century of Spanish
Cinema* (Albany: SUNY Press), 143–60.

Lázaro-Reboll, Antonio (2012), *Spanish Horror Film* (Edinburgh: Edinburgh
University Press).

Lee Six, Abigail (2010), *Gothic Terrors: Incarceration, Duplication, and Bloodlust in
Spanish Narrative* (Lewisburg, PA: Bucknell University Press).

Lee Six, Abigail (2012), 'Introduction', *Journal of Romance Studies* 12/1, 1–9.

Lemma, Alessandra (2012), 'A Perfectly Modern Frankenstein: Almodóvar's
The Skin I Live In (2011, Sony Pictures Classics)', *International Journal of
Psychoanalysis* 93, 1291–300.

Lezard, Nicholas (2002), 'A Spanish Gentleman', *Waterstone's Book Quarterly* 4,
28–30.

López, Diego and David Pizarro (2014), *Silencios de pánico: historia del cine fantástico y de terror español, 1897–2010* (Barcelona: Tyrannosaurus Books).

Lowenstein, Adam (2005), *Shocking Representation: Historical Trauma, National
Cinema, and the Modern Horror Film* (New York: Columbia University Press).

McGrath, Patrick (1997), 'Transgression and Decay', in Christoph Grunenberg
(ed.), *Gothic: Transmutations of Horror in Late Twentieth Century Art* (Boston/
Cambridge, MA: Institute of Contemporary Art/MIT Press), 158–3. (The
pagination for this reference runs backwards.)

Meddick, Judith (2010), 'The Telling of Memory in *La sombra del viento* by
Carlos Ruiz Zafón', *Romance Studies* 28/4, 246–58.

Mighall, Robert (1999), *A Geography of Victorian Gothic Fiction: Mapping History's Nightmares* (Oxford: Oxford University Press).

Minguell, Jordi (2010), 'Ojos que no ven, Sitges que no siente', *El País* 7 October, <http://elpais.com/elpais/2010/10/07/actualidad/1286439449_850215.html> (last accessed 22 August 2015).

Mira, Alberto (2010), *The A-Z of Spanish Cinema* (Lanham, MD: Scarecrow Press).

Mirzoeff, Nicholas (2002), 'Ghostwriting: Working Out Visual Culture', *Journal of Visual Culture* 1/2, 239–54.

Monleón, José B. (1990), *A Specter is Haunting Europe: A Sociohistorical Approch to the Fantastic* (Princeton: Princeton University Press).

Montaner Frutos, Alberto (2000), 'De libros y de enigmas: la trama bibliográfica de *El club Dumas*', in José Manuel López de Abiada and Augusta López Bernasocchi (eds), *Territorio Reverte: ensayos sobre la obra de Arturo Pérez Reverte* (Madrid: Verbum), 214–61.

Morgan, Jack (2002), *The Biology of Horror: Gothic Literature and Film* (Carbondale, IL: Southern Illinois University Press).

Navarro, Antonio José (2002a), 'Jaume Balagueró', *Dirigido* 316, 32–3.

Navarro, Antonio José (2002b), 'En el corazón de las tinieblas', *Dirigido* 316, 30–1.

Navarro, Antonio José (2005), 'La Fantastic Factory: Terror Made in Spain', in Carlos Aguilar (ed.), *Cine fantástico y de terror español 1984–2004* (San Sebastián: Donostia Kultura), 221–59.

Newman, Kim (2007), 'Goya's Ghosts' *Empire* 4 May, <http://www.empireonline.com/movies/goya-ghosts/review/> (last accessed 17 Nov 2015).

Newman, Kim (2013), 'The Old Dark House' in James Bell (ed.), *Gothic: the Dark Heart of Film* (London: BFI), 96–102.

'"Los ojos de Julia", con Belén Rueda, inaugura Sitges' (2010), *El Norte de Castilla* 8 October, <http://www.elnortedecastilla.es/v/20101008/cultura/ojos-julia-belen-rueda-20101008.html> (last accessed 22 August 2015).

Olivares Merino, Julio Ángel (2011), *Jaume Balagueró: en nombre de la oscuridad* (Madrid: Akal).

Olney, Ian (2013), *Euro Horror: Classic European Horror Cinema in Contemporary American Culture* (Bloomington, IN: Indiana University Press).

O'Neill, Phelim (2011), 'Julia's Eyes – Review', *The Guardian* 19 May, <http://www.theguardian.com/film/2011/may/19/julias-eyes-review> (last accessed 22 August 2015).

O'Regan, Tom (2004), 'Cultural Exchange', in Toby Miller and Robert Stam (eds), *A Companion to Film Theory* (Malden, MA: Blackwell), 262–94.

Page, Benedicte (2004), 'Barcelona Gothic', *Bookseller* 5109, 24.

Parmiter, Tara K. (2011), 'Green is the New Black: Ecophobia and the Gothic Landscape in the *Twilight* Series', in Giselle Liza Anatol (ed.), *Bringing Light to* Twilight: *Perspectives on a Pop Culture Phenomenon* (Basingstoke: Palgrave Macmillan), 221–33.

Pérez Morán, Ernesto (2009), 'NO-DO', in Equipo Reseña (ed.), *Cine para leer enero-junio 2009* (Bilbao: Mensajero), 262.

Pérez-Reverte, Arturo (1998), *El club Dumas* (Madrid: Alfaguara).

Pérez-Reverte, Arturo (2000), 'La vía europea al best-séller', in José Manuel López de Abiada and Augusta López Bernasocchi (eds), *Territorio Reverte: ensayos sobre la obra de Arturo Pérez Reverte* (Madrid: Verbum), 361–7.

Perona, José (2000), 'Historias de libros en tres novelas de Arturo Pérez-Reverte', in José Manuel López de Abiada and Augusta López Bernasocchi (eds), *Territorio Reverte: ensayos sobre la obra de Arturo Pérez Reverte* (Madrid: Verbum), 368–88.

Perriam, Chris (2003), *Stars and Masculinities in Spanish Cinema: from Banderas to Bardem* (Oxford: Oxford University Press).

Perriam, Chris (2011), 'Javier Bardem: Costume, Crime, Commitment', in Ann Davies (ed.), *Spain on Screen: Developments in Contemporary Spanish Cinema* (Basingstoke: Palgrave Macmillan), 114–28.

Pollock, Griselda (1980), 'Artists Mythologies and Media Geniuses, Madness and Art History', *Screen* 21/3, 57–96.

Pollock, Griselda (2001), 'A Hungry Eye', in Ginette Vincendeau (ed.), *Film/Literature/Heritage: a Sight and Sound Reader* (London: British Film Institute), 32–7.

Ponga, Paula (2010), 'Belén Rueda: el terror es el miedo al daño físico', *Fotogramas* 26 October, <http://www.fotogramas.es/Peliculas/Los-ojos-de-Julia/Belen-Rueda-El-terror-es-el-miedo-al-dano-fisico> (last accessed 22 August 2015).

Punter, David (1996), *The Literature of Terror: a History of Gothic Fictions from 1765 to the Present Day*, vol. 2, *The Modern Gothic* (London: Longman).

Punter, David (2005), *The Influence of Post-Modernism on Contemporary Writing: an Interdisciplinary Study* (Lewiston, NY: Edwin Mellen Press).

Punter, David and Glennis Byron (2004), *The Gothic* (Malden, MA: Blackwell).

Quintana, Àngel (2014), 'Anchors in Time: Historic Memory and Representation', *Hispanic Research Journal* 15/1, 10–21.

Ramblado, Cinta (2008), 'The Shadow of the Dissident: Reflections on Francoism in Carlos Ruiz Zafón's *The Shadow of the Wind*', *Clues* 26/3, 70–85.

Ramos Alquezar, Sergi (2011), 'Le fantastique espagnol, une aproche historique du genre', in Marie-Soledad Rodríguez (ed.), *Le fantastique dans le cinema espagnol contemporain* (Paris: Presses Sorbonne Nouvelle), 33–50.

Resina, Joan Ramon (2008), *Barcelona's Vocation of Modernity: Rise and Decline of an Urban Image* (Stanford, CA: Stanford University Press).

Ribeiro de Menezes, Alison (2014), *Embodying Memory in Contemporary Spain* (New York: Palgrave Macmillan).

Roas, David and Ana Casas (eds) (2013), *Visiones de lo fantástico en la cultura española (1900–1970)* (Benalmádena: E. D. A Libros).

Robey, Tim (2009), 'The Twilight Saga: New Moon, review', *Telegraph* 19 November, <http://www.telegraph.co.uk/culture/film/filmreviews/6606699/The-Twilight-Saga-New-Moon-review.html> (last accessed 2 January 2016).

Rodríguez Marchante, Oti (2002), *Amenábar, vocación de intriga* (Madrid: Páginas de espuma).

Ruiz Tosaus, Eduardo (2008), 'Algunas consideraciones sobre *La sombra del viento* de Ruiz Zafón', *Espéculo* 38, <www.ucm.es/info/especulo/numero38/soviento.html> (last accessed 15 January 2013).

Ruiz Tosaus, Eduardo (2009), 'Motivos, símbolos y obsesiones en la narrativa de Carlos Ruiz Zafón', *Espéculo* 41, <www.ucm.es/info/especulo/numero41/motivzaf.html> (last accessed 15 January 2013).

Rubín de Celis, Andrés (2009), 'NO-DO', *Cahiers du Cinéma España* 24, 42.

Ruiz Zafón, Carlos (2008), *La sombra del viento* (Barcelona: Planeta).

Ryan, Lorraine (2009), 'Terms of Empowerment: Setting, Spatiality, and Agency in Carlos Ruiz Zafón's *La sombra del viento* and Dulce Chacón's *Cielos de barro*', *Clues* 27/2, 95–107.

Sala, Ángel (2010), '¿Cine gótico español? Un viaje a las mazmorras del subdesarollo y otros infiernos', in Antonio José Navarro (ed.), *Pesadillas en la oscuridad: el cine de terror gótico* (Madrid: Valdemar), 321–50.

Sánchez, Yvette (2000), 'De bibliófiles culpables y lectores inocentes en *El Club Dumas*', in José Manuel López de Abiada and Augusta López Bernasocchi (eds), *Territorio Reverte: ensayos sobre la obra de Arturo Pérez Reverte* (Madrid: Verbum), 423–35.

Savater, Fernando (2003), 'Riesgos de la iniciación al espíritu', *La Ortiga* 42–4, 155–69.

Seitz, Matt Zoller (2007), 'The Inquisition in Spain: Expected and Even Hailed', *New York Times* 20 July, <http://www.nytimes.com/2007/07/20/movies/20goya.html?_r=0> (last accessed 17 November 2015).

Smith, Andrew (2013), *Gothic Literature*, 2nd ed. (Edinburgh: Edinburgh University Press).

Smith, Andrew and William Hughes (eds) (2013), *EcoGothic* (Manchester: Manchester University Press).

Smith, Patrick (2011), 'Julia's Eyes DVD Review', *Daily Telegraph* 8 September, <http://www.telegraph.co.uk/culture/film/dvd-reviews/8750931/Julias-Eyes-DVD-review.html> (last accessed 29 August 2015).

Smith, Paul Julian (2001), '*The Others*', *Sight and Sound* 11/11, 54.

Smith, Paul Julian (2006), *Spanish Visual Culture: Cinema, Television, Internet* (Manchester: Manchester University Press).

Smith, Paul Julian (2012), *Spanish Practices: Literature, Cinema, Television* (London: Modern Humanities Research Association/Maney Publishing).

Sooke, Alastair (2015), 'Goya The Portraits: Must-See National Gallery Exhibition', *Telegraph* 23 October, <http://www.telegraph.co.uk/sponsored/culture/national-art-pass/11947400/goya-portraits-exhibition.html> (last accessed 1 December 2015).

Spooner, Catherine (2006), *Contemporary Gothic* (London: Reaktion).

Spooner, Catherine (2014), 'Twenty-First Century Gothic', in Dale Townshend (ed.), *Terror and Wonder: the Gothic Imagination* (London: British Library), 180–205.

Steen, Maria Sergia (2008), '*La sombra del viento*: intersección de géneros y *bildungsroman*', *Espéculo* 39, <www.ucm.es/info/especulo/numero39/sombra.html> (last accessed 15 January 2013).

Stone, Rob (2007), *Julio Medem* (Manchester: Manchester University Press).

Thau, Eric M. (2011), 'The Eyes of Ana Torrent', *Studies in Hispanic Cinemas* 8/2, 131–43.

Torrecillas, Tonio (2012), 'Belén Rueda se pone los pantalones', *El País* 24 November, <http://smoda.elpais.com/articulos/belen-rueda-se-pone-los-pantalones/2737> (last accessed 9 August 2015).

Triana-Toribio, Núria (2003), *Spanish National Cinema* (London: Routledge).

Triana-Toribio, Núria (2014), 'Residual Film Cultures: Real and Imagined Futures of Spanish Cinema', *Bulletin of Hispanic Studies* 91/1, 65–81.

Trotman, Tiffany Gagliardi (2007), 'Haunted *Noir*: Neo-Gothic Barcelona in Carlos Ruiz Zafón's *La sombra del viento*', *Romance Studies* 25/4, 269–77.

Tudor, Andrew (1989), *Monsters and Mad Scientists: a Cultural History of the Horror Movie* (Oxford: Basil Blackwell).

Tudor, Andrew (2002), 'Why Horror? The Peculiar Pleasures of a Popular Genre', in Mark Jancovich (ed.), *Horror: the Film Reader* (Hoboken, NJ: Taylor and Francis).

Twitchell, James (1985), *Dreadful Pleasures: an Anatomy of Modern Horror* (New York: Oxford University Press).

Úbeda-Portugués, Alberto (2005), 'Alejandro Amenábar: selección de declaraciones', in Carlos Aguilar (ed.), *Cine fantástico y de terror español 1984–2004* (San Sebastián: Donostia Kultura), 141–55.

Vallín, Pedro (2013), 'Pedro Almodóvar: "Esta es mi película más gay pero también, más candorosa"', *La Vanguardia* 4 March, <http://www.lavanguardia.com/cine/20130304/54367976785/pedro-almodovar-pelicula-mas-gay.html> (last accessed 6 January 2016).

Veldman-Genz, Carole (2011), 'Serial Experiments in Popular Culture: the resignification of Gothic Symbology in Anita Blake Vampire Hunter and the *Twilight* series', in Giselle Liza Anatol (ed.), *Bringing Light to* Twilight: *Perspectives on a Pop Culture Phenomenon* (Basingstoke: Palgrave Macmillan), 43–58.

Vidal, Belén (2012), *Heritage Film: Nation, Genre and Representation* (London: Wallflower).

Vidal, Belén (2014), 'Introduction: The Biopic and its Critical Contexts', in Tom Brown and Belén Vidal (eds), *The Biopic in Contemporary Film Culture* (New York: Routledge), 1–32.

Vidler, Anthony (1992), *The Architectural Uncanny: Essays in the Modern Unhomely* (Cambridge MA: MIT Press).

Vincendeau, Ginette (2001), 'Introduction', in Ginette Vincendeau (ed.), *Film/Literature/Heritage: a Sight and Sound Reader* (London: British Film Institute), xi–xxv.

Waddell, Terrie (2006), *Mis/takes: Archetype, Myth and Identity in Screen Fiction* (London: Routledge).

Waldron, Darren and Ros Murray (2014), 'Troubling Transformations: Pedro Almodóvar's *La piel que habito/The Skin I Live In* and its Reception', *Transnational Cinemas* 5/1, 57–71.

Warner, Marina (2000), *No Go the Bogeyman: Scaring, Lulling and Making Mock* (London: Vintage).

Warner, Marina (2002), *Fantastic Metamorphoses, Other Worlds: Ways of Telling the Self* (Oxford: Oxford University Press).

Warner, Marina (2006), *Phantasmagoria: Spirit Visions, Metaphors and Media into the Twenty-first Century* (Oxford: Oxford University Press).

Warner, Marina (2014), *Once Upon a Time: a Short History of Fairy Tale* (Oxford: Oxford University Press).

Warwick, Alexandra (2007), 'Feeling Gothicky?', *Gothic Studies* 9/1, 5–15.

Wheeler, Duncan (2014), 'Back to the Future: (Re-)Packaging Spain's Troublesome Past for Local and Global Audiences', in Duncan Wheeler and Fernando Canet (eds), *(Re)viewing Creative, Critical and Commercial Practices in Contemporary Spanish Cinema* (Bristol: Intellect), 207–33.

White, Rob and Paul Julian Smith (2011), 'Escape Artistry: Debating "The Skin I Live In"', *Film Quarterly* October, <www.filmquarterly.org/2011/10/escape-artistry-debating-the-skin-i-live-in/> (last accessed 29 January 2014).

Williamson, Milly (2014), 'Let Them All In: the Evolution of the "Sympathetic" Vampire', in Leon Hun, Sharon Lockyer and Milly Williamson (eds), *Screening the Undead: Vampires and Zombies in Film and Television* (London: I. B. Tauris), 71–92.

Wright, Sarah (2013), *The Child in Spanish Cinema* (Manchester: Manchester University Press).

Wright, Sarah (2014), 'Ana Torrent as Palimpsest in Elio Quiroga's *NO-DO (The Haunting)*', in Duncan Wheeler and Fernando Canet (eds), *(Re)Viewing Creative, Critical and Commercial Practices in Contemporary Spanish Cinema* (Bristol: Intellect), 155–64.

Zamora, Jorge (2008), 'Femmes fatales/femmes formidables: mimetismo y subversión en *El club Dumas o la sombra de Richelieu* de Arturo Pérez-Reverte', *Anales de la literatura española contemporánea* 33/1, 153–73.

Zurián, Francisco A. (2013), '*La piel que habito*: A Story of Imposed Gender and the Struggle for Identity', in Marvin D'Lugo and Kathleen M. Vernon (eds), *A Companion to Pedro Almodóvar* (Chichester: Wiley-Blackwell), 262–78.

Index